IT GOES WITH THE TERRITORY

IT GOES WITH THE TERRITORY

Memoirs of a Poet

Elaine Feinstein

ALMA BOOKS

ALMA BOOKS LTD
London House
243–253 Lower Mortlake Road
Richmond
Surrey TW9 2LL
United Kingdom
www.almabooks.com

First published by Alma Books Limited in 2013
Copyright © Elaine Feinstein, 2013

p. 67, lines from Wallace Stevens's 'Sunday Morning' reproduced with kind permission from Pollinger Ltd. All rights reserved.

Photograph of Jill Neville © Getty Images
Photograph of Fay Weldon © Jonathan Dockar-Drysdale

Elaine Feinstein asserts her moral right to be identified as the author of this work in accordance with the Copyright, Designs and Patents Act 1988

Printed and bound by CPI Group (UK) Ltd, Croydon, CR0 4YY

HARDBACK ISBN: 978-1-84688-301-9
EBOOK ISBN : 978-1-84688-306-4

Contents

IT GOES WITH
THE TERRITORY

PRELUDE

Last week, I went to St Martin-in-the-Fields on Trafalgar Square and listened to a performance of Bach's Christmas Oratorio, directed by my son Martin. I came out buzzing with the tenderness and exhilaration of the music. It seemed to me, at that moment, that for all my eccentric dedication to a writing life, I have not too seriously harmed any of my three sons. Good fortune is unpredictable, but none of them will ever have to brood over what they failed to attempt.

I am not so sure about the damage done to my marriage. My desire to make poems and stories was as intense as any adultery, and the demand to put that ambition first is not readily forgiven in a woman. Still, poetry strengthened me in the face of more traditional infidelities and harsh words. And all our attempts to separate over fifty years came to nothing.

My childhood hardly equipped me for the life I wanted to find, but it was a happy one, and gave me an optimism I have never entirely lost. Jean Rhys once said that if she could live her life over again she would rather be happy than write. It is not a choice any of us are ever offered.

– Elaine Feinstein, January 2013

CHAPTER I

Foreign Roots

All four grandparents came from Odessa, a port on the Black Sea coast of Ukraine, and settled in the north of England some time in the last decade of the nineteenth century. They were all Jews, though the two families were remarkably disparate.

Dad's family loved the old rituals. I remember candles on Friday nights and crackly *matzot* on Passover. When my father told me the story of the Hebrews escaping from slavery in Egypt, it was as if he remembered the events himself. I must have been about four, and it was the most thrilling story I had ever heard. The following year I could read most of the English words in the Haggadah myself and found it something of a disappointment.

My mother's family, on the other hand, assimilated into English middle-class life in one generation. Two of her brothers went to Cambridge and learnt to speak a perfectly inflected standard English. None of them believed in God or his protection, and found my father's beliefs tiresome, though they were far too polite to say so.

As a child I gave the matter little thought, until one day in 1937 I was given a brusque awakening. I remember the smell of wet coats hanging up on the low hooks of the Cloakroom, so it was probably just after lunch. I had won one of the silver medals the Form Teacher awarded every week for good work. As I was pulling off my coat, with the medal proudly pinned to my tunic, a red-faced girl, whose name I can still remember but won't use, came up to me and sneered: "My father says you are nothing but a dirty Jew." I was in floods of tears as I told my father after school, and I heard my parents talking about what action to take long after I had gone to bed.

Those were the years when Mosley's Fascists fomented riots among the unemployed in London and Manchester, though I don't remember my parents fearing violence in Leicester. What I did overhear, once I had begun to listen for it, was their alarm about what was happening in Germany. I remember my father refusing to buy me a balsa-wood aeroplane, powered marvellously by an elastic band, because it was made in a wicked country. He read the *News Chronicle* every morning and believed England had a quite different sense of fair play. The man I married many years later, however, saw another side of England. He grew up in Stepney, in Blackshirt territory, where he was taunted "Go back to Palestine!" and had his head banged against the paving stones of the schoolyard.

My own earliest memories are of a small house on Groby Road, Leicester – a road which led to the outskirts of town, past the cemetery, towards a quarry where children were not allowed to play, although there were fascinating pebbles, some of which held fossils. Dad's father often came to stay with us in Groby Road after his wife died – his children shared the care of him – and I was told to call him Zaida. He was large and affectionate, with a ginger beard and deep laughter lines round his blue eyes. His yellow handkerchiefs smelled of snuff and the strong peppermints he carried in the pockets of a cardigan, which always sagged at the back. I liked to sit on his knee while he told me stories about the sunny streets of Odessa. He had been sent there to study after he lost the top joint of his first finger while minding a circular saw.

Zaida was always a dreamer. And he loved to study, particularly relishing heated argument over the meaning of rabbinic texts on a Saturday afternoon. He did not say much about his childhood in Belarus, or the hostility of their Ukrainian neighbours, though I remember he had wistful stories about young girls and boys playing hide-and-seek in the great forests.

He could read Russian, but he spoke Yiddish as a mother tongue. It was, I know now, a language used not only in the shtetls of the Pale but across the whole Jewish world from Russia through

Germany to Paris, London and New York. It was a language rich in poems and stories. The poet Peretz Markish found it a genuine lingua franca, which brought him audiences wherever he travelled after the Russian Revolution. What took him back to Russia, fatally, was learning about the Soviet encouragement of Yiddish culture, especially Solomon Mikhoels's Yiddish theatre. Markish never wrote poetry in Russian, but Akhmatova herself translated him, and mentioned with delight his image of a dry leaf blown in the wind as "scuttling like a brown mouse". Stalin had him shot on the Night of the Murdered Poets in 1952. These days, of course, as Isaac Bashevis Singer said when collecting his Nobel Prize, "Yiddish is the language of ghosts".

The language was never spoken between my parents, but my father often used Yiddish phrases. For the most part they went along with a shrug. Not all of them find their place in Leo Rosten's remarkable book, *The Joys of Yiddish*, and friends in London who are more knowledgeable than I am in this area are puzzled by them. Perhaps they were local to Zaida's early days in Belarus, perhaps my father simply mispronounced the words.

If he was overtaken by a speedier car, he would say: "*Layf und freizach*". This, he told me, translated as "let him laugh and enjoy himself". Or he would say, when he wished me to regard someone who troubled me as insignificant, "*Khob im in bod*". This he translated as "We have him in a bath". I was bewildered by the nature of this encouragement. "Look," he tried to explain, "when you have someone in a bath they are helpless." Since he frequently used the words about some figure in authority, I was unconvinced. My headmistress was clearly not in the least helpless.

Yiddish is written in a cursive Hebrew script, running from right to left – not the heavy square alphabet of the prayer book, but a sinuous, almost Arabic flow of letters. I still know them, because Zaida asked me to use them when writing to him in Manchester, even though I could only transliterate English words. Since then, I have occasionally used the script to disguise my thoughts in diaries.

I never heard my mother use Yiddish. She was happy to observe religious customs which she came to believe in devoutly, but all her words were English. She had a number of superstitions learned from my grandmother, whom I hardly knew. She was afraid of white blossom brought into the house, for instance, and threw salt over her shoulder when it was spilt. Challenged about that last habit, she confessed uneasily that it was to blind the eyes of the Devil. I cannot imagine her discussing these matters with her brothers, or indeed my father, who would have dismissed them as *narishkeiten* (nonsense).

We were not, by present-day standards, particularly observant. Even my rabbinical Zaida never expected his wife to wear a *sheitel* (wig). My mother, in her hat and tweed coat at a bus stop, looked like any other Midlands housewife. My father, built like a sportsman, was accepted without demur at Glen Gorse Golf Club. Still, D.H. Lawrence, who wrote in his letters about disliking rich Jews at the seaside, would probably have detected him as foreign quickly enough. There were not many immigrants to provincial Britain in those days. And Jews looked "different" even to writers like Jean Rhys, a Creole from the West Indies, who always felt like an outsider herself.

* * *

My mother was particularly proud of two brothers, Joseph and Maurice, who took First Class degrees and went on to make a place for themselves in the English establishment. Both were thin men, with narrow faces, though Jo became redder and more corpulent as he grew older. Even Grandfather Solomon listened to Jo, I was told. He had served in the First World War and, soon after he came down from university, persuaded Solomon that the family name should be changed from Goldstein to Compton. The change was a sensible move towards acceptance into gentile society.

As it happens, my father already had a surname – Cooklin – which did not sound particularly foreign. The name has always puzzled me. I was told the origin was the Russian word for doll, *kukla,* and I liked the idea: perhaps some earlier generations had been involved in making dolls, or perhaps even puppets. In Turkey, puppet masters were storytellers, and very often Jews.

A wish to find the tale had some basis in fact led me to investigate the *donmeh* (Muslim converts) of Istanbul in the late Seventies, and what I discovered fed *The Shadow Master,* a novel I was writing then. A less romantic origin is likely, however. Alan Sillitoe, a friend of later years who loved maps, discovered the village of Kooklin in Belarus, not too far from the village where my great-grandfather Hatskel is said to have worked as a factor for a local landowner. Somewhere along the line, the traditional way of naming a child – as in the synagogue, by calling him the son of his father – had been lost in favour of using the village where the family had settled. In Odessa, which I visited in 2005, I found several families in the telephone book with the same surname, though none of them, it seems, were related to me. All denied any Jewish roots.

My father's Manchester sisters had a tough independence which went back to the old shtetl world, where women often earned a living for the family while their husbands studied holy books. One ran a wood shop and could even handle a circular saw. They welcomed my mother warmly; indeed, his sisters liked to tease my father she was far too good for him. She was uncomfortable with their praise, and quietly miffed by their comments about my olive complexion, skinny body and habit of retreating into a book. For my part, I found their huge bulk and the noise in their big house, alarming. They piled too much food on my plate: *latkas,* stuffed meats, roast potatoes. I could never eat much of it.

* * *

My mother taught me to read at four, and like many only children I read avidly. Discovering as much, she wrote to her brother Jo, then Director of Education at Ealing, describing this unexpected passion and asking him to suggest a list of suitable books. He replied loftily that it really didn't matter what I read, as long as I was reading. So no one objected to my choices. I enjoyed Lewis Carroll – not just *Alice*, but *Sylvie and Bruno* too, intrigued rather than put off by the moral puzzles – and Rudyard Kipling, especially the story of the gallant mongoose Rikki-Tikki-Tavi. I read *Jane Eyre*, which my mother had once enjoyed, but also and with equal eagerness my father's Hopalong Cassidy cowboy books. Other novels on those shelves were more puzzling. One, I remember, was highly charged in ways I did not understand. A cloth was thrown over a child's cot so that something unspecified could go on without the child seeing. Nobody stopped me reading whatever I wanted.

Fortunately for me, my mother did not always take Uncle Jo's advice. When she wrote to ask about the best schools in Leicester, Jo wrote back that she should save her money since, if I had any intelligence, it would come out whatever school I went to. My mother rejected this opinion and chose an excellent junior school at the other side of town, for which I needed to wear a dark velour hat with a smart crest on it and a navy-blue coat.

Most of the girls there came from middle-class backgrounds, but it was a world in which my mother could pass easily: her whole upbringing had fitted her to do so. And it was always she who came to the end-of-term parents' days – in tweeds, court shoes and wearing gloves. She was, my form teacher told me after I had earned a reprimand for some disgraceful behaviour, a "perfect lady", who did not deserve such a daughter.

Dad was not enthusiastic about open days, but he collected me from school every day in his Armstrong Siddeley; the big, heavy car smelt attractively of real leather and had a walnut dashboard. It was somehow redolent of the man who drove it. I watched for him driving up the hill towards me from a curved metal seat in the school railings.

He was often a little late, but always reliably turned up, until one day, when I was six or seven, he failed to appear. I stared down the hill, looking for the V-shaped nose of his car with complete confidence, long after all the teachers had left and the school gates closed. It was then I began to panic, as I wondered how to pay for two trams to the other side of town if he failed to appear. The conductors, surprised to see such a young child on her own, let me travel free, but I was snivelling by the time I walked up Groby Road to the family door.

An ambulance was standing outside. When my father saw me, he looked at his watch in astonishment, then got into the ambulance to join my mother. Seeing this, I burst into wild tears, and the cousin who had been called in, perhaps to look after me, thought I was distressed to see my mother taken away. I was too ashamed to explain, if indeed I allowed myself to know, that I was weeping because my father had put my mother *first*. In fact, a fetus had lodged in one of her fallopian tubes and she had haemorrhaged badly. She was lucky to be alive, but there were to be no more children.

I have never written much about my mother, though images of my father run through all my novels. She was a good, kind woman who dabbed my spots with calamine lotion when I had chicken pox and tried to turn me into a respectable young lady. But I had no wish to turn into someone who wore tweed suits and gloves. I wanted to climb trees and scuffle through brambles on patches of wasteland. I absolutely didn't want to turn into her – and until now I have never tried to imagine what it was like to *be* her.

She looks shyly pretty in her childhood photographs – everything about her slight and feminine: slender wrists, delicate lips and small nose. Her court shoes were size three. Unlike my father, who left school at twelve, she had a grammar-school education. Did she think wistfully of finding some use for her intelligence beyond typing Dad's business letters? I don't know. I never thought to ask.

At sixteen, when the Great War was at its height, she took a job in an office and enjoyed it. Her nickname in those days was "Goldie" – and I have letters from girl friends who seem to have made a pet of her. An autograph album suggests a young soldier felt some affection for her, too, though I have no idea what happened to him. She married my father in her late twenties, and must have felt keen to do so, since she pretended to be a year younger than her age: she was thirty-one when I was born.

For my quiet mother, my father's working-class ease and lack of embarrassment about bodily functions was part of his attraction. She once confided that he was the only man with whom she felt no anxiety about admitting her need for a lavatory. She did not often talk to me so intimately.

She had small pearly teeth, and my father once told me that it was her smile he had fallen in love with, though he spoilt the praise by adding "of course, she wasn't bonny" – meaning that she wasn't plump and sturdy in the manner of his sisters. On his side of the family women were laughing, bossy creatures who had all married rather less powerful men.

I only began to look at my mother as a separate being when she was in her early middle age. By then, she wore rimless glasses, and her body was held in by pink cross-laced corsets. I understand now how she came to be wearing those corsets and grimace at my unthinking, barely repressed mockery of them. My mother had rhesus-negative blood. As her first child, I survived a difficult birth, but the pregnancy set up antibodies which destroyed every other fetus she carried. And there were several. It was her defining tragedy, though she never spoke of it. She felt a failure in relation to the wives among my father's relations who had large families. She remained brisk, bustling and cheerful nonetheless.

Even now I think of her fridge with awe: the savoury fish, fresh-cooked and balled in jelly inside glass containers, the meat washed and salted, ready for roasting. She devoted the same meticulous attention to her domestic world as her sister Annie gave to running a hospital. The most insignificant articles were given their appointed places.

Quite early on, a steely determination grew inside me not to resemble her. Underneath that round black velour hat and behind the shyly smiling face of my first photograph was a fierce spirit of which my mother would certainly have disapproved, had she guessed how I daydreamt of a more adventurous life.

Meanwhile, Dad stole my affections. As soon as I started school, he made my breakfast – poached eggs on toast – while she rested. And on holidays he enjoyed fairgrounds and seaside piers, roller-coaster rides and booths where you could win fluffy toys. He watched patiently while I tried to lower a penny mechanical crane over trinkets lying in piles of coloured pebbles, never scooping up so much as a boiled sweet. In a treasure hunt one afternoon on Skegness sands we were luckier: we won a miniature boat with white sails. He was triumphant.

Unquestionably, in a worldly sense, my mother married beneath her. My father was enjoying a brief period of prosperity at the time of their engagement, but her Compton family would not have been impressed. I don't know if her parents took any pleasure in finding that she had married inside the Jewish community. Of their seven children, most did not marry at all. Of the sons who did, none married Jewish girls. None of them showed much desire to be fruitful and multiply. There were only three cousins I know of, in comparison to the plethora of cousins on my father's side of the family.

My mother was closest to her younger brother, Frank, who wore a dark-blue blazer, was captain of his golf-club team and had something of the appearance of Bing Crosby, with a charming smile barely repressed at the centre of his lips. My father used to tease Frank about the length of time he spent in the bathroom flossing his teeth, or the meticulous care he took defrosting the windows of his car before setting off on the drive north. Secretly, I liked Frank's superb white teeth, the way he always smelt of lavender and his blue two-seater sports car.

Maurice, a permanent under-secretary at the Ministry of Agriculture and Fisheries, visited more rarely, and Uncle Jo only stayed in touch by letter. None were family men. Maurice had a happy marriage, but I remember him saying the world was too brutal to bring a child into it. He had a son nevertheless. Frank never married. Uncle Leslie's first marriage ended in divorce, and he let my mother's sister Annie bring up his daughter.

My father was unimpressed by their academic success, and for a long time I accepted his poor opinion of them. My father liked to dismiss Annie – a handsome, sophisticated woman, then matron of a hospital near Durham – because she had never married. To be a spinster in those days was to be counted a failure. I observed her lilac underclothes, therefore, with some perplexity. In turn, Annie remembered my mother's delicate prettiness as a girl, and was disappointed in my stronger, more masculine features, once sadly remarking that my looks resembled those of my father's family.

Grandfather Solomon was a small, clean-shaven patriarch, with starched triangles to his white collars and a single rose-cut stone in his tiepin – a cold scary man, albeit a shrewd one. I cannot remember anything he said, or even the sound of his voice. My mother liked to tell me that when he first arrived in Liverpool he had to carry sheets of glass around the city on a bicycle, but by the time of her marriage he was a wealthy glass merchant and owned property across Liverpool.

The year after I was born, my father had to sell his three wood shops in Liverpool and begin again. My mother's family quietly noted this business failure. However, Dad was a resilient man. The manager of Barclays Bank gambled on him and financed a lease on three floors of a rundown piece of Leicester, where he set up a small factory. Solomon's initial reservations about his business acumen, however, began to harden into active disapproval. Some time in the early years of the marriage, he decided to disinherit my mother, though we didn't discover that until he died in 1941. He divided his estate between his other children, though for some reason he left a little money to me.

All through my childhood, I thought of my father as rich because he drove a big car, took us to grand hotels and expensive restaurants and enjoyed giving presents. "Izzy," my mother would reproach him, because she did the firm's books and knew their financial situation to a penny. He laughed while I gazed up at him with complete trust.

Once, though, in the Maypole grocery shop close by our Groby Road house, I was shaken by a brief glimpse into what it meant to run out of money. I can still smell the sweet tea and smoky odours of bacon sides and hear my mother say nervously to the shopkeeper: "We're going off on holiday this evening. Will next Tuesday be all right?" And I remember tugging at her sleeve and reminding her it was *next week* we were leaving for Devon. Her face went pink with embarrassment. Then I realized with horror that she'd been lying because she couldn't pay. She didn't take my hand as we walked silently home together along Groby Road.

* * *

My father once told me about an ill-fated venture of Zaida's, which took the whole Cooklin family off to Canada to set up a farm. Perhaps Zaida was thinking of southern Russia, where fruit and vegetables grow easily. Perhaps it was a wish to live directly from the earth. Unfortunately, the land he was allocated by the Canadian government was close to Montreal, where snow and ice cover the ground for more than six months of the year. The family found themselves surrounded by distrustful Ukrainian Catholics, by no means delighted to discover a Jewish family in their midst. They were amused at Zaida's efforts rather than helpful. The whole enterprise was a financial disaster.

Dad, who was four when the family arrived in Canada, described some moments of sheer magic nevertheless: he liked to tell me how his mother threw boiling sugar out onto the snow, so that the sizzling liquid made a delicious brittle toffee. And he remembered looking up at the huge trees, which had to be cut and sent downriver as timber, and the awe their height inspired in him, even though he was felled by an errant branch of one of them.

His handwriting was clumsy, and usually sprawled all over the page – yet, after my mother died, he wrote me several letters from a two-week holiday in Israel, which were filled with childlike wonder. He had a genuine sense of the numinous. When I confronted him in my last years at school with evolution and astronomy, he was not so much assertive of his own beliefs as humbled. "What can we little human beings know of all that?" he said.

A poet friend, to whom I showed an early draft of this chapter, asked me: "What did your father actually *do*?" Not so easy to explain. He was trained as a cabinet maker and worked in the family business until he started his own. He was always boss of his own shop. The idea of a *career* as the Comptons understood the word was quite alien to him.

Dad liked what he did. He once made me a doll's house in which the small furniture was crafted with the same carefully made joints as real chairs and tables. His workshop in Clinton Street, however, rarely made use of such skills. There, he and his workmen made household objects such as kitchen chairs, breadboards or rolling pins.

His office was barely separated from the main area of the factory. I sometimes sat in it, impatiently, listening to the whine of circular saws and hating the smell of boiling glue – restlessly pushing about the wood shavings that covered the floor while he finished dealing with a problem. He liked to work at the bench alongside his workmen, though since he had to find the wages for them every week, in cash, what was made had to be sold. Selling was not what he enjoyed. He employed Mr C. for that. My mother thought he should look more closely into the expenses Mr C. claimed. Dad ridiculed the idea, saying they were a perk of the job.

CHAPTER 2

A Quiet War in Leicester

The war marked my way of seeing the world and my place in it for ever. When it began I was an eight-year-old tomboy stupidly excited by the drama of underground shelters, blackout curtains and the absence of streetlights. When it ended, I was a teenager with an after-school life of Saturday nights at the Palais de Danse, illicit cigarettes and delicious sexual games in parked cars. I also had a precocious, damaging knowledge of human cruelty, taken from newsreel footage of British tanks entering the camps: bones, bulldozers and emaciated children in striped pyjamas. So that's what it meant to be Jewish. Or, more exactly: that's what might have happened to me.

We were still in Groby Road in 1938. My father dug an Anderson shelter in the garden: a dank, unhealthy place, he decided. He was glad to leave it behind when, in early 1939, he struck a deal with a builder for a patch of land in Stoneygate, the smarter south side of the city, and there designed his own detached house on a corner of Elmsleigh Avenue. I remember the delight he took in walking round the foundations, looking at plans, then arranging for his workmen to put in wooden floors and solid-oak doors, the way he chose the colours of the walls to match the huge tiled fireplaces: russet-gold in the dining room, pale-lilac in the front sitting room.

It was a source of some irritation to him that, once we were there, I preferred to play in the patch of wild ground beyond our fence, where there were pear trees to climb and grass came up to my armpits. My younger cousins sometimes joined me in the games I invented. We made bows and arrows which we shot into the redcurrant bushes, or crawled on the ground like Indian trackers with dry powdery earth hurting our eyes.

I was still only eight on 3rd September 1939, but I picked up the urgency of my parents' attention as we listened to the radio together. I struggled to understand the words, though they sound readily enough in my ears now in the often repeated cadences of Chamberlain's voice. "I have to tell you no such assurance... This country is now at war with Germany." I remember my father's great sigh, which had a puzzling measure of relief in it, as though something hidden were at last out in the open.

The next day he arranged for heavy sandbags to be put around the wash house, which he fitted with bunks and electric light. This was sensible enough, unless there was a direct hit, but by now I understand him well enough to guess his other motives for building our refuge there. He did not want an ugly tin shelter to wreck the look of the garden, which had been landscaped to his plan: Victoria plum trees, a sunken lawn surrounded by a rockery; alpine shrubs with tiny flowers, pots of lavender on the terrace. He wouldn't want an Anderson shelter spoiling that.

Even before the outbreak of war there was air-raid practice in school, and when the alarm sounded we formed orderly lines and walked over the hockey pitch into concrete bunkers, all of us carrying satchels of goodies in case we were forced to stay in the shelters for a long time. I particularly relished the packets of Sun-Pat raisins my mother tucked into mine. Even now the taste of those fruity blobs evokes a memory of under-the-earth smells and a heart-pounding excitement which never became terror, because there were in fact no daylight raids on Leicester.

That first winter of the war nothing much seemed to be happening, but our domestic landscape changed radically. My parents took in two children: Ilse, from Breslau, a plump girl with round spectacles, a couple of years older than I was, and Stanley, much younger, evacuated from the East End of London. He was a pretty child and very polite. He did not talk much about his family, and I don't remember him getting letters from them, but he must have missed them. He went back to London, Blitz or no, a year or so after he arrived.

Ilse's father once owned the largest department store in Breslau, and had arranged for his two children to be sent abroad when he was taken into a concentration camp in late 1938. He was strangely fortunate in being held there for only a few months before he and his wife were able to take a boat to Chile. I had no idea then how unusual their escape was. Ilse's brother, Hans, went to Scotland to work on a left-wing commune as a farm labourer. When he came to visit Ilse, a couple of years into the War, I found him alarmingly well-read; he had plainly enjoyed a privileged education. He was eager to argue about politics, especially the evils of capitalists, among whom he included his own father. I resented him including mine among his villains, pointing out that Dad lived from the work of his hands as much as any worker. He sighed at my lack of comprehension.

Wartime changed Leicester into a cosmopolitan city. The provincial Jewish families of Leicester found European strangers living among them: German doctors and dentists who had retaken their exams after coming to England, entrepreneurs who arrived with valuable patents and set up factories, Viennese ladies living in shabby rooms who loved Mozart and Beethoven. In general, German refugees were far more cultured than the people they found themselves among, and were still very proud of being German, which local Jewish families found annoying.

Soon there were Canadian and Australian servicemen in the street alongside patriotic Poles and de Gaulle's Free French. In the last year of the war, there were wealthy Hungarian refugees, too, who had thought themselves altogether part of Budapest high society before the Arrow Cross began to investigate their Jewish ancestry. At the other extreme were market traders who had evacuated themselves from the East End to the safer Midlands – Leicester always had a huge and celebrated market in the centre of the town – their children were lively, fearless and not altogether respectable; they wore suits with padded shoulders and combed their hair into DA haircuts.

There had been some discussion in the first weeks of the war about sending me by ship to Canada in case the Germans invaded. My father was opposed to the idea, because there were submarines in the Atlantic, and when we heard that a ship had been sunk, with children aboard, that was decisive. I was pleased, because the thought of going so far away made me feel lonely, and I could not imagine a situation in which he could not protect me. We knew so little then.

Parents did not like to leave children behind when they went out for the evening, so on a Saturday all five of us went to Variety shows at the Palace Theatre in the centre of town: Murray and Mooney, Max Miller, naked women standing on plinths in beams of coloured light – art, my father explained – who were not allowed to move, but were legal as long as they stood perfectly still. Innocent days. At nine, I didn't really understand the jokes, but I can still remember the moonlight and the stars and the laughter on the long walk home up London Road.

Did my mother enjoy the entertainment? Certainly she expressed no disapproval. Still, most of the songs she sang to me had melancholy stories in them, like 'The Isle of Capri'. She was also very fond of Gilbert and Sullivan, and regaled me gleefully with songs from *The Mikado*.

> I've got a little list…
> And they'd none of them be missed.

We had a wind-up gramophone in an oak case, which held favourite records of current popular music. However, my father's eldest sister Eva, who lived in London, was gifted musically and had made sure all her four daughters played a musical instrument. One of them, Ruth Pearl, went on to become a classical violinist. During the first years of the war, she came to Leicester to play with the Reginald Jacques Quartet for ENSA. We went to listen to a concert: Mozart, Haydn and Schubert. I can't remember what I thought of it, except that it went on a long time.

A friend of Ruth, Miss Railton, happened to be teaching music at my grammar school, and my father set about arranging violin lessons for me. These were not a success. Any stringed instrument requires hours of dedicated practice, which I hated, and my parents hated even more. They wanted me to learn, but the sounds my playing produced were excruciating to them, so I was isolated farther and farther away, until it was possible for me to mutiny, put the violin down and quietly read a book. Miss Railton could hardly believe that any relation of Ruth could make such slow progress. I took Grade 3, played the *Messiah* in one school orchestra performance, then begged to be released.

The following year, when the wailing sound of the sirens began at night, I was suddenly very frightened. The bombs on Leicester were mainly dumped by German crews who had failed to find the munitions factories of Coventry, but they were still deadly, and someone we knew was killed in a raid nearby. My mother prepared thermos flasks of tea, and at first we went into the wash house and shivered there, obediently, half asleep, until the all-clear. A small electric fire was connected to a plug in the kitchen. After a time, we all began to sleep through, sirens or no, though I sometimes lay awake until I heard the all-clear.

Dad was too old to be conscripted as a soldier – though a cousin and an uncle were sent to Egypt, and another cousin by marriage fought as a pilot – and business boomed as Dad's machinery was converted to making wooden clothes pegs, for which there seemed suddenly to be an insatiable demand. This was because the industrial manufacture of plastic was useful to the war effort.

We read about the progress of the war and listened to the news with anxiety, though Dad was never in any doubt England would win. When France fell, he declared that country had always been a *kurova*, a rude Yiddish word for prostitute. Even when the war seemed to be turning ineluctably against the Allies in North Africa, he still persisted proudly: "The English always win the last battle."

One day in June 1940, Zaida – who had come to stay on a sofa-bed in our front room for a few weeks – walked up the stairs with the *News Chronicle* in his hands to tell me that Hitler had invaded Russia. His face radiated delight. "God has *fertummelt der kopfs* (muddled up their heads). The two monsters will destroy one another," he announced. I objected strongly to him comparing Hitler to Stalin, whose noble Communist ideals had been explained to me by Miss Adams, my new English teacher.

He sighed. "It's all the same, Elainela."

"But it isn't," I argued crossly.

"It was all part of Stalin's *plan*," Miss Adams explained a day later. "The pact with Hitler was a trick to give Stalin time to build tanks and planes."

But the German army pushed deep into Russia nevertheless, and it looked as if they were both wrong.

Once America entered the war, my father began to bring back loose-limbed, casual young soldiers who turned out to be Jewish to eat with us on a Friday night. The young men enjoyed my mother's cooking and sometimes brought presents from their stores for her. It became apparent that American soldiers had very different rations from English servicemen or the rest of us. I was not surprised. In those years, everything about America was glamorous. I kept my radio tuned to AFN even while doing my homework, enjoying the relaxed voices of the presenters as much as the music. I read Raymond Chandler and used to daydream of becoming an elegant woman in his dark world.

When was it I began to spend all my Saturday nights at the Palais de Danse? I cannot have been more than fourteen, but I have no memory of my father voicing any objections, though he must have known it was a place of shivery sexual excitement. I went with a crowd of friends on a tram on dark winter evenings. Not with friends from school, but children of my parents' friends, the ones who came round to play poker on a Saturday evening and brought their family with them. Looking back now, I am surprised my mother did not protest.

I remember standing with a row of girls combing my hair in front of a mirror. I can still smell the powder and the pancake, and see the breasts that stuck out like pencil points underneath close-fitting jumpers. Everyone wore heavy red lipstick and thickened their delicate skins to look older for the Yanks, meeting one another's eyes in the lacklustre glass with a haughty blankness learnt from photographs in fashion magazines.

How I envied them, those girls whose hair hung down each side of their faces so fashionably. I could never assume their expression of arrogance, however hard I tried. My boneless face changed expression with every thought I had. My eyes were too large. My mouth was twenty different shapes. And in repose? It was never in repose. My own hair was a dark-brown bush. There was a lot of it, but it was too fine and flopped in curls all over my face. For all that, I was never a wallflower. I was an athletic dancer, and I knew how to match my feet neatly to the rhythm as an American arm threw me out and pulled me back.

In this after-school life the people I most wanted to like me cared only about clothes, gambling and sex. The girls I knew best were children of my parents' friends. One was the daughter of a famous publican who promoted boxing matches. Another went to the Wyggeston with me: a pretty girl with an enviably tiny waist. We shared intimate sexual secrets, humour and hypochondria. The boys we liked most were the confident children of market traders who did not go to good schools.

Sexual games in those far-off days of the Forties were frustrating for boys, but oddly pleasurable for girls, though we naturally feared to become pregnant. Our boyfriends' own needs taught them all manner of subtle fingering more conducive to women's pleasure than the direct encounters of later generations, who could take reliable contraception for granted.

The first boy I saw regularly was a Londoner from the East End, with broad Slav cheekbones and a lovely smile. He was quick-witted, though he had little education. When he went into the Air Force, I took up with a fair-haired, very slender young man much older than I was, who worked in his father's firm but aspired to the Variety stage and indeed found a place on it after we parted.

When I look back at photos of my adolescent face, I no longer dislike it as I once did. At the time, I longed to erase the laughter lines, which ran from nose to mouth. Now what I see is the absence of anything sly or malicious or hidden – though, in fact, there *was* something important I was hiding: a secret ambition I never attempted to bring into my after-school life and which none of my friends shared.

My first poems were made up as I bounced a tennis ball in Groby Road, and then against our garage doors in Elmsleigh Avenue. I showed one to my form teacher in the junior school and she puzzled over my handwriting until I took the book back and said, "It's a *poem*. It sounds like this."

The excitement of seeing that poem in the school magazine hooked me for life in an addiction as dangerous as any other. I was soon sitting up and reading poetry aloud by the one-bar heater in my bedroom wall. While other girls dreamt of princes or Hollywood stars, I dreamt of dead poets.

My first novel was written when I was about twelve on plain paper. I remember securing the pages together with my mother's stapler. I can't remember the story, but when my mother was curious, I let her read it. She expressed some dismay at the title – *The Gatecrashers* – and wanted me to understand that a gatecrasher was a very bad thing to be: the word meant pushing into a party when no one had invited you. I was impatient with her criticism. To break into some other and more exciting world was exactly what I wanted.

I was not a very dutiful school pupil, and was often in trouble, sometimes sent to the headmistress for not having gym shoes or forgetting my homework. I daydreamt in class and sometimes scribbled my own thoughts when I should have been taking notes. Examinations suited me much more than course work.

Some time, as I went through Wyggeston Grammar School, Miss Adams sent my poems to a friend of hers – L.A.G. Strong, then a well-known novelist and poet – and his response convinced her that, for all my erratic behaviour, my talent deserved encouragement. An early story about a ship in a bottle won a prize open to the whole school, and Miss Adams began to include me in a group of girls in whom she placed particular hope. None of her band of favourite girls was without ambition. One was an aspirant actress, another a lovely girl with hazel eyes who wrote about wildlife in the Norfolk sands at Blakeney Point. They became my first literary friends.

With this new set of intimates I cycled into the countryside at weekends. We lay on the grass, stared up at the sky and wondered how it was possible to imagine either infinite space or any end to it. We talked about God too, a topic I rarely considered in those days, although my father liked my mother and me to go to the synagogue on a Saturday. Somehow, God did not seem to live there. I found it very boring up in the women's gallery, and spent most of the service staring over the brass bars at handsome male cousins.

What I remember most vividly was standing on the steps outside. Children who had not lost their parents had to withdraw from the service during *Yizkor*, the prayer for the dead. Some frolicked together, without inhibition. Some went round the corner for a smoke. In my formal coat and hat I longed to join in.

Two of my cousins held aloof from all this. One was bookish and quite brilliant, though he found himself called on to take over the family wood shop when his father fell ill and was trapped there. For a time he was engaged to an elegant girl who could sing and play the piano at the same time, the way movie stars did in films. His mother disapproved of her profoundly, and urged him to find someone more suitable. He never married, but he had some remarkably interesting girlfriends thereafter, and although he continued to live at home, I remember being shown a flat in Charles Street where he could lead a life of his own.

VE Day felt like the end of the war and was celebrated with street parties all over England, but what I remember best are the conga chains in the centre of town, the wild kissing of complete strangers, the sense that real life could at last begin. The war in the Far East, however, continued. There were men still dying in brutal Japanese prisoner-of-war camps, but I don't think I knew about that.

When victory over Japan came, we were away in the north, staying for a week in my Aunt Annie's hospital near Durham. It was a surprisingly enjoyable holiday. There were tennis courts, and Annie was a tough opponent.

As matron, she was an imposing figure. Nurses scuttled about as she approached. Even my father was a little muted in her presence – and once, when my parents took an afternoon nap, she told me about her years in France. I decided she had enjoyed a far more interesting life than my mother, and said so. She was delighted by my interest, and after her retirement became an indulgent friend, putting me up in her Blackheath flat whenever I needed a place to stay in London.

During that holiday, my father and I walked down to the local shop to buy a newspaper. The bomb on Hiroshima was a huge headline in all of them. Nobody could explain to me what it meant to harness the power of the sun, but one thing was clear: the war was over.

* * *

I always preferred the dramatic life I found in books to my own safe home, and perhaps such ingratitude deserved punishment. Things certainly began to change soon after the war ended – and not for the better. The domestic comfort I had taken so foolishly for granted began to crumble around me.

Looking back now, I can see how inevitably the disaster unfolded. When the lease on my father's factory in Clinton Street expired, he was sent a huge bill for dilapidations which he indignantly refused to pay. The rent remained low, however, and a more calculating man would have seen the advantages of negotiation. Instead, he confidently bought a plot of land on the south side of Leicester, where there was planning permission for new factories. Once again there were drawings to pore over, foundations to tramp around and euphoria. Unfortunately, it soon became clear that my father's architect had seriously misjudged the cost of the building. Moreover, everything took far longer than he promised, and my father's capital began to melt away. Even when the machinery was in place, problems continued. Import restrictions were beginning to be lifted, and the Czechs made far cheaper bentwood chairs than we could. First the factory had to be sold – then, most unhappily, our home in Elmsleigh Avenue.

When I first read Thomas Hardy's *The Mayor of Casterbridge* just before taking the examinations for Higher School Certificate, I immediately recognized my father in Henchard – not as drunk or surly, but as a stubborn man who made decisions based on emotion rather than reason. I cried when Henchard's planned feast was ruined by rain, as if my own father had suffered the disappointment. And Farfrae was the epitome of all the virtues of my mother's family: he was clever and calculating, perhaps cold too, but with a quicksilver gaiety of his own.

All my childhood I had a recurrent nightmare. In it, my father was gallantly fighting off a man with a shiny knife, holding the blade away from his throat, with one big hand securing the man's wrist. But the man with the knife was stronger. I always awoke screaming before the blade reached my father's neck, but the terror of it remained with me.

Astonishingly, my father didn't go under when he lost his factory. I marvelled at his spirit. Money, he conveyed to me, came and went inexplicably, and shouldn't be taken too seriously. He still had a cabinet maker's skill in his hands. My mother too seemed surprisingly sanguine, though she must have felt the loss of our home more than she let me see. If she was afraid for our future, she didn't show it. "Your father will think of something," she said. And indeed, after one false start in the import-export business, so he did. He set up a workshop for converting large tables into others that would fold up and take less room in a small house. He muttered sometimes about the lovely solid oak he had to mutilate, but soon he was laughing again, mocking his own sales patter:

"Fix your table, lady?"

Just a few weeks ago one of my Leicester cousins, a retired GP now living in London, told me that the Leicester Synagogue I remembered from my childhood was being sold, and that they were also seeking buyers for the Communal Hall, which my father had arranged to purchase for the community in his prosperous years. As I remembered that he had laid the foundation stone, I felt something of a pang. When the Hall was opened, a plaque had been put into the wall to thank him.

The neighbourhood is now largely Asian; the dwindling Jewish population has moved away to London. For the most part, the immigrants from the sub-continent are colourfully dressed Hindus and Sikhs, but Muslims are likely to take over the synagogue itself. It was a very pretty building as I remember it, with a small cupola, then painted green inside. The Communal Hall holds more of my post-war adolescence: Maccabi, ping-pong, vinyl records, melodies from old musicals and my father, then a powerful figure who was still able to make things happen.

* * *

Ilse continued to live with us until there was a boat to take her across the Atlantic. She left some time in 1947, before we had to sell Elmsleigh Avenue. I think now I was never friendly enough to her, though we sometimes cuddled in the same bed. Her English improved, but she had no interest in books, and left Sir Jonathan North Secondary Modern School as soon as it was legal to do so. She seemed positively to enjoy clearing tables, putting cups back in their appointed places or getting up early to set fires. My mother, who would have been very happy to have a much larger family, poured so much affection over her that I became quite jealous.

Ilse continued to write letters to us all for many years after she had returned to her parents in Chile. She sent us photographs both of her wedding and her young children. Sometimes I wrote back to her, guiltily, but, lost in my own changing life, less and less frequently. Her own letters stopped gradually.

News began to seep out about the harsh conditions suffered by displaced persons in their European holding camps. Nearly all were malnourished, many dying. Nobody wanted them. Many had spent the war in fear for their lives, hidden or imprisoned, often grieving for murdered relatives. They were understandably reluctant to be repatriated to their old homelands, but refugee quotas to the countries of Western Europe were deliberately restricted. Most were Jews, but Latvians, Lithuanians and Poles were equally reluctant to find themselves under Soviet rule.

What preoccupied the Foreign Office most, however, were the numbers of Jewish displaced persons who wanted to make a life in Palestine. It was a shock to find out they were prevented from doing so by our own British Navy. Had we not elected an honourable Labour government? My father told me grimly that Ernest Bevin himself had announced a White Paper in November 1945 expressly designed to prevent any further immigration.

I was sixteen and found it difficult to accept the simple explanation: Britain was a colonial power whose vast Empire was beginning to wobble. In spite of the old Balfour declaration of approval for a national home for the Jews, the British had no wish to unsettle the Arab inhabitants of Palestine, still less those in surrounding Arab countries. The good will of Arabs in the Middle East was essential to secure British supply lines, especially to India. There were other factors, naturally. There was a long history of English sympathy for a romantic vision of Arab life since the days of

T.E. Lawrence, especially in the Foreign Office. Two years after the end of the war, 850,000 displaced persons were still huddled in camps.

Looking back now, I am chiefly amazed by my innocence. The family belief in British decency had been confirmed by war-time heroism, Churchill's oratory, a daily reading of the *News Chronicle* and sheer ignorance about events in the British mandate of Palestine. But 1946 and 1947 were dramatic years in the life of that little strip of land at the edge of the eastern Mediterranean.

All through my childhood a blue-and-white tin with the map of Palestine drawn over it stood on my parents' sideboard. My parents dropped spare change into it. We had several such charity boxes: one for orphan children, another for the Red Cross. We had no wish to go and live in Palestine ourselves. We were British, and had no need to do so.

An ex-serviceman friend – not, I think, Jewish (though he later went on to fight for the newly formed State of Israel) – told me, there was a Jewish underground which charted old boats to bring DPs willing to take the risk of sailing through the British blockade. Haganah was the acceptable face of this paramilitary, underground group, while Irgun Zvai Leumi was a far more ruthless organization which blew up civilian buildings in protest at British actions.

My friend, the novelist Aharon Appelfeld, was brought to Palestine as an orphan on one of Haganah's boats; he had survived in the forest with the help of strangers from the age of eight. He kissed the ground of Palestine when he arrived. Others were less fortunate. The British Navy turned them back, and some of their rickety boats sank.

When the news began to trickle out about these miserable events, I was at first simply indignant. Then the situation became more confusing. On 12th July 1946 the Irgun kidnapped two British soldiers off-duty in Netanya and held them as hostages against the lives of three captured Irgun fighters in Akko prison. On 29th July those Jewish captives were executed. The next day, the two

British NCOs were hanged from a tree in an orange grove outside Netanya.

English newspapers were filled with the story and photographs of the murdered sergeants. In Britain, over a period of about four days, synagogues and Jewish-owned properties were attacked by mobs in Liverpool, Manchester, Glasgow and Brighton. In Palestine, the British Army went on the rampage.

The sixth form of Wyggeston Grammar School naturally took up the issue. Many of the girls had brothers serving abroad, and to them the situation seemed totally clear-cut. As the only Jewish girl in the class I felt I had a duty to explain that survivors of Hitler's camps were understandably reluctant to return to homelands which had collaborated with the Nazis, that no one wanted them in the West, and that it was natural for them to dream of Palestine. The girls listened, unconvinced, but without any obvious hostility. The civilized tone of that debate consoles me for much that has happened since.

* * *

In 1947, I remember being part of a group of friends who planned to heckle a meeting of Colin Jordan in Charles Street near Leicester's Clock Tower. Jordan was already a name on the right for his unashamed admiration of Hitler. My boyfriend was on leave from the RAF, and had arranged to meet a group of ex-servicemen who had come down from London to express their opposition to Jordan's politics. He was a tailor's apprentice, born in the East End, and Jewish himself, which perhaps explains why my father approved of him but not why he allowed me so much freedom. I think with one part of his brain he always treated me as the son he never had.

I remember shaking with adrenalin as our little group stood where the meeting had gathered. I can still see the Clock Tower, the streetlights, the sparks from the trams. The crowd was large and enthusiastic, which I found surprising. Hadn't we all been fighting Hitler and fascism together? But the anger of the first speaker had nothing to do with Hitler. His passion was directed against the dismantling of the British Empire. The Jews came into it only because boatloads of them were trying to take refuge on British territory. He was not in the least concerned, I have to say, with the rights of the indigenous Arab population, whom he distrusted and disliked equally. His point – and the crowd cheered him wildly – was that the English had won the war and did not deserve to lose their colonies.

I don't think Jordan ever showed up at the meeting. Our heckling was drowned in the roar of approval around us. After a while shouts died down, and the crowd moved on before the pubs closed. There were no police that I could see. There were not many of us, and we were lucky not to get our heads kicked in.

CHAPTER 3

Dreaming of Elsewhere

My headmistress – a disapproving beak of a woman – warned me not to set my heart on going to Cambridge, as no one from the school aspiring to read English had ever succeeded in getting in. Scientists, yes. Classicists, perhaps. Even, sometimes, a historian. But not to read English. So I was not optimistic about my chances as I took the entrance examination. Indeed, even when I was summoned by Newnham for an interview, I was far from hopeful. There were only two colleges in Cambridge open to girls in those days.

Eating in Clough Hall, Newnham College, a week later, alongside girls who wore no makeup and seemed altogether at ease with one another, my confidence was further diminished. Could this possibly be my world? After dinner, I retreated to my allotted room, which was shabby, cold and scary; the rain on my window kept me awake like the tap of fingernails. Before my interview the next morning, I was sleepless and wretched and had several fresh spots on my cheek.

Two women dons were waiting for me. I remember Miss Welsford best. She was a short woman, with square shoulders and girlish features, and she sat on a floral, loose-covered armchair with both her legs tucked underneath her. She asked me whether I knew that my literature paper had been my best.

I didn't, and said so. On the contrary, I still felt unhappy about it. When I confessed to Miss Adams that I had chosen to write on Milton – about whom I had received no tuition whatsoever – she shook her head over my perversity. What did I know about seventeenth-century poetry or politics? It was a whim, of course; I had just read *Paradise Lost* and was excited by the roll of the Miltonic lines, the defiance of the fallen angel Lucifer and the way the animals bounded out of the earth at their creation. "I hoped you would write about Keats," Miss Adams said glumly.

"Who are your favourite poets?" Miss Welsford asked me.

"Gerald Manley Hopkins," I began and then hesitated, remembering the dismissive comments about Romantic poetry overheard at breakfast. "And John Keats," I confessed reluctantly, adding, "I know he's not exactly…"

"If you don't like Keats now," she said, amused, "I don't know when you will. Tell me. How would you convince readers that Hopkins was a great poet?"

I had to think about that.

"Maybe I would get them to listen to his poems read aloud," I said, eventually. And then I tried in a rush to explain the lyric daze induced by repeated words in 'The Golden Echo and Leaden Echo'. It was a completely unprepared account, and I flushed miserably as my voice faltered to the end of it.

On the train home I was still embarrassed by the kindness with which I was soon afterwards dismissed. There were other interviews, but I can't remember them. Rain lashed the train windows. Hollows in the fields were flooded. Resolutely, I put the failure out of my mind. A London college was a perfectly good option. When I told Miss Adams my story, she thought I might prefer it, though she did not say why.

When the telegram came to tell me I had won an exhibition to Newnham, I could not at first be found, because I was hiding in the school washroom to avoid a freezing hockey pitch. Indeed, when I heard my name called out several times, I considered remaining in the cubicle. Then I emerged sheepishly in case something was seriously wrong. I still remember my incredulity, then the elation and, almost at once, a puzzling half-thought: Cambridge will be my escape. But escape from what, exactly? Mine had not been an unhappy childhood.

My mother had her own ideas about what I needed, of course. She sometimes took me along to meet friends in Ratcliffe Road with whom she liked to play bridge. I was restive and bored there. She once gave me a book she had loved as a child: Sarah Tytler's *Queen Charlotte's Maidens*, but I don't think I ever read it through. I had never placed myself on the class ladder with the shrewdness of Larkin and Amis, or I might have thought of raising my position on it. Most of my life I had lived in a detached house at the corner of Elmsleigh Avenue, with an oak staircase, huge tiled fireplaces and a Welsh girl to keep it clean. I had no sense of underprivilege.

Even so, I had occasional hints of a larger and bolder world. A friend I came to know only because as a Roman Catholic she was excused from attending prayers as I was lived in a huge house with an untidy garden in a street of old trees. I was mainly astonished by the number of dogs there. In spite of the size of the house, I did not think of her as wealthy, because the furniture was so shabby; I could hear my father's voice saying, "I wouldn't give it house-room." Yet I remember her speculating whether she might have to "come out" when her parents returned from India. Were they a military family? She often made fun of their attachment to the Raj. We laughed together easily, without my quite understanding how remote from her usual circle I was. I never met her parents, but I guess they would have found me as totally alien as a group of Angela Thirkell's villagers encountering a hapless Central European refugee.

I did not in the least envy her the society she might enter, because my own ambitions were quite other. My daydreams centred on a table at La Coupole. Or a dive in 42nd Street. Writers and jazz musicians inhabited the world I thought of as glamorous, and I had not the least idea the doors of it could be opened by anything other than talent.

Fortunately for me, I was arriving in Cambridge at a particularly propitious time. Before the war, even if admitted, I would have known myself as much an outsider as Amy Levy, the precocious Jewish poet, who was a Newnham undergraduate in the 1870s. I doubt if that instinctive prejudice altogether disappeared after the Second World War, but it was never voiced in my hearing, and in

1949 I did not even recognize the invisible snobberies of the English class system. Gatecrashers in the gardens of privilege like myself received the same deference from college porters

Most colleges after the war made an effort to widen their intake with students from state schools. And in 1949 I was far from being the only Jewish student at Newnham reading English. The major scholar of my year was Audrey Harris. And in the ancient colleges, undergraduates were no longer boys straight from public schools. Many were ex-servicemen in their early twenties who had fought in the Far East, or Americans who had driven tanks under Patton. There were Fulbright Scholars, too, and Bevin Boys who had gone down the mines. I was not as exotic as I would have been ten years earlier.

Cambridge in 1949 was an enchanted city. There were cows on Midsummer Common as we walked through to lectures in Mill Lane, a golden light on the Wren library, walls as yellow as Florence, and a whole landscape smelling of leaf dust. Heffers bookshop on Petty Cury had knobbly glass windows bending forward over a cobbled street. The shop gave out free wall calendars and maroon leather diaries to every member of the University – limitless credit, too, which I soon enjoyed recklessly. A British Restaurant from wartime years, still run by the WVS, stood on the first floor at the other end of the street. On the upper floors were rooms to let with a dubious reputation. A few years later Ted Hughes stayed there for a time in the early days of his relationship with Sylvia Plath.

When my parents first delivered me to Newnham with my baggage I was jubilant rather than apprehensive. Perhaps I felt a twinge of unease as we met Miss Robertson, the tutor of Old Hall, in the corridor. She greeted my father in a voice whose vowels I had never heard except in a theatre. I suddenly became conscious of my father's own speech, which retained a Scouse lilt. Still, hands were shaken with perfect dignity, my parents were welcomed to sherry in a high-windowed room overlooking the gardens, and if they felt troubled in her presence they gave no sign of it.

I could not fail to be aware soon enough that I was stepping into an Englishness which went back into the thirteenth century, though Newnham itself had only been founded in the nineteenth. It was a world in which there was little concession to comfort, perhaps rather like a boarding school. My own room was on the ground floor, close to the Hall, where meals were served. The shared washing facilities just across the corridor were unheated. There was nowhere to hang clothes, and only an oak coffin to hold my jumpers and underwear. There was a grate to make a fire and a scuttle for collecting coal. We were expected to make our own fires. I welcomed all this, as a sign I was entering a completely new life.

Loyal bedders looked after men's college rooms and washed up their dishes. Newnham undergraduates were given no such help. In Old Hall, we had an unhappy middle-aged Lithuanian refugee who was responsible for clearing the ashes from the grate, but not for bringing in fresh coal and wood. Mainly, she needed to talk. She complained bitterly of the Russian occupation. I was not yet ready to be sympathetic to her description of Communists as oppressors – Miss Adams's voice still commented within me – and I secretly thought she had probably been a Nazi sympathizer.

Christianity was everywhere: in the music, the churches and the minds of most students of the Humanities. English Literature of the past, in particular, transported all of us into a world centred on a Christian God. In our first week we had to write an essay on John Donne, and even as I devoured his love poetry, I absorbed his blackest fears; his thoughts about the inevitability of death filled me with terror. I shivered, reading Donne's 'Hymn to God the Father', and longed for that reassurance in the last verse so altogether denied to me.

> I have a sin of fear that when I have spun
> My last thread I shall perish on the shore.
> Swear by your self that at my death your Son
> Shall shine as he shines now and heretofore.

When thou hast done that, thou hast done
I fear no more.

Soon afterwards, Bunyan's *Grace Abounding to the Chief of Sinners* brought me to wonder, with a great knock of horror, where I stood myself. I began to look into the New Testament. Most dons were believers, especially visiting lecturers like C.S. Lewis, who later moved from Oxford to become a Professor of Medieval Literature. And, most persuasively of all, there was T.S. Eliot. Mine is not a temptation likely to be felt by any student living in the secular twenty-first century. But in 1949 I entered a world where belief was the norm.

My thoughts felt altogether treacherous – much more disloyal than Uncle Frank's amused scepticism about Jewish rituals or Uncle Maurice's dislike of a God who was so casual about human pain. If I succumbed, I would be joining the very culture which had murdered my people for their faith from the Spanish Inquisition onwards. When I went home on my first vacation I confessed the attraction guiltily.

My father was more bewildered than angry once he had checked that there was no romance involved. Zaida was in Manchester, and never very good over the phone anyway, so he invited our local Rabbi to speak to me. Sadly, Rabbi T., though a good-hearted man, was a refugee from the Czech Tatra mountains. His appointment to the synagogue had been based on the sincerity of his orthodoxy rather than his ability to reason with adolescents. He knew nothing of the literature that troubled me. Only snatches of our conversation remain in my memory.

"Did you know that Lord George Gordon converted to Judaism in 1787?" he asked me at some point.

I could not see the relevance of this. I wanted to know what Judaism said about damnation. He blinked, before explaining that there was no such concept in Judaism, only *Gehinnom*, a much more shadowy possibility. He didn't think there was a very firm promise of heaven either. I brought out an Orthodox Singer's prayer book, which I had consulted since coming home. He had to agree that the life to come was often mentioned in it, but he thought Judaism had borrowed the concept from Christianity in the Middle Ages.

"So what does happen after death? In your opinion?" I demanded, as if he could speak for the endlessly argumentative rabbis down the ages.

"Who knows?" he replied.

And he shrugged.

Without any intention to do so, those two simple words – or was it the shrug? – were reassuring. He had seen a lot of death, had Rabbi T. He didn't know what awaited us beyond, but neither did Bunyan. Nor did sweet-voiced poets like George Herbert. Nor, I thought flinching, did Jesus Christ himself.

Returning to Newnham, I tried out some version of this last thought on Jilly, the prettiest girl in Old Hall, who was a firm believer. She was appalled at the blasphemy. What about the stone rolled away from the entrance to the cave? How about the people who saw Christ when he was risen? And the martyrs through the ages? Did I really think they were all liars? I realized in that moment that it was impossible to argue with stories. But I must have continued to be troubled even in my third year, working on the Tragedy paper with Miss Welsford. I remember maintaining that there could be no tragedy in a Christian universe, since everything is put right after death. *One short sleep past, we wake eternally.*

* * *

A set of witty and frivolous young men, who could play at being Sebastian Flyte, centred on King's College. It was not a circle I entered. Once, walking along King's Parade with my friend Michael Podro, we passed close enough to hear the high-camp voices and delighted laughter of Mark Boxer and his admirers. I remember making fun of Boxer's green velvet jacket and his air of *fin de siècle* decadence. However, Michael had been at Berkhamsted School with Boxer and liked him.

"Is he homosexual?" I asked, not without a certain excitement.

Michael said. "It's fashionable in that set to look as if you might be, whether you are or not."

I thought they must then be rather silly.

Michael patiently explained. "Mark likes to belong to a circle of people who enjoy power and influence in English life. He told me long ago it was the only interesting place to be."

I remember the conversation, but I can't recall what I thought about it. I knew E.M. Forster was still in residence at King's, and that Dadie Rylands and Noel Annan had been friends with the Bloomsbury Group. A year or so later, Boxer was rusticated for publishing a blasphemous poem while Editor of *Granta*, and might well have been sent down altogether without powerful friends in college. But I don't think I translated even that knowledge into a web of London connections. Michael's own father was a scholar of many languages, who had worked on several books with Robert Graves, and, as a personable young man, Michael had already discovered circles of his own.

He had come up a year later than I did, so I thought of him as much younger, though in fact there were only a few months between us. He had a long aquiline face, with a high forehead and humorous lines running down his cheeks. He dressed with a careful attention to colour and texture. He was immensely clever and knowledgeable, but inclined to idiosyncratic obsessions. I remember his allegorical reading of *Measure for Measure* held him in thrall for a whole term, and he could not help explaining his insights in sentences of such complex syntax his listeners became impatient. He was formidably articulate, but I was never afraid to argue with him, largely because I had done so much better than he did in Part 1 of the Tripos. His complexity served him ill in examinations then, but later in life, when he moved into Art History under Gombrich, it brought him First Class Honours and eventually a chair. He had already painted a remarkable portrait of himself, which hung on the wall of his rooms on Jesus Lane, so I was not surprised to find him turning to Art History after his English degree. Nor was it his only painting which showed talent.

In May 2011, travelling back from a friend's eightieth-birthday party in Lewes with Michael's widow, Charlotte, I enquired what had happened to that painting, with an impulsive thought of buying it. She told me that Michael had destroyed it in the last months before his death. He had not told her why.

I wondered about that. On the walls of his lovely house in Swiss Cottage he had several Auerbach paintings and drawings of great value. He would not want his adolescent work to hang alongside them. Or perhaps he did not like *any* images of himself? There is a famous depiction of him asleep on a train in a painting by R.B. Kitaj, *The Jewish Rider,* which Michael hated, as he once told me, perhaps because he felt it undignified to be caught dozing. Or perhaps he found the echo of the Holocaust painful. For all his Sephardic name, he was as much an Ashkenazi Jew as I am.

At Downing, he attended seminars of F.R. Leavis and could do an excellent imitation of his adenoidal voice and overpowering certainties. Leavis and his wife Queenie devoted their lives to setting the standards by which serious writing ought to be judged and were contemptuous of King's College's literary pretensions and social exclusiveness. We were advised in Newnham not to fall under the spell of F.R. Leavis, however impressed we might be. I went to his seminars nevertheless. In those days, Leavis had worldwide influence through his critical magazine *Scrutiny*, but the English Faculty disapproved of him.

Each week I was supervised with Audrey Harris, the major scholar in English of our year. Audrey was a shy girl with thick black hair, a low voice and a formidable brain. Her parents were observant Jews, but very different socially from mine. Her father, a senior civil servant, worked for Inland Revenue, and the family had been evacuated to Colwyn Bay during the war; her mother, a tiny, bustling woman, fussed over Audrey devotedly. Audrey was now their only child: her brother had died young. Some of Audrey's fears – notably an anxiety that she could bring harm to someone by wishing for it – may well go back to that calamity. Like his wife, Mr Harris was short and neatly dressed. The two of them travelled up by car every fortnight to bring boxes of goodies to their daughter. Food was austere at Newnham in those days. Meat was still rationed, and dinner often no more than scrambled eggs and peas. The Harrises brought tinned food, and their own ration of sweets. Their gifts, more surprisingly, also included copies of magazines such as *Woman* and *Woman's Own*, which Audrey read avidly: even the astrology columns interested her. Everyone teased her about this – including, I fear, myself. In her own quiet way she took no notice of us. She read anthologies too, I remember, which we were discouraged from doing: we were not supposed to come at poets only through their most popular work.

Audrey and I had many faults in common. As spoilt only children, we were unused to looking after ourselves, and our rooms were the most sluttish in the college. Also we were hypochondriac, superstitious and determined to make our mark. Both of us published in *Granta* in our first year: my contribution a short story based on a deal with Lucifer, hers a witty poem of which I can still remember the first lines:

> The gin ran out at twenty-five to two
> Drunk by some men we didn't know we knew.

Both of us began writing a novel in our second year. Audrey set hers in a ballet company. I insisted that writers had to write from direct experience, but she ignored the criticism. Mine was set among the market boys of Leicester – an uncultured, lively bunch of adolescents living on their wits with a fund of jokes and insults, who had to get up in the dark to buy the produce they laid out every morning. They were based rather loosely on Londoners I knew from my adolescence at the Palais, so I had the voices right, though of course I was inventing a world I had entered as little as Audrey had a ballet school. My plot turned on an innocent youngster who was shopped to the police over clothing coupons.

Writing my novel became a curiously companionable activity. The story seemed to write itself, and friends used to drop by to read the pages as I finished them. I didn't feel at all secretive about it. After all, wasn't I planning to publish? I'd written to Heinemann and Macmillan, who encouraged me to go ahead. I wrote on a little Olivetti typewriter, and the tale was so absorbing, it displaced for a time the enthusiasm I put into my weekly essay.

I told two friends at St Catharine's about my novel, one a handsome boy from Birmingham who had taken a First in English Prelims. He took some pleasure in ridiculing my folly. I had met them both the year before I went up – in fact, in the company of a Leicester friend who was, I think, showing them off to me. I fell instantly in love with the one who gibed. And when I went boldly round to call on him in my first term I still found him immensely attractive, even though he was much beset with sin and Catholicism. This sounded exciting, though he scornfully explained that although the English thought that *sin* meant sex, in fact it was a state of being. He dismissed my novel unseen. Nothing written so quickly could be any good.

I sent if off happily enough, nevertheless, and hoped I had left myself enough time to work for the Tripos. The MS was returned to me just after I had taken the examinations. Neither publisher accepted it, though Macmillan bothered to say that the dialogue was good. With a stupidity I was often to repeat when disappointed, I burned the thin, many-times-corrected pages one by one in the grate. It is an act I've sometimes regretted. I am not sure Audrey finished her early novel, but those she wrote later in life drew directly on her own experience.

Audrey took a Double First and married John Laski, a Trinity mathematician and brother of Marghanita Laski, the novelist, celebrated as a TV panellist on *What's my Line?* John had, he admitted cheerfully, a physical resemblance to Lytton Strachey, and an equally high-pitched voice. He once explained to me that it was part of the marital deal that he should rescue Audrey from the constraints of her parents. She certainly changed under his direction. She began to wear high-fashion clothes and to speak with great assurance. I thought him something of a bully, however, as I listened to him instructing her to sit up straight, as Touchstone did in *As You Like It*.

Audrey played Hecuba in my Newnham College production of *Trojan Women,* which I directed in my third year, concentrating on the brilliant dramatic interludes, while Alix Lee rehearsed the choruses, arranging the girls in poses reminiscent of dancers on a Grecian urn. Probably Audrey was the only girl in the cast thoroughly to enter her part. She could have been a marvellous actor, and it seemed natural that she went on to teach drama at the Central School, where Dawn French and Jennifer Saunders were among her pupils. What she really wanted, however, was to be taken seriously as a writer. And so she should have been. John told me that she was not valued highly because she made writing look too easy. She published five elegant novels, nevertheless, notably *Night Music*, in which she craftily explored John's character through the nightmares of a central figure who takes an experimental LSD trip.

When I saw Audrey in hospital, just before she died in 2002, she reminded me of an occasion when I tried to help her lose her shyness. Somehow it had become part of the legend she invented around me. She told me that I had once recommended her going to the Copper Kettle on the King's Parade and waiting for a nice young man to begin a conversation. There were, after all, ten men to every woman in the University, and a pretty girl sitting alone must attract some attention. I promised to follow along half an hour afterwards to rescue her if it was necessary. Or at least that is what she told me I said. I have absolutely no memory of this incident and remain appalled to hear of my own arrogance.

In Old Hall I made friends with two very different girls. Peggy was from Yorkshire. She had large sea-blue eyes, an upturned nose and a superb shape. She had been brought up by her mother alone, with little money to spare, so she had to work on the buses or the Post Office during the vacations – unusual then, though my grandchildren may do as much now. What we had in common were a street sophistication, a love of popular music and the Rex, an off-limits dance hall where we could dance with a few remaining Americans from the nearby base.

She puzzled me, nevertheless, because although very intelligent, she seemingly had no wish to achieve anything: she just wanted an exciting life. The night she first slept with the Editor of *Granta*, she came into my room late to tell me about it. I was not too pleased to be shaken awake, but when she told me the news I sat upright. She said it was very tiring – and no, she hadn't had an orgasm – but it was wonderful and she would certainly do it again.

After we were both living in London she continued to have interesting boyfriends. One of them gave her Kingsley Amis's *Lucky Jim* before publication, and she pressed it into my hands. What she particularly liked in the central figure of that novel was a clue to her whole being. I remember her saying, "He doesn't pretend to care about Mozart and culture. Just drink and sex." She found the lack of pretension likeable, but it was more than that. She relished the rejection of ambition.

My other close friend, Jill, was an outdoor girl with a lovely skin and small, even features who liked to ride to hounds. She it was who retained her Christian faith against all arguments. Like Peggy, she had lost her father some years earlier. He had fainted after giving blood, fallen over and cracked his skull. The story haunted her.

When I described my own adolescence, she found it altogether astonishing. I remember she once said to me: "You aren't interested in anything you can do in daylight!" She wasn't quite right about that, but nights were for fun, and what I wanted to do in daylight was work.

Was I homesick in all this? Yes, I was: I missed the warm claustrophobic air of the Leicester shtetl I had left behind so eagerly, particularly a close girl friend who had been a companion through all my revision for matriculation and then, inexplicably, abandoned school just before the examinations.

So it was I let Audrey take me, in my second term at Newnham, to the Jewish Society in the shabby synagogue on Thompson's Lane. The buildings have been refurbished since, and now mainly attract students whose beliefs are deeply orthodox. In the late Forties and early Fifties, however, the society was a heterogeneous group of often irreligious boys and girls, some actively hostile to the old rules and for the most part socialist. One went on to be a Labour MP and later a Member of the House of Lords. A contingent had left South Africa because their parents opposed Apartheid. There were scientists, lawyers and historians; one who read Moral Sciences with distinction and went on to become a Liberal rabbi in London. Several Jewish girls from Newnham read English, but I can remember no Jewish men with literary aspirations who were attracted to the Society.

And yet there were many such men in the University at large. The Shaffer twins, Peter and Tony, edited *Granta* one after another. They were only four years older than I was, but altogether more knowing, schooled at St Paul's and easily winning scholarships to Trinity, Tony to read Law, Peter to read History. They were quick-witted, iconoclastic, immensely worldly and had already published a detective novel together under the pseudonym of Peter Anthony when I met them in my first year. They cannot have been identical twins. I found Peter alarmingly clever, while Tony was more genial. Indeed, he let me use his superb set of Trinity rooms for my birthday party in October of my second year. Neither young man worked very hard for the Tripos, and neither excelled there, but both were inordinately successful in later life, Peter with *Amadeus*, and Tony with *Sleuth* and many screenplays. Both won awards, and Peter was knighted. Somehow the glow of future success was already around them. Their younger brother, Brian, a biologist, was the only one to make an academic career, and perhaps it bored him. He loved puns and word games. When he went on to edit *Granta*, he gave it his own idiosyncratic style: I remember he brought out one issue cut up inside a beer bottle. Later in life he put much energy into conceptual art.

Their background was similar to that in Peter Shaffer's *Five Finger Exercise,* which gives an unkind portrait of a wealthy family, never named as Jewish, in which the mother is overly eager to improve their social standing. To this end she affects a culture she does not deeply care about. In real life, however, such parental pressures offer real advantages.

I don't remember any American Fulbright Scholars drawn to Thompson's Lane. When the one I knew best asked me what on earth I found there, I said lamely that it reminded me of home. He raised his eyebrows. His own home, he assured me, did not sing Grace over food. "Nor did mine," I retorted crossly, unable to convey how the people there nevertheless felt like family.

It wasn't only American men who attracted me. There was a brilliant girl from Columbia University, a New Yorker taught by the great art historian Meyer Shapiro. She lived in the Central Hotel, just near the Arts Theatre on Market Square. The hotel was subsiding: the doors hardly closed, and smoky odours rose up the stairs from a café on the ground floor. No matter. I had never heard anything to compare with her fluency, or seen anyone smoke with such a deep drag of nicotine into her lungs. Or indeed have such a story to tell.

She knew so much about art and New York which I longed to share. Only a few years older than me, she had lived a much wilder life. I was particularly fascinated by her account of a failed relationship with Norman Podhoretz, whom I knew tangentially. I could not now give you her story, but it was infused with the drama of passionate love and male betrayal. The only evening I spent with Podhoretz himself – against a tree in Sidgewick Avenue, as it happens – he assured me that her version of events was totally inaccurate, and that he had been in love all the time with a pretty blonde who lived in Sidgewick Hall.

Podhoretz took a First in Part 2 of the English Tripos with great ease, and had an essay included in *Scrutiny* before he returned to New York. There in due course he became the Editor of *Commentary*. For a time he was at the centre of New York society. With some candour, he chose the title *Making It* for his autobiography, which came out in 1968. Many of us mocked the self-congratulation of that title, missing the irony and perhaps disguising from each other how much we wanted such success for ourselves.

When I looked at the book again recently, I recognized the shameless glee of the introductory chapter – but reading on, I made out the shrewdness of his observation, especially on the different ways the class ladder operates in England and USA. In New York, he had been instantly recognizable as a Jewish child of an immigrant family in Brooklyn, because class had something to do with style and manners. Not so in Cambridge, where he became simply an American postgraduate whom the College minions readily called Sir.

* * *

I had German measles when I took Part 2 of Tripos, but I was not particularly ill, and doubt if it made any difference to how I performed in the examinations. Still, I had worked for a First and was miserably disappointed when I only got a 2.1. Miss Welsford – one of the examiners it turned out – told me that two of my papers had been given a First, but she had not been able to persuade the other examiners about the rest. Her support did not console me. She offered me the opportunity to stay up at Newnham, promising that she could get a grant for me to do so. A few years later I would have grasped such a chance eagerly, but then, I foolishly refused it. I was still a spoilt child.

Instead, I decided to read for the Bar in London – to learn a trade, as I thought of it – and to put the charms of a literary life out of my mind. The Inns of Court would allow me to take Bar Finals in two years. And I could live for that length of time on £500 left to me by Grandfather Solomon. I gave no thought to the likely difficulties of entering Chambers as a woman in those days. And although I almost immediately met a handsome young solicitor and was soon engaged to marry him, that was not to prove the lasting relationship of my life.

* * *

When I came down from university in 1952, my mother thought I should meet my Uncle Jo – Joseph Compton that is, then Director of Education in Ealing. Her motives were complex, I imagine. As far as I recall, Jo had never visited us, but my mother continued to write to him, with a certain pathos, to give him news of my examination successes. He wrote back civilly, though without particular warmth. I don't think he liked my father, and I rather doubt if he felt much love for my mother. Still, she was very pleased whenever he wrote to her.

Perhaps she imagined some invisible sophistication acquired at university would impress her brother. She may have hoped he would take me to the Savile Club, of which he was a member, and there introduce me to his circle of literary friends. Although still uneasy about my general bearing, she may have dreamt he would be impressed by my cleverness. If my mother imagined he would help me in any way, however, she was altogether mistaken.

To be candid, this was my own fault. In worldly terms, Cambridge taught me little. I never learnt to imitate the girls I lived alongside, whom I found dowdy, and I did not recognize the names of great English families. As a social climber I was a non-starter. I made fun of the public-school voice of boys who were to be the toffs of tomorrow.

Once, when I met Miss Chrystal, a white-haired don who wore her hair in the style of a Mozart wig, she reproached me, saying,

"You are one of the best-looking girls in College, and should take more care of your appearance." At the time, I thought she was referring to my torn trousers and old sweater, but she probably had my dressed-up self in mind. I still wore absurdly high wedge shoes, pencil-slim skirts and dark-red lipstick.

When I went to see my uncle Jo at his office in Ealing, I am embarrassed to remember that I wore a pair of long dangly earrings. I met a man in his early fifties with a florid face who looked like a librarian. As soon as I spoke, he heard the Midland accent I had never tried to lose and was appalled. The dismay was as visible in his face as if it had been written above him in a cartoonist's balloon: "What is Cambridge coming to?" His own voice was rounded and deep: he had a life-long involvement in the encouragement of poetry spoken aloud. Yet surely he can't have left me standing up? I have a clear memory of him perched on the edge of his desk, rather like Philip Larkin, to whom he bore some resemblance.

As we exchanged pleasantries, I began to make out that whatever his opinion of me, he nevertheless wanted to impress me. Why else would he, almost at once, have mentioned his friendship with Compton Mackenzie?

"We share a name," he said, laughing at his own good fortune. I thought he was very pleased with himself, this red-faced man in a formal suit, securely on his own territory. He meant his own surname, of course.

Now, I had never read Compton Mackenzie – not even *Sinister Street*. I had probably attended more of F. R. Leavis's seminars than was good for me, and knew that Mackenzie was definitely not in the canon. Someone had told me that Mackenzie shared a publisher with D.H. Lawrence, and had tried unsuccessfully to persuade his editor to suppress Lawrence's story 'The Man Who Loved Islands'. I found that amusing, and foolishly made some dismissive remark.

Uncle Jo was not pleased. His narrow face, already red, deepened in colour.

"I suppose you prefer D.H. Lawrence?" he asked.

"Well, Lawrence is a genius, surely? In the letters and poems as well as the novels."

It was something I was prepared to argue, but it was not the response he wanted. I could see he was angry for reasons I could not quite understand. I suppose he expected me to be more respectful in offering opinions of my own. But then he said something really interesting:

"It may be so, though I find much of what he has to say pretty tedious. But writing isn't everything, you know. And however you rate Compton Mackenzie's novels, he always knew how to live!"

It was a distinction Lawrence might have made, and a preference he might have shared, and for a moment I was impressed by my uncle's judgement. The next moment I felt hot with shame and anger, decisively snubbed. That exchange was all I could remember when I found myself about half an hour later outside on the stone steps of Ealing Education Department.

Did he ask me if I had any plans? Did he ask me if I wanted to write myself – or had written anything? Did I tell him about anything I had done? I can't remember. I knew I had screwed up meeting him, and that it could never be put right. Nor was it. I never saw Uncle Jo again, though my mother continued to write letters about me until he died in 1964, just before I published my first book of poems.

Just now I looked up the achievements that had brought him his CBE. He was a Chairman of the Poetry Panel of the Arts Council and contributed to journals of Education, particularly those concerned with the teaching of English and the reciting of poetry. After his death in 1964 he left money to endow the Compton Trust, which the Arts Council administered to help poets.

I know very little else about him. Either he did not marry or he chose not to mention the fact to *Who's Who*. A few days ago, I found that two of his books could be bought on the Internet, and I acquired copies. One was an anthology of poems for schoolchildren – a safe, pleasurable mix of ballads, Christina Rossetti and

A.A. Milne. The short preface revealed little of the man. The other book was more promising, since it offered accounts of explorers and adventurers who had visited places altogether exotic in those days before cheap travel. Once again, his own preface was no more than a page and a half, though the selection itself was more interesting.

A few days ago, I mentioned my uncle to the poet Alan Brownjohn over lunch. He remembered Jo from the years he had spent on the Arts Council Poetry Panel. He knew about the Compton Trust for poets too. Alan thought him a pleasant fellow, precisely spoken, dressed formally, a little too formal in manner perhaps, but kindly enough. As I walked away from the China Garden in Finchley Road I thought how people change in relation to the people they meet. Alan, a young and rising poet, was treated with a respect Uncle Jo saw no reason to give me.

My aunt Annie nursed Uncle Jo in his last illness – he died of bowel cancer – and was full of admiration for his courage. When the pain was too bad, he went to his bedroom and read a book. "He preferred poetry," she told me.

Do I owe my passion for poetry to Uncle Jo and the Comptons? I feel reluctant to admit the likelihood. If so, my mother was the unconscious conduit. Or perhaps not in the least unconscious? I remember suddenly a box holding brownish newspaper reviews of my books. She must have longed for me to conquer a world she had renounced on marriage.

CHAPTER 4

NW3

My attachment to Gray's Inn ended a few months after taking Part 1 Bar Finals, soon after my engagement broke up. I now understood that, far from learning a trade as I had imagined, I would need a substantial second income to keep me going until I could find Chambers willing to take me – and that even if I did I would only earn a pittance. I wanted to continue living in London, so as an interim measure I decided to become a supply teacher.

Wistfully, at the same time, I also enrolled as a postgraduate student at Birkbeck College and began a dissertation under Professor Geoffrey Tillotson on popular nineteenth-century fiction by women writers – Ouida and Marie Corelli among them – who had explored women's erotic fantasies. It might have become a useful piece of early feminism if I had ever finished it, but I could only work at night, and I minded losing touch with my lodestone, poetry.

In 1954, I rented a room in a basement flat on Hampstead Hill Gardens, NW3. My landlady, Gerda Böhm, was a good-looking Polish woman who often sat as a model for her nephew Frank Auerbach, already a distinguished painter. She was bored, and perhaps lonely; certainly, we often talked for hours in the kitchen, and as she explained her nostalgia for the bohemian life she had enjoyed in Warsaw before the war, she gave me permission to have boyfriends to stay whenever I wanted. I saw her then as a woman far more interested in recapturing her former world than in her husband, who was often away.

One day she set off with huge excitement for a week's visit to Poland, her first since the war. On the day of her return, Arnold – my then boyfriend – and I came in from the Everyman Cinema to discover her husband sitting up rigidly in a chair.

Arnold found a doctor's number in a book by the telephone, but we both knew the man was dead. When Gerda arrived from the airport she was greeted by police and collapsed in shock. Arnold and I slunk away to my room to drown in sex, which seemed to be the only answer to death.

I had only exchanged a few words with Gerda's husband, but the discovery of his dead body disturbed me profoundly. I remembered it whenever I put a key in the front door of the flat. And Gerda and I grew nervous with each other. Shortly afterwards, I decided to look for other accommodation. I soon found a flat in Belsize Park, with high ceilings, mahogany furniture and several large rooms. At only seven pounds a week it would be very inexpensive to rent if a group of us moved in together. I arranged the lease, and Arnold moved in with me without much discussion, just as we had slipped into bed together almost as soon as we met. As for Gerda, she found a new circle of friends and did not come back into my life for some thirty years, when my world had fallen into serious disarray.

No one who knew Arnold later will remember him as he was when we first met. He was profoundly shy. He thought more quickly than he spoke, often left his sentences unfinished or let them change direction as some fresh insight modified his first words. He was tentative but eager, ready to talk all through the night when there was something to learn. I saw he was without malice, trusted him completely and took no account of the clues to a fractured inner world – the bitten nails, for instance, and an intermittent twitch which made one side of his face appear to wink. This tic vanished in any case as we settled in together. His smile was always charming and mischievous.

Some nights, however, he lay on his back, wanting to explain his sense of disabling under-privilege. His Stepney childhood in a street where Blackshirts held nightly meetings was a part of it, his loneliness in evacuation another, but he spoke most frequently of his bullying father, Dave, an unemployed tailor whose skills with a needle were no longer much needed in a world of sewing machines.

Dave was a bitter man whose spectacles had thick lenses which gave him an insectivorous look. He had always controlled the house radio, and turned off any *yockishe* (non-Jewish) music whenever he heard it. Arnold liked to sing in choirs, loved Bach and was once picked as a schoolboy to sing in a concert which fell on a Jewish holiday; Dave refused to allow him to take part. His mother, Rosy, bravely tried to persuade her husband without much hope of success; she was no match for Dave's sarcastic tongue: he often reduced her to tears. Arnold was very proud of photographs of her as a slim pretty girl sitting next to his father on the sands: "Beauty and the Beast," he liked to say. His brothers and sister agree that it was Arnold who came in for the worst of Dave's bullying.

* * *

In the last two years of his life, Arnold learnt to use a computer and began to sketch out notes about his childhood and adolescence. He recalls a market, close to his home, with barrels of pickles and the singeing smell of chickens; the horsehair in the chair seats of his grandparents' house and cut-up squares of newspaper hanging from a loop of string which served as toilet paper in their outside lavatory.

Dave is a less villainous figure in these notes than I expected. Arnold remembers being carried on his father's shoulders, going with him to the local cinema, or being taken up White Horse Lane for a drink of milk and vanilla soda water. He has an early memory of a factory where his father once worked, which had a floor covered with coloured scraps of cloth and silky, shiny material for linings. One night his father, thinking he was asleep, pulled the bedclothes up round him; Arnold was surprised to find that recalling the gentleness of that gesture still moved him.

But the unhappy memories are there too. He writes with an omnipresent sense of opportunities missed:

My mother borrowed a violin from her brother Harry, who once played it in a silent cinema. She sent me with a sixpence taken from the shopping money to a group violin lesson in the school building. I went in and found them playing in unison on the open strings. This was not their first lesson. I stood around baffled until someone took my money and suggested I just watch. I had no idea what was happening. I sat bewildered. I got home, gave my account to my mother and that was my only violin lesson ever.

Reading this, I remembered how in the last years of his life, when ill health had forced his retirement from work as a scientist, he bought a cello, took lessons twice a week and began to practise several hours a day. I marvelled at his progress, and to this day cannot hear his favourite Bach partita without remembering his gallantry and persistence. As a child, his eager enthusiasm was often disappointed.

Once I rolled balls at a fair in Tring and won a magical pair of white doves in a cage. My father sold them back immediately without thinking to ask my permission.

When I first met Dave himself, however, he went out of his way to impress me. He even brought out his school reports from a drawer in a kitchen cupboard to show me the red marks of the Grade A he had received when he was fifteen. Leaving school at that age was a far worse blow to him than leaving at twelve for my father, who moved off without regret into the wood trade and soon started up his own business. At fifteen Dave set about looking for a job, but there were no jobs, and found no way of using his intelligence.

It was Arnold's fear of wasting his own intelligence that preoccupied me. After university he took a job as an industrial chemist at British Oxygen, which he left to work for a PhD at Acton Technical College. Unfortunately, the topic he had chosen was not a way into biochemistry as he'd hoped. He was convinced he would never now have the chance to work in the field he wanted. I eagerly took on the task of rescuing him.

In the early months of that Belsize commune, Arnold and I were unusually happy together. As I write this now, I realize our way of life was the true *elsewhere* I had imagined all those years earlier in the washrooms of the Wyggeston Grammar School. A friend observed with some accuracy that we were like two playing cards propping each other up. We were both impractical, but our different kinds of knowledge complemented one another. I understood about application forms and referees. He taught me how to set up a tent in a rainy Cornish camping site, to hitch-hike down to Spain, to jump-start an old banger we bought together. And at his side, my circle of acquaintance widened to include strange people. He valued strangeness.

Late at night one week in 2009, some years after Arnold's death, I made out the voice of Gustav Metzger on the radio. Astonishingly, he was still alive and articulate at eighty-four. Tate Modern had recently bought one of his works of art. When we knew him first, fifty years earlier, he had a stall in Cambridge Market Square, near David's second-hand bookshop, which Arnold liked to visit while he was working in Colloid Science, Free School Lane. In my memory Metzger was a wizened little man, a Jewish refugee from Eastern Europe, probably Poland, who thought art had to represent the destructiveness of the world around him.

Metzger did not smoke or drink alcohol, coffee or English tea, which in those days I thought faddish. He carried his own supply of green tea around with him. He was a vegan and indeed ate almost nothing when he called on us, which may account not only for his emaciation but also his longevity, if research on underweight rats has any relevance to human beings.

Arnold liked him, mainly because, as I say, he was always taken with people who were odd, and partly because, at the time, Metzger was interested in liquid crystals, which made unpredictable patterns of intense colour. It was one of these that Tate Modern bought in

2005. A skilled physical chemist before he became a molecular biologist, Arnold enjoyed collaborating on slides for a demonstration Gustav was to give at a university lecture hall. Arnold took making those slides very seriously, and was mildly irritated that Gustav did not. By the time of the lecture, Gustav had moved on to an interest in setting fire to sheets of nylon curtaining, and his demonstration of the magical properties of liquid crystals was merely perfunctory.

By 1966 Gustav's concern with environmental issues generated far wilder projects. An early exponent of happenings, he was driven around London – he did not drive himself – with a transparent jar on the roof which held either hens or rabbits. Exhaust fumes were funnelled into it so that people could see the danger of allowing cars to pollute the street. It generated massive publicity for the concept of auto-destructive art, but it seemed a little unfair on the hens.

Less eccentrically, Arnold introduced me to classical music. At a party a few days after we first met, he wooed me by playing Telemann on a wooden recorder directly to me. It was not my kind of music then, but I could see how much it mattered to him, and I was impressed by his dexterity. He had found by then a musical world at Morley College, where Michael Tippett introduced him to early music.

* * *

Among the friends who came to share the flat in Belsize Park with us in the Fifties was Donald Hope, an Oxford graduate, by then studying at the Slade, introduced by my old friend Michael Podro. Donald was a tall, bony man – so thin a cartoonist would have shown his elbows as spiky. He had a shock of black hair above his forehead and a rather straggly beard. His voice was surprisingly high-pitched, but he had a gift for shaping anecdotes, particularly stories against himself, with a ribaldry I had almost forgotten since my Cambridge days.

He shared the room he took in our Belsize Park Gardens flat with another painter. This was an economy Donald had no need to practise, I judged soon enough. But he liked to live austerely. I remember he had a teapot with a cracked lid which he stubbornly refused to replace. I once asked him why, and he explained that to do so would involve choosing a new one, which in turn would have been a declaration of preference for a completely mundane object – and that would embarrass him. His own taste was in fact immaculate once he allowed himself to set up a home of his own: but at this time he was hopelessly in love with a girl whose face he described as an Ingres painting.

He made a joke of his lack of success with her, and I liked his ability to find unhappiness funny. There had already been disasters in his life. He had taken a drug, perhaps Benzedrine, to stimulate him during Oxford Finals. This allowed him to feel so little under pressure of time that he sent in sheets of blank pages. I think he was given a pass degree. I am not sure now what subject he was reading – Classics, I suspect, to judge from later brilliant translations of Catullus and Horace – but he knew more English poetry by heart than anyone I have ever met. Perhaps as a Wykehamist, he had learnt much of what he knew at school. Donald wrote wonderful letters in a black italic hand, as fluent as his speech and always uncorrected. In those days he had no need to find a job. What indeed would a better Oxford degree have added to his life?

Arnold and I puzzled him, I think, because the only Jews he knew were public-school boys like Michael Podro, whose family home was a splendid double-fronted house with a magnificent library. At some point Donald's mother, intrigued to think Donald was living in a "Polish ghetto" – her phrase – invited us for a weekend to their country cottage, hoping to understand her son's fascination with unsuitable friends.

The Hopes were related in some way to the Pakenham family, but had made their money from the manufacture of window frames. His mother, a remarkably animated woman, phrased her anecdotes as cleverly as Donald – indeed his voice rather resembled hers. We laughed a good deal over dinner, but I probably drank too much, and back in Belsize Park I felt like apologizing to Donald for our lack of wit. However, he seemed delighted that we had not hit it off with his mother.

Michael was by this time living in a flat in Albany Street, with a Slade student who had the fine-boned beauty of a Greta Garbo. His own eloquence was undiminished. Arnold listened to him closely and learnt a great deal about the philosophy and history of art. He began to ask probing questions, too. Some of these brought Michael to a pause, and one day he confided to me that Arnold had a genuinely original mind.

Other friends in the commune, whom I remember less vividly, worked out our share of the rent, gas and so forth, so Arnold and I were solvent there as we rarely were thereafter. In other ways, we were less in control. I don't remember how we came to have a baby's plastic tub in the bathroom, but that was where Arnold put his used socks, covering them with water and soap powder, feeling he had at least made a start. I suppose he hoped I would know how to deal with them. I think I threw them out.

While he worried away about his mistake in choosing Acton Technical College for his PhD, I determined to find some alternative route, without much idea about how. I could see that his scientist friends from Queen Mary College were content to rub along in one capacity or another for the rest of their lives. It seemed to me he needed to meet more dedicated scientists.

* * *

In June 2011, meeting Liebe Klug at a birthday party in Lewes – Lady Klug now – she reminded me how I had brought Arnold round to meet Aaron and herself when they were living in Adelaide Road, just round the corner from Belsize Park Gardens. Aaron is a quiet, powerful man. He went on to become the head of MRC

Molecular Biology and to win a Nobel Prize, but always remained softly spoken and thoughtful. Liebe was then an unusually glamorous woman, her beautiful legs always poised on high heels. She had the slim, muscled body of a dancer. That evening, I watched her perform an electric tango – not with Aaron, but another friend who danced superbly. Arnold and Aaron were absorbed in conversation the while. On the strength of the success of that evening, I determined to take Arnold back to meet other Cambridge friends doing research in biochemistry. They would know what he ought to do.

Soon after an idyllic first visit to Cambridge, Arnold and I entered a second-hand jeweller's, and he placed a square blue sapphire on my engagement finger. Then we visited Leicester together. As a general rule, my father did not find any of my boyfriends good enough for me, so I was surprised to find that, apart from grumbling about Arnold's shabby clothes, he was careful to offer no unfavourable comment. My mother, who had found my solicitor extremely suitable, found little to say either, other than that Arnold seemed very kind. Of course, I was by then twenty-six, almost an old maid in those days.

My earlier engagement had gone so very publicly wrong – my father had organized an event to celebrate it, which included the Lord Mayor and every member of the family – I wanted no other party. My parents, however, were very eager to make a wedding for us, and this was planned for July.

Some time in late May I began to feel sick every morning. As my periods stopped simultaneously, we naturally recognized the most likely explanation. No twenty-first-century woman would see this as much of a problem. After all, the date of the wedding was set, and the likely father had put a blue ring on my finger. But in those days it was a serious matter to be pregnant outside marriage, and I wasn't looking forward to seeing my mother's stricken face.

It seemed sensible, in any case, to consult a doctor who lived close by before doing so. He agreed on the probable cause, and I peed into a glass vessel and went home forlornly to wait for the result. In those days, urine was injected into rabbits to see if they ovulated. In a few days' time I went back for the result – and to my immense relief the doctor beamed at me: I was not pregnant.

I was profoundly relieved, though I couldn't help wondering a little about the absence of periods, since yet another key date had elapsed. "Stress," he suggested. "Do you have any particular stress?" Indeed I did. My parents were now planning a white wedding. There were dress fittings, a going-away dress and so forth. More surprisingly, they had to arrange a bus to bring the whole Feinstein family to Leicester, since that was where the wedding was to be held.

Meanwhile I was typing out letters to possible referees, and filling out forms for Arnold to apply for an MRC grant to do a PhD in Cambridge. "You can do anything on a page," he teased me. "Hopeless in the real world."

* * *

A month after the wedding we took rooms in Cambridge, over the bridge in Mill Road, and Arnold became a sprayer of woodworm killer on Church property, while we waited to hear about the research grant. Spraying was an exhausting job, though he liked the people he worked with. One of them explained how the patented remedy for killing woodworm was completely useless, since it was directed at the holes where the insects come out. The work itself was boring and quite possibly a health risk.

Meanwhile, since I no longer felt sick, I set about finding a job myself. Deighton Bell on Trinity Street were looking for someone to run their New Fiction Department. The interview went well, and two days later the job was mine. It was the best thing that had happened to me in several years. And to clinch our happiness, Arnold, to his astonishment, found that he had been given a grant to write a PhD at Colloid Science on something to do with immunoglobulins and hay fever.

The following weekend, perhaps because there was at last good news to report, we went back to visit my parents. As I took off my coat, my mother scrutinized me narrowly and without particular approval.

"Well," she said. "And I thought you were going to be so clever."

My face showed complete incomprehension.

"You are pregnant," she said flatly.

I sighed. I usually managed to keep the knowledge out of my mind, and I really didn't want to worry her, but I had to explain that I had been to a doctor and he had said I was not.

To my surprise, she laughed aloud, approached, and pressed a hand down just below my waist.

"Try another doctor," she suggested.

I remembered that, before she married, her sister Annie had once let her help out on a maternity ward, but I could hardly trust her diagnosis.

As it happens, the two rooms we were renting – a bedroom and a kitchen – were part of a doctor's home. She had been very kind when we discovered mice behind the cupboards, and did not once suggest it had anything to do with our habit of leaving dishes unwashed overnight.

So I joined her practice and reported my symptoms. And she too laughed when I voiced my doubts. "I'll send off a test if you like, but really there's no question in my mind. Due in February I should think."

I have to say that the date did not at first alarm me. It seemed a long way away – and it was such very good news that I wasn't dying. I was a little surprised, though, to find that my shape began to change as soon as I knew I was pregnant. I was absurdly skinny in those days – but almost at once I began to bulge, as if I had somehow given my stomach muscles permission to do so. After a few weeks, the manager of Deighton Bell, who had been rather pleased with my enthusiasm, noticed my new shape. He gave me the sack forthwith, as he was allowed to do in those days.

I was disappointed to lose a job I liked, but Arnold's grant had come through, and everything was going to be all right. I read Grantly Dick-Read on natural childbirth, learnt to breathe deeply and relax – as healthy primitive women were said to do – and booked a bed in Mill Road Maternity Hospital.

My son was born on 24th February 1957, after a simple enough labour, only spoilt by a placenta which did not come out as it should. The baby was a handsome, perfect boy – my small, pert breasts functioned easily to provide milk, and after about a week I was back home in our newly rented cottage in Panton Street, close to Arnold's lab. I was happy, energetic and in love with my child.

One evening, about ten days after my return from hospital, my temperature rose unexpectedly as I was trying to make some kind of order in the bathroom. Then blood began to stream down my legs into a pool on the floor. By great good fortune I was not alone when I called out in panic – Arnold had looked in to check on me – and an ambulance came quickly. I remember being taken downstairs on a stretcher, staring up at the blue stars overhead, which looked remote and indifferent to my fear. The baby was sleeping quietly in his carrycot next to me. When I arrived at the hospital, I was rushed on a trolley down a corridor to the operating theatre. I woke with my left wrist strapped to a board and a drip in my arm The surgeon who removed the placenta had left a swab inside me, and the resulting haemorrhage was nearly fatal.

CHAPTER 5

Portugal Place, Cambridge

Our tiny Panton Street flat, with its rickety stairs and sprawling wires, was certainly close to the centre, but it was hard to manage with a child. After little more than a year, we began looking for somewhere larger we could rent once again with a group of friends.

Portugal Place is a paved alley in the centre of Cambridge, just across the street from St John's College. In 1959, we became part of another commune, this time in Francis Crick's fairy-tale house. Its oddly shaped rooms were tilted, the nursery boldly painted red, the huge kitchen below pavement level floored in stone. A single golden helix hung outside the front door; the other strand belonged to Jim Watson, with whom Crick had discovered the structure of DNA a few years earlier.

We did not then know Francis and Odile except by reputation, but we soon formed an impression of an unusually likeable couple. As we were setting out our books on our first day there, we came across a cache of discarded papers. These included the typed copy of a bawdily witty poem and a cautious letter of reference from our own bank. More conventional landlords would have been alarmed by the tone of that reference. I can still remember one sentence: "He is in receipt of a small university salary, which he completely spends." Later, when we were living in La Jolla, we saw more of the Cricks and understood they were in no way ordinary.

In Portugal Place we soon acquired some of their friends. A couple from Molecular Biology remained on a staircase to the left of the main house and perhaps it was through them that we met John Gayer-Anderson – the Obscene Potter, as he was known – who held wild parties at his large house in Waterbeach, often attended by distinguished molecular biologists, London novelists and some of the prettiest au-pair girls in Cambridge.

We had accidentally stumbled into a bohemian world, permissive sexually and humanly liberal. Odile was a painter, who liked drawing nudes from life, usually of beautiful girls; she was responsible for the witty scrawl of a naked woman on the bath, but also for a detailed sketch of the helical structure of DNA. When we knew them in La Jolla, California, many years later, Crick was a Professor of Neuroscience at the Salk Institute. He was a tall, thin man with pale hair and a lean face, always ready to break into a huge bray of a laugh; Odile was a quiet, amused presence, and perhaps because of her French background never showed a trace of jealousy for all Francis's open infidelities.

Francis loved poetry. In Cambridge, nevertheless, I remember that at one of Gayer-Anderson's dinner parties he argued that Milton's *Paradise Lost* had to be rejected, not only for the theology but because the poem perpetuated cosmological errors. He was thinking of the planets hanging on chains around the earth. One of the guests at that dinner was Arieh Sachs, a good-looking Israeli from Jerusalem who was writing a PhD about Samuel Johnson; he argued eloquently for Milton. But Francis was not open to persuasion. He was militantly opposed to Christianity and resigned his Fellowship at Churchill, I am told, when the College decided to build a chapel there.

Many years later, Arnold was a Fellow of Gonville and Caius College when the post of Master to follow Joseph Needham, the great Sinologist, was discussed. Francis Crick was sounded out as a possible successor to Needham. I doubt if he was much tempted – and the rumour was that Odile would not hear of it. She had no wish to become a respectable Master's wife, with all the formality involved. In any event, the offer was not accepted.

* * *

In 1959, undergraduates who wanted to live bang in the centre were eager to join us in our Portugal Place commune. Among them was David Leitch, who looked like Hemingway, our idol of those years, and already had the nerve and fluent pen which would take him to Vietnam for the *Sunday Times* and make him one of the Insight team pursuing Philby. He and his friend Peter Papaloizou (later Loizos) were supervised by the poet Donald Davie, whose lectures were among the few I made a point of attending; he was using the material that went into *Articulate Energy: An Inquiry into the Syntax of English Poetry*.

Both David and Peter admired the poetry of the New Movement and patiently explained the development of one of Thom Gunn's poems to me. Their point was that the sonorous last line of 'On the Move' had been *earned* by the meticulous argument that preceded it. In return, I brought them Wallace Stevens's 'Sunday Morning'.

They had no acquaintance with Stevens. The first English selection of his poems had only been published by Faber in 1953, not long before his death, and had not yet dazzled Cambridge. I think Donald Hope introduced me to his poetry. Stevens was traditional in form, and rich in language, but he argued metaphysics with the stuff of this world.

> Complacencies of the peignoir, and late
> Coffee and oranges in a sunny chair,
> And the green freedom of a cockatoo
> Upon a rug mingle to dissipate
> The holy hush of ancient sacrifice.

David and Peter took my remarks to Donald Davie, who startled them by agreeing that Stevens was indeed a major poet, and evincing some curiosity about me. Impulsively, I invited Donald and his wife Doreen to dinner and, though I had little enough to offer them, the evening went surprisingly well. Donald was a man of impish good humour, his face not unlike that of the young Yeats; Doreen was downright and sharp-witted.

We may have talked about Stevens, but I don't remember it. The conversation centred on Ezra Pound, since Donald was at that very moment engaging with him seriously, and was a little puzzled at my willingness to forgive him his monstrous anti-Semitism. Pound had been released from his asylum in 1958, just a year earlier, and the issue was fresh in our minds. I had always admired 'Cathay'. Naturally, I was aware of those Cantos, which speak with loathing of "kikes" – Pound's preferred word for Jews – but my indignation was confused by a sad knowledge of how many English writers I admired shared his prejudice, including Eliot. I had no wish to reject all of them. What I loved in 'Cathay' was Pound's ear for syllables, the precision of each one set against another and the slowness his lines demanded when read aloud, so that the subtlety could be savoured.

Ezra Pound is arguably the most influential poet of twentieth-century Modernism, and the general case against him is widely known. He had chosen to live in Italy since 1924, under Mussolini, and remained there during the Second World War. He broadcast for the Fascist government from Rome. When the Allies defeated the Italian Fascists, Pound was imprisoned in a detention camp in Pisa in 1945, and subsequently brought to trial as a traitor in the United States. In 1946, he was acquitted of treason, on the grounds that he was too mentally ill to plead, and shut up in St Elizabeth's Hospital in Washington.

During his confinement, the jury of the Bollingen-Library of Congress Award gave him a prize for *The Pisan Cantos*. It is his most poignant work, and there were many voices, including that of Robert Lowell, raised on its behalf. The prize was not won without controversy, however, and Pound's winning it from a lunatic asylum may well have confirmed the distrust of the common reader for poetry in general.

I had not then read the text of Pound's broadcasts, or I might have felt less secure in my opinions that evening. I was euphoric as it ended, but too shy to imagine pursuing the friendship until I had some occasion to do so. This soon arose, however.

David Leitch knew most of his year's literary stars. Through him in 1959 I was offered the chance to edit an issue of the University magazine *Cambridge Opinion*, while the usual editors worked for their final examinations. I accepted eagerly, because I knew exactly what I wanted to do with it. The issue was to be called: *The Writer out of Society*. And I was going to look across to America for my outsiders.

Since I was born in the north, with grandparents who were Jewish immigrants from Odessa, and moreover a woman, I felt myself altogether at the edge of the English literary world, and I had begun to take a perverse pride in being on that periphery. It seemed an appropriate, even an honourable position for a poet.

So it was I briefly became a conduit, more or less by chance, for an American avant-garde not yet much known in England, all of them acknowledging the influence of Ezra Pound and several of them as Jewish as I was, outsiders themselves, but ebullient, unfrightened figures.

While still living in London I had picked up the poems of Allen Ginsberg in an early City Lights Pocketbook edition of *Howl* (1955). In Cambridge he was not yet a celebrity, though three years later he would pack the Oak Room in King's College. Indeed, he was not yet well known in Great Britain, though an obscenity trial had brought him notoriety in the USA. In 1959 his name told against him. It suggested a *tailor*, someone said – in fact his father was a distinguished minor poet. I enjoyed Allen's breathless unpunctuated paragraphs and the witty short lyrics, and wrote to him in my new eminence as editor. I received an enthusiastic reply, and was able to include the first UK publication of 'Walt Whitman in a Supermarket' alongside an amusing letter from Gregory Corso.

Allen was generous to me. Soon afterwards, he sent me the addresses of a whole network of other American poets more or less unknown in Britain. Among these was Charles Olson, and some time during our stay in Portugal Place I began to correspond with him. More exactly, I sent him a letter with a few bald questions, signing it, as I remember, E.B. Feinstein, obviously wishing to conceal the fact that I was a woman. Olson's response was rapid and overwhelming. His letter was no less than his latest take on poetics, his first shot since 'Projective Verse' many years earlier. This letter has, of course, often been republished since Grove Press first elicited it from me. At the time, I was mainly puzzled by it. For a while, it silenced me. On the other hand, I loved the poems which Olson included along with the letter.

For all the steely, purposeful sound of *Prospect*, the magazine came about as a result of this literary accident. I now knew there was nothing arcane about bringing out a small magazine. The same printer used by *Cambridge Opinion* was pleased to work for me, and demanded no money up front. Those who had trudged around the colleges and bookshops placing copies of *Cambridge Opinion* were happy to do so again. I had no financial backing, and one of the few local firms willing to advertise in that first issue was Jack Carter, whose shop in an elbow of Portugal Place rented out dinner suits for balls and feasts, and also sold second-hand clothes which we occasionally bought. A few publishers also bought space, charitably.

It was not my intention to use *Prospect* as a vehicle for my own poems, which at that time were little more than lines drifting across the page, waiting to find a shape. The first issue of *Prospect* in the summer of 1959 included only poets I admired. There were three lyrics of Denise Levertov, a poem of Paul Blackburn and a short story of Harold Pinter, who had stayed with us overnight after an evening at the English Club. Crucially, there was a brilliant essay from Donald Davie, 'Remembering the Movement'. Although often associated with Kingsley Amis, D.J. Enright and Thom Gunn, I had very fortunately caught Davie in transition. His rejection of the poets with whom he was most commonly grouped was as arresting as a political change of heart.

> Ours was writing which apologized insistently for its own existence... In the interstices of our poems – in the metrical places wasted on inert gestures of social adoptiveness... "no doubt", "almost", "perhaps"... you can see the same craven defensiveness which led us when we were challenged or flattered or simply interviewed to pretend that the Movement didn't exist.

The presiding spirit of that first issue of *Prospect,* however, was Charles Olson, an altogether more controversial figure, whom many still see as both pompous and incomprehensively venerated by groups of poets as obscure as himself.

The first Olson poem I published was entirely direct. It made me imagine the rocky coast, the ocean and the men from Dorset who first saw the shore of Massachusetts, even though I knew nothing of Gloucester, the fishing village where Olson had grown up, still less of the Widow Babson, whose "progeny and property / is still to be found and felt on Main / and Middle Streets".

I knew nothing of John White – a local clergyman who had written the history of Gloucester – but nevertheless I attended.

> and the snow flew
> where gulls now paper
> the skies
>
> where fishing continues
> and my heart lies

Looking at the poem now, that last line seems less than perfect, but the second poem from the same sequence was as sharp as an etching. The scene is the same, but the narrative moves confidently from John White's days into Olson's own.

a Plantation a beginning

I sit here on a Sunday
with grey water, the winter
staring me in the face [...]

Fourteen spare men the first
year who huddled
above Half Moon beach

or got out of the onshore
breeze by clustering
what sort of what shacks

around the inshore harbor side
of Stage Head where now lovers
have a park and my mother

and my wife were curious
what went on in back seats
and Pat Foley

was furious some guy
on all four legs
crawled

about to get a better view

The bareness, the lean particularity excited me, but also the intoxi-cation induced by the absence of all punctuation – and line endings which suggested the pauses of a man thinking aloud. There were no metaphors to tease out, no clever arguments, just statements made in a voice that was nonetheless peculiarly lyrical. All the poems which went into my first books *In a Green Eye* (Goliard Press) and Faber's *Poetry Introduction 1* aspired to that condition. That last publication came about with the support of an ally whom I had not yet met: Ted Hughes.

I never met Olson. I never went to Buffalo. I wasn't even at the famous party given for him in London by the heiress Panna Grady. Apart from a taped recording of a famous reading at Buffalo which I listened to, years later, with Andrew Crozier from Essex University, I knew Olson's voice entirely through the notation of it on the printed page.

* * *

I had an early encounter with Harold Pinter when he came to the English Club to give a talk as part of a lecture series given by new English playwrights. Arnold Wesker, and perhaps John Arden, had already featured. As I remember, Pinter's short play *The Dumb Waiter* was performed, fairly stolidly, and there were questions from an audience who affected bewilderment.

Now, one of the bonds that had formed between Arnold and myself was a love for Pinter's *Birthday Party*. We had seen it at the Cambridge Arts Theatre before it went off to London, only to close after a week. We liked the rhythms of the dialogue, and both of us, in our different ways, could identify with the characters. Arnold felt himself very much like Stanley, while I felt my (not altogether satisfactory) mothering of him had a resemblance to Meg's. Talking to Pinter much later in life, I found he had little sympathy for Meg, in fact, and disliked Beatrix Lehmann's performance accordingly. Arnold enjoyed the command of East End vernacular and the essential Jewishness of the play.

At the English Club in 1959 a girl from Girton asked questions which Pinter refused to answer. I can't remember what they were, except that they were hostile and spoken in the chilly voice of an ADC actress. To my surprise, Arnold rose to his feet as the session was coming to an end – he was still a little shy – and voiced his irritation at the level of questioning. He wanted Pinter to know that there were people present who admired his plays and would be very unhappy if he stopped writing them. Afterwards, Pinter came over to talk, and since he had nowhere to spend the night came back to sleep in Portugal Place, on a couch in the upstairs living room. He wrote afterwards with the story I included in *Prospect*.

By the second issue of *Prospect* it had become obvious I could not handle the magazine on my own. Tony Ward, a burly young comrade of David's, suggested himself as an assistant editor, and he became a close friend. He was handsome in an Elizabethan style, with thick curly hair and a dark-brown beard. There was a strong resemblance to Holbein's Wyatt, but his expression was less querulous. A butcher's son from Lincolnshire, he was proud of his muscular build, and once remarked casually that he could lift a car. Unlike David Leitch, Tony never hit anyone – he was afraid that if he did, he might kill them. But he had more energy than he knew how to use: sometimes he played rugby, sometimes we all stayed up talking into the first light of morning. We formed a strong, almost familial bond. When we moved from Portugal Place to Adams Road (then Sherlock Road and, after that, De Freville Avenue), Tony moved with us.

In Adams Road, where we rented the grand house of an Economics professor on sabbatical, Arnold and I began to write a film column together for *Cambridge Review*. Tony came to the cinema with us, and Arnold and Tony then argued endlessly, long after I would have liked to go to bed. My job was to put the consensus into some kind of shape, then drive the piece round to Heffers to meet the deadline. The wrangling was good-humoured fun, but I was fretful because I had to get up early.

* * *

I knew another house in Adams Road from my third year as an undergraduate: Geoffrey Roughton – a friend from Trinity – held parties in the large ballroom of No. 9. His mother, Alice Roughton, was one of the most remarkable Cambridge figures of her day. She and her husband, then Professor of Colloid Science, occupied separate parts of the building. She ran her own rooms with eccentric generosity, letting Hungarian refugees live there after the failed Budapest uprising, often alongside Latin American communists, psychiatric patients and waifs and strays of every kind, including – for one memorable week – the entire Feinstein family.

Alice worked as a psychiatric doctor at Fulbourne. She kept hens and goats and made her own sausages for Sunday evenings, which unusual people continued to attend several decades later. While renting 4 Adams Road from the Economics professor, I relied on her resident au pairs to help look after my children. There were two sons by then.

Prospect did not remain in my hands beyond Issue 5: we were too short of money, and indeed Tony Ward was named as editor for Issues 4 and 5 (and must have written the editorial for No. 4, which makes use of an elaborate metaphor drawn from rock climbing). I had begun to take on unrealistic amounts of supervision for the English Tripos, and was also travelling to Knebworth and Stevenage for the WEA. There was no time for writing, or indeed for much life of any kind. At one moment in our increasingly frenetic trajectory through Cambridge houses to rent, we found ourselves living alongside the printer to whom we owed a great deal of money. It was decisive. I was relieved to hand over the title to Jeremy Prynne, who kindly picked up the overdraft.

* * *

The longest and closest relationship built through *Prospect* was that with Tony Ward. Of all the precocious talents I have known, Tony's was the strongest. At twenty-two, he had an entirely fresh prose voice, with a flow of language and as sharp a response to the physical world as D.H. Lawrence. Bamber Gascoigne, then scouting for Constable, was so impressed by the manuscript of Tony's first novel, *The Tent of God*, that he took it away with him to place in London (the novel was eventually published by MacGibbon & Kee in 1963). In the future lay two more novels, both well received, and an opera at the Coliseum, written with David Blake, about Toussaint Louverture. There are three other novels which only exist in manuscript.

Tony married Nicole Jouve, a pretty French girl from the École Normale Supérieure in Paris. She was a devout Catholic from a professorial family and altogether more scholarly than he was; I remember how she helped him with the footnotes to his thesis on Walter Pater. Jeremy Prynne, who had always found Tony immensely engaging, surprised me once by suggesting Nicole was the finer intelligence. This was no problem for Tony – at least not then. He was very proud of her.

When Tony was appointed to a lectureship at the University of York, he and Nicole bought an enormous house in Butterwick, a village about half an hour's drive from York, with a paddock and, quite soon, a horse. Tony learnt to ride to hounds and became friendly with the local gentry. The Wards made their home very beautiful, and our whole family stayed with them many times.

The marriage changed its dynamic, however, when Nicole also joined the staff at the University and then began to publish short stories herself. Some of these made powerful use of her relationship with Tony. I remember Tony was in tears once as he told me: "I write about her as if she were an angel, and she writes about me as a drunken lout." I can't remember my response, but I knew a writer's treachery from my own experience by then.

Nicole had once been part of a small circle of writers around Éditions Des femmes, and her stance was in part political. Her second book, *The Street Cleaner* (about the Yorkshire Ripper), revealed her own loneliness as a Paris intellectual in North

Yorkshire, and her resentment of the casual dismissal of women she found there. Tony read the book as a personal attack.

Even before his children had grown up, Tony began to drink heavily, had many affairs and, at last, he and Nicole separated painfully. He continued to write, but he had no agent and refused to pay a secretary, or even to type in double spacing. This last obstinacy probably cost him the chance of publication.

He was in his fifties, living with a much older woman, when he contracted a disease of the liver. It was she who rang to tell us that he was in hospital, and she sounded urgent. I said we would go up and see him. Arnold was reluctant. He and Tony had quarrelled on a holiday they had taken with one of Tony's sons, but I hoped he would feel differently once he saw Tony again.

As we arrived, Tony was being wheeled around a hospital ward, and was surprised as he saw us, and wondered what we were doing there.

"I'm not dying, am I? I don't feel as though I'm dying," he said.

He certainly didn't look well, but I didn't think he was about to die either. The woman he was living with, the widow of a general, was very tender with him: she left tactfully at six so that Nicole could visit. It was when I saw Nicole that I knew how serious the situation was. She had lost a great deal of weight, and the strain of her present situation showed on a face that had always been calm or amused.

When we got up to catch our train, she suggested we stay over. The children were no longer living at home, and the big house felt empty to her. That evening she broke down in tears as she explained the possible scenarios and her own wretched loneliness. And no, she wasn't writing. She didn't have the heart for it.

The funeral was a true Irish wake, the first I had ever attended, with an open coffin at once fascinating and alarming to me, since Jewish tradition forbids any close contact with dead bodies. I looked at Tony lying on a pillow and thought him simply asleep. I told him how sorry I was that I hadn't managed to find a publisher for his huge, sprawling masterpiece of a novel, with its nod to Melville's *Moby Dick*. I cried. David Leitch came up from London on a late train and looked very shaken. I knew Tony's older brother, Gilbert, from his visits to Cambridge, and indeed from his presence in Tony's first novel. He was a sculptor, and Tony adored both his work and the robust enjoyment he took in being alive. I remember the summer Tony took Gilbert to one of the Potter's parties. His amorous exploits there earned him the nickname "Come-into-the-garden Ward".

The coffin was in a separate room, and I watched Gilbert go in to talk to Tony several times. Once, he came out muttering: "It wasn't his turn."

* * *

As I look back from 2013 at myself as a skinny girl in the early Sixties, at once opinionated and shy, some of my convictions now trouble me. Allen Ginsberg was a generous, friendly figure, and he always remained an exhilarating presence in front of large audiences. I still admire both *Howl* and *Kaddish* and his early short lyrics. Nevertheless, Allen's insistence on spontaneity and his disapproval of poets redrafting their work were mistaken, and his later political poems against the Bomb lack the edge of his early work.

His own enthusiasms were wholehearted and genuine. He was more interested in beauty and human discovery than his own celebrity. One morning, later in our acquaintance, he disappeared early from his couch. It turned out he had gone to the Fitzwilliam Museum and persuaded the curators to bring out their Blakes for his inspection. The following day, when he should have been in London for an interview with the BBC, he decided to visit the Molecular Biology laboratories first, and Arnold arranged it. Allen could well have been an embarrassment in that nest of Nobel Prize winners, but in fact he impressed them with serious questions. Allen was far more interesting than the usual caricature often presented to us. Still, I no longer feel a prude in questioning his compulsive promiscuity, his unscrupulous recommendation of drugs, the destructiveness of his influence on minds less robust than his own.

Politics, however decently felt, damaged the work of other poets I admired in the early days of *Prospect*. Denise Levertov's early Welsh gift, shown for example by her verses about clothes on a washing line between lemon trees, was sacrificed to political indignation. Those who opposed the Vietnam war usually did so from safety, and their poems lack the grim power of those written by soldier-poets who fought in the two World Wars or joined in the Spanish Civil War with fervour. Poets write best about what they experience in their own flesh.

A more awkward question is: how much do I continue to read Charles Olson? My own poetry no longer shows much evidence of his influence. I still admire the way Olson followed his own intellectual passions, but some of the admiration I once felt for *the Mayan Letters* evaporated after a visit to Mexico City. There I went round a magnificent museum where figures of the Aztec and Mayan gods were displayed. Both seem equally ferocious, and I looked vainly in the streets for the soft and gentle descendants of the Mayans he described.

I think now my attitude to Pound in Portugal Place was overly complacent. The first decade of the twenty-first century has given me plenty of occasion to ponder my false sense of security. Pound and his opinions seemed in 1959 to belong to a past, albeit recent, which everyone condemned. I no longer feel quite so sure of that as I watch crowds marching with an occasional placard blaming "the Jews" – meaning the bankers of course – for the recession. Mobs of the righteously indignant do not make me optimistic.

I remember with disquiet reading Ginsberg's interview with Pound in Rapallo, where Pound claimed his hatred for the Jews was only equivalent to a loathing of the profit motive. Sadly, that equation is easy to turn on its head. History and habit are very powerful. Hungary has a significant extreme-right party; Greece has the Golden Dawn, there is vandalism throughout Europe: even a few physical attacks in London on Orthodox Jews wearing the gear of medieval Poland. You may say it was ever thus – but that is my point. I have lived most of my life in a rare island of time when such behaviour was *not* acceptable, and I did not appreciate my good fortune.

Thom Gunn, a poet for whom I have a profound respect, argued in a selection of Pound's verse made a few years ago for Faber that if we are prepared to "forgive Hazlitt for his admiration of Napoleon, then we should be prepared to do likewise for Pound's delusions about Mussolini". The snag about this seemingly humane proposition is that Pound's essential culpability did not lie in his adulation of Mussolini, but in his own words. During the war Pound broadcast at least 120 times on Radio Rome from 1941 to 1943. Many of these talks condone, indeed encourage murder. It is worth pointing out that no one asked Pound to make any such broadcasts. His admiration for Mussolini was not reciprocated: he was not close to him and, indeed, from all accounts, Mussolini had little respect for him.

Just a couple of years before Ezra Pound died in Venice, Nadezhda Mandelstam's *Hope against Hope* was published and captured the imagination of the Western World. As I try to recall the quality of excitement with which we read the story of a group of brave people in Stalinist Russia – and the love between them – I realized that part of the fascination lay in their central assumption, that *poetry matters* – that it was a spiritual strength, just as a belief in God might be, and in some ways related to that. As I came to reflect on how rarely such claims were currently made for poetry in contemporary Western society, I began to wonder if some part of the reluctance to do so went back to our bemused response to the voice of Ezra Pound.

CHAPTER 6

The Opening Field

My career, if it can be called anything so purposive, was having a slow start. For two years I worked as a sub-editor for Cambridge University Press, a job that mainly demanded attention to detail and a natural orderliness. Neither quality had ever been my strong point. When I met Anne Phillips at a Newnham College feast recently – she was Chief Sub-Editor in my years at CUP – she reminded me of other frustrations: I wanted to relate to the authors – and that really wasn't my job.

Nevertheless, I did so, illicitly. I learnt a good deal from the file of correspondence with David Holbrook before sending him queries about wording in his *English for the Rejected*. And I exchanged letters with Maurice Cowling, the trenchant historian of Peterhouse, who thought Britain's stand against Hitler was an error of judgement which cost Britain its Empire. Cowling punctiliously thanked me for my comments and suggestions when his book came out, whatever amusement they occasioned in him. But indeed such exchanges were not part of my remit.

The best thing about my time at the Press was working in the Pitt Building in the centre of Cambridge. Arnold and I were by then living in Babraham, a small village beyond the Gogs, in a house rented to us by the ARC, where Arnold worked in the Immunology Department. The rent was so low we could take on the purchase of a car and I was able to employ a live-in au pair, though doing so ate up a good deal of the spare money I generated.

I began to have lunch in the roof garden above the Arts Theatre with Jeremy Prynne. He was as unusual and eccentric a figure as anything out of Dickens: a tall, thin man with black hair slicked back behind his ears and a chin as long as Fred Astaire's. He usually wore a dark jacket of velvet corduroy. Although he often chuckled, he always had the air of being about to challenge you with the question: "Well now, what have you to say for yourself?"

Those of us who knew Jeremy at that time conjectured he was a descendant of William Prynne, the seventeenth-century Puritan who had his ears cut off for pamphlets written about the Archbishop of Canterbury. I have no idea about Jeremy's ancestry, but he had a similar contempt for metropolitan authority. He wrote no polemics, but he had no need to do so. He was Director of Studies at Gonville and Caius College, and could pick the brightest students reading English to educate as his disciples. He was already beginning to surround himself with a loyal group of young men fascinated by his presence as much as his literary certainties. He is now a guru not only among poets of the so-called Cambridge School, but admirers such as Iain Sinclair, whose studies of cities have a passion for local detail. There are now specialists in Prynne studies at universities all over the world.

At the time he rescued me by taking *Prospect* out of my hands, he was not yet in correspondence with Charles Olson and other Black Mountaineers. He is a thorough man, and once he decided there was something to learn there he set about doing so. He had only written one book of poems, published by Routledge Kegan Paul, and these were so very far from his developing aspirations that he does not now allow them into the canon of his *Collected Poems*. Since retiring from his post as Reader at the University of Cambridge a few years ago, he now spends a good deal of the year living and teaching in China.

When we began having lunch together, I had already written several of the poems that would go into *In a Green Eye*, and Jeremy took two of them for his first issue of *Prospect*. (It was his last, too, as it turned out.) Other poems of mine more influenced by Olson's Projective Verse went into the *The English Intelligencer*, mimeographed sheets printed on Gonville and Caius's

Roneo machine, edited by Andrew Crozier and Peter Riley and circulated to perhaps twenty-five poets, including Tom Raworth and Tim Longville. These formed the centre of a group of poets mesmerized by Prynne's mockery of the smug and unadventurous poetry of the mainstream.

Prynne always kept the door to his rooms in Caius College open, and it was tempting to enter them, to see if anyone else had decided to do the same, or if there was no one there, shamefully, to read the letters he left open on his desk. There was one from George Oppen, I remember – or was it Charles Reznikoff? – whose poems about people in his own Jewish family were already a powerful influence on my own work – it was an American Objectivist anyway.

Prynne's own poetry was always difficult, but at that time it was flawlessly musical, however antagonistic he became later to the lyric voice. I remember discussing his poem 'The Western Gate' – it went into *The White Stones*, but I read it in *The Intelligencer* I imagine. We spoke about it over the phone, and I questioned the pessimism of lines I particularly liked. He replied sharply that there were many lines he might have changed in the poem, but not those.

The explosion

is for all of us, and I dedicate the results
to the fish of the sea and the purity of
language: the truth is sadder but who
would ask me to hope only for that?

The group of poets who have collected around Prynne over the last three or four decades may be referred to as the Cambridge School, but few live in Cambridge. Many, though not all, were taught by Jeremy; they hold widely disparate political and aesthetic views, and not all are poets. Essentially, they see themselves as drawing strength from the English Modernism of Basil Bunting and David Jones, while responding to the voices of the Black Mountain movement. They like to use vocabulary from industry, business and science. All of them offer a resistance to media-based literary fashions, prized in London.

Their complex ideology involved a search in geography, geology, myth or politics, for a way to set personal lives into a living continuum with the past. My own poems were often written directly out of my life: a maternity ward envisaged as a landscape of men at war, the inner world of my own sons, Martin on a lonely swing, Adam with his dreams of another self.

* * *

I was the only one of my generation of Newnham English graduates who worked outside the home once they had children. In 1961 I was decidedly *pre-feminist*, a loner – a monster even, as I wrote in 'Patience' some years later.

Patience

In water nothing is mean. The fugitive
enters the river, she is washed free;
her thoughts unravel like weeds of
green silk: she moves downstream
as easily as any cold-water creature

can swim between furred stones, brown
fronds, boots and tins the river holds equally.
The trees hiss overhead. She feels their shadows.
She imagines herself clean as a fish,
evasive, solitary, dumb. Her prayer:
to make peace with her own monstrous nature.

And why a monster exactly? It was because my need to write poems led me to neglect all household chores. It never occurred to me to share domestic responsibilities with Arnold. His career was flowering as we had planned, and I had no wish to encumber his progress. At least I was now earning enough money to pay school fees – Adam sailed into the Perse with ease at seven – although I was harassed and exhausted at the end of every day, while women who stayed at home had more time to play with their children

* * *

Some time in 1961, when I was still working at the Press, Allen Ginsberg came to read at King's College. We drove in to hear him. He looked a little frazzled. His beard was blacker and bushier than I remembered, and his face was unhealthily moist. An American, Tom Clarke, then a post-graduate at the University of Essex and poetry editor of the *Paris Review,* was protecting him from the press of interest, and we only found seats with difficulty. Most of the undergraduates had to stand.

Allen was always a spell-binding performer, and he read several short poems before one about the lion he found in his kitchen. The audience laughed at the unexpected mix of terror and domestic detail, but Ginsberg glared at them.

"This is a deeply religious poem," he declared. "I can't go on without more wine."

It was Arnold who went off to the buttery to get a fresh bottle. Tom Clarke, however, shook his head at our innocence.

When the wine was opened, Ginsberg began to read again as persuasively as before.

We had offered to put him up, so after the reading we stood around while Allen signed books. It was clear we were in for a long wait. Each undergraduate was allowed a conversation. Ginsberg had begun to enjoy himself.

Tom advised us to go.

"He thinks he's going to get laid," he told us. "It's not going to happen, but that's what he thinks. Go home. Let's all have coffee tomorrow."

I can't remember now where I showed Allen my poem 'Calliope in the Labour Ward' – perhaps he was standing in front of a wall covered with children's paintings – and a poem of Adam's about a snake, which Allen read out in his huge dark voice to the startled seven-year-old. In fact, I think I was sitting in the back of a car with him when I showed him 'Calliope'. He particularly liked the last verses.

> grunting in gas and air
> they sail to a
> darkness without self
> where no will reaches
>
> in that abandon less
> than human
> give birth
> bleak as a goddess

"A lot of people would have avoided that word 'grunting'," he remarked, with approval.

Encouraged, I brought my poem 'Drunken Tuesday' to Prynne, which he liked, while suggesting I cut the first two verses.

I did not send either poem to the London papers and magazines which published poetry. It didn't occur to me. I did not enter them for competitions. Nor did I put a collection together. This last was not as eccentric as it would be nowadays. Even if I had put a manuscript together, it would not have been eligible for either the Somerset Maugham or a Gregory Award, since I was already thirty. When I became a judge of the Gregory Awards alongside Dannie Abse, much later in life, we laughed together at the strangeness of becoming judges while skipping the usual stage of winning prizes ourselves. Poets were much less worldly in those days. (Not Sylvia Plath, however, who was energetically sending out both Hughes's poems and her own a few years earlier.)

Some time in the same year Tom Clarke took my poem 'Bodies' for the *Paris Review*. It was my first publication in an important magazine. When it appeared months later, it was facing a poem of Robert Duncan which has always been one of my favourites: 'My Mother Would Be a Falconress'.

* * *

There were more disturbing events in the outside world that year. Some time in 1960 a group of undercover Mossad agents had kidnapped the Nazi war criminal Adolf Eichmann in Buenos Aires and taken him to Jerusalem to stand trial. It was controversial, naturally, since Argentinian territory had been violated, but the enormity of Eichmann's crimes seemed to justify it.

I was unprepared for the length and detail of the evidence that filled the newspapers day after day once the trial began in 1961. In some ways the printed words of the transcriptions troubled me even more than those post-war pictures of the camps. In the witness box, accounts of survivors who had seen their families murdered through a dutiful obedience to this courteous little man, now safe behind his glass screen, were particularly distressing – the death marches most of all: parents had walked on stubbornly till they dropped, fathers gagging the children they carried so they would not cry out and be shot. In the face of such terrifying testimony, the dignity of court officials, judges and barristers was gravely impressive. I did not write about any of this, but I always understood how Sylvia Plath came to use such imagery drawn from the camps in her *Ariel* poems. It was in the air we breathed.

* * *

I was teaching in Hockerill Training College, Bishop Stortford – a paradise after the Press – when I heard that Donald Davie had been appointed as Chair of the Comparative Literature Department at the newly formed University of Essex. We had been out of touch in the intervening years, though we had occasionally exchanged letters. Boldly, I rang him to ask whether he could take me on as a research assistant or some such, and he said he could. Indeed, he found a grant for me in return for a lecture a week.

The university was then no more than a single white tower set in Wivenhoe Park near Colchester. There was a lake with swans. The building was altogether pristine, with interesting modern features – paternoster lifts, for instance, you could step into without any need to summon them; you stepped out at the floor of your choice, and the lift proceeded over the top and down the other side. I glimpsed Robert Lowell, sadly in a depressive phase, and Ed Dorn, Donald Davie's new discovery, whom he had appointed as supervisor for my thesis.

In the Sixties, Dorn was a figure of some glamour. He was a slim-bodied, handsome Westerner resembling the angel cowboy from his poem *Gunslinger*. His slow-spoken, drawling sentences were far removed from New York. Since those days, English and American poetry have moved far apart. However, Prynne's most recent *Collected Poems* is dedicated to Dorn's "brilliant, luminous shade". Olson had brought Dorn to Black Mountain, and in *Geography* the lessons from Olson are easy to hear, but Dorn's voice is his own. Poems like 'On the Debt My Mother Owed to Sears Roebuck' are unmistakably American. I read that poem first in Donald Allen's mainstream anthology *The New American Poetry, 1945–1960*. But it was the sound of poems from *The North Atlantic Turbine*, particularly one about the Inuit peoples called 'Thesis', that first delighted me with its unexpected propositions and seductive rhythms.

Thesis

Only the Illegitimate are beautiful
and only the Good
proliferate only the Illegitimate
Oh Aklavik only you are beautiful
Ah Aklavik your main street is dead
only the blemished are beautiful only
the deserted have life made
of whole, unsurpassable night

The music of this opening, and the magical evocation of a deserted city in the far north-west of Canada which follows is evident enough – but what did I think the poem was actually saying about the Illegitimate, the Good and the Beautiful? Did I ever tease it out? I am not sure. I read it now as an authentication of the Inuit tribe, whose customs had evolved to survive in the permafrost. Many years later, when I lived for a couple of months above the Arctic Circle in Tromsø, I recognized the daze of whiteness which pervades the poem.

The first book of Dorn's *Gunslinger* came out in my second year at Essex and was rather different. The cast of characters included the eponymous hero, seemingly immortal, a talking horse addicted to marijuana, a brothel owner named Lil and a narrator whose consciousness is not the centre of the story. These cartoon figures inhabit the landscape of an arcane allegory, although the poem is littered with jokey asides and outrageous puns which undercut the metaphysical questioning.

I found it completely impossible to explain to Arnold what this poem was about, and I think he began to distrust my judgement altogether. However, he accompanied me to a reading at Better Books on Charing Cross Road out of curiosity. And as we watched Dorn crossing Charing Cross Road towards the bookshop, with his graceful first wife Helen, Arnold murmured, "Oh, so there *are* some figures with dignity in your world, then." He had come to be sceptical about any group I joined. And in later life, whether we ate with Yevtushenko in Peredelkino or Brodsky in New York, it was one reason he always felt entirely equal to the occasion. I think any sense of their greatness was reduced by the connection to me.

I was shy in my first tutorial with Dorn, and since my thesis was barely begun, I handed over a clutch of my poems as an introduction. He took them away without reading them, and I can't recall now what we spoke about. Two weeks later he told me casually that Tom Raworth and Barry Hall would be publishing them in a book from Goliard, soon to be part of Jonathan Cape. Tom and Barry had founded the Goliard Press together a couple of years earlier. Their books were hand-set and beautifully designed, and they were also producing others for Stuart Montgomery's Fulcrum Press, including the first edition of Basil Bunting's *Briggflatts*.

I saw less of Tom Raworth than I would have liked while I was at Essex, though I do remember meeting him one evening in a London flat, with Barry Hall, where I smoked my first joint, later returning to Cambridge much the worse for it. Tom had spent many years in Mexico, and he was attached to the Spanish Department. When I look at his early poems, especially those in *The Relation Ship*, the music feels not unlike my own.

In a Green Eye came out in 1966. I don't think there were any reviews other than a very generous piece by Donald Davie in *Wivenhoe Park Review*. Nevertheless the book was noticed by a wide network of poets, including Tom Pickard, who invited me to read at Morden Tower in Newcastle in Spring 1967. I think I first saw Pickard's own poems in an issue of Jon Silkin's *Stand*, and was particularly struck by a poem in which Pickard described a street cleaner remaining "his own man". That was the true voice of the counter-culture outside London, genuinely defiant of the class system. Some of that assurance can be found in Richard Hoggart's writing, and was always there in D.H. Lawrence.

I remember the Morden Tower occasion vividly – travelling north was like going back through the seasons, losing buds and leaves and birds as I went – until the train swung over the bridge across the Tyne and I recognized a great city. Morden Tower was built into the old Newcastle wall. You reached it up stone steps and then entered a room smelling sweetly of either hay or hash, where a crew of poetry listeners lay about on carpets and cushions, some in one another's arms. It was almost my first reading, and I enjoyed the sharp exhilaration of it. Walking back to Tom and Connie's hut across windy fields was exciting too, though I was a little afraid of taking off like an untethered kite, and very grateful for hot sorrel soup, which was made from leaves picked from those same fields.

It was the beginning of my life as a travelling poet. I read at Better Books soon afterwards, though I can recall little of the occasion. From my reading at the Oxford English Club, I remember only the mischievous, bouncy figure of the young Michael Schmidt, who has been my good friend these many years.

To announce *In a Green Eye* Barry Hall published a sheet of flecked Japanese paper with two green figures of mandrake roots above my witch poem 'Song of Power'. I still have it. At the time those images of mandrake roots made me uneasy: I so much didn't want to be part of the fashionable world of pagan magic and Indian gurus. It was absolutely not the power I wanted to invoke.

Very clearly I recall the origin of that particular poem. On the days when I did not have to be in Colchester, I used to cycle to school with one child on a seat in front of me and another holding on at the back. As we were usually late, I cycled fast, and my long hair, down to my waist – and probably tangled – streamed behind me. Hence the central witchy image at the heart of this poem.

It was always Martin who had to fight those jeering children – Martin, the slightest of my boys, whose sharp-tongued retorts often got him into trouble.

For the baiting
children in my
son's school class who
say I am a witch:
black is the
mirror you give me

drawn inward at siege
sightless, mumbling:
criminal, to bear three
children like fruit
cannot be guarded
against enemies

Should I have lived sterile?
The word returns me.
If any supernatural power
my strangeness earns me
I now invoke, for
all Gods are

anarchic even the Jews'
outside his own laws, with
his old name
confirms me, and I
call out for the
strange ones with wild hair

all the earth over to
make their own coherence,
a fire their children
may learn to bear at last
and not burn in.

* * *

In Essex, I gave one lecture a week about the nineteenth-century American passion for the organic metaphor, from Emerson through Whitman into Ginsberg's insistence on a spontaneity drawn from the improvisations of jazz. In his case, there was also the influence of Jack Kerouac to consider. No doubt, far behind all this, lay John Keats: "If poetry come not as naturally as leaves to a tree, it had better not come at all", or Shakespeare, who "never blotted a single line". I remember claiming it as the true Anglo-Saxon tradition.

But I was about to move out of it.

I have already mentioned Nadezhda Mandelstam's *Hope against Hope*, which fired the literary world with veneration for the intensity of Russian poetry and the love great poets felt for one another in the face of oppression. It was in her book I came across the name of the poet Marina Ivanovna Tsvetaeva for the first time, though she disappears early in Nadezhda's story, partly because she went into exile and partly because she was never accorded the same reverence as Anna Akhmatova by Madame Mandelstam. So it was only when I began to read an English translation of Boris Pasternak's autobiography and came across the sentences which describe his admiration for her as a poet that I registered her importance. He declared:

"Tsvetaeva soared over the real difficulties of creation, solving its problems effortlessly and with matchless technical skill [...] I was overcome by the immense lyrical power of her poetic form, which had sprung living from her experience [...] stanza after stanza in its vast periods of unbroken rhythm."

Eagerly, I looked for translations of her work, but there were none. There was, however, a short account of her life by Simon Karlinsky, which included passages of her poetry in Russian with facing text literal versions. Her poems were tough in spirit, with an immense register of emotions. 'Poem of the End' is about the bleakness of rejection at the end of a love affair.

As I puzzled my way through the verses Karlinsky quoted and read about her tragic life, I was overwhelmed with a sense of her greatness. I had not taken many women poets to heart in the same way. I revered Emily Dickinson, certainly, but for all the ferocity of her language, her quiet, reclusive being puzzled me. I did not then know Elizabeth Bishop and had read little Marianne Moore. Among contemporary poets, I failed to see the strengths of Elizabeth Jennings, and responded more intensely to the early poems of Denise Levertov. I liked Christina Rossetti and Stevie Smith well enough, but their lives, without marriage or children, were so unlike my own I could not identify with them.

Long ago, Donald Davie pointed out in *Under Briggflats* that I recognized myself in Marina Tsvetaeva, even though my life was not marked by the same tragedies of exile, poverty and state murder. "In both [...] the usual tensions of wife, mother and poet were written dangerously large." Her personality attracted me exactly because we shared so many faults: eccentricity, impracticality and the lack of domestic graces. I recognized her sense that the work she still had to write demanded her total dedication. I was drawn by the intensity of her emotions, the honesty with which she exposed them and her stamina in doing so.

She was the daughter of a professor of fine arts at Moscow University, and grew up in a childhood of some comfort. Her mother, Maria, was by far the most powerful presence in the household – a gifted musician who had been forbidden to become a concert pianist by her own father and forced to renounce the man she loved to marry a widower much older than herself. She turned all her energies towards educating her elder daughter, Marina, insisting on hours of music practice and sternly refusing any words of praise. It was an austere childhood.

Maria died of tuberculosis when Marina was only fourteen, expressing complete indifference to the world she was leaving: "I only regret music and the sun," she told her daughter. Marina reflected: "After a mother like that, I had only one alternative: to become a poet."

At the age of eighteen she was sufficiently well known to be invited to Max Voloshin's Crimean dacha, where she met her future husband, Sergei Efron, the orphan child of early revolutionaries. The first two years of their marriage were probably the happiest of a life soon disturbed by the massacres of the Great War, Revolution and Civil War. Sergei – usually called Seryozha – fought for the White Army, influenced by Tsvetaeva's idealist vision of loyal courage. Tsvetaeva was left alone in Moscow with two small children through the Moscow famine. Her younger daughter, Irina, died of starvation in an orphanage, where Tsvetaeva had placed her so she could nurse her elder child Alya.

Seryozha went into exile after the Bolsheviks triumphed. When Tsvetaeva heard that he was still alive and living on a Czech grant in Prague, she set out with her surviving daughter, Alya, to join him. She was initially welcomed among the émigrés, but Seryozha was already suffering from tuberculosis, the Czech grant left them very poor, and she lacked the domestic talents which can make poverty bearable. Nevertheless, she wrote some of her greatest poetry in Prague, much of it relating to a love affair with Konstantin Rodzevich, who broke off their relationship to begin a new one with Moussa Bulgakova (no relation to the playwright), who had a little money.

In the Russian Department at Essex, Angela Livingstone – a gentle, fair-haired scholar who dressed in delicate colours – sometimes put me up overnight. She had already worked with Donald Davie on the translation of Pasternak's essays, and very generously made literal word-for-word versions of lyrics 1, 6 and 8 of Tsvetaeva's 'Poem of the End' for me. I also began to learn Russian, though I put far more effort into transmuting those literal versions into English poems.

I began to see form as a matter of a spoken voice flowing down the page, pushing against a stanzaic structure. In making these versions I took many risks, often simplifying her images, making her thought more direct, less jagged.

I replaced Tsvetaeva's excited dashes with 2-em spaces, as in Black Mountain typographical poetry, indenting her lines to avoid the static sense of regular stanzas, always working to preserve the onward rush of her voice.

* * *

While I was working on Tsvetaeva, my Aunt Annie died and left me the equivalent of two years' salary in her will. I don't think either Arnold or I considered my giving up work to write full time. Instead, we decided to buy a big square house opposite the Coach and Horses in Trumpington. I was pregnant at the time, and gave birth to my third son, Joel Francis, not long before the move.

Suddenly, we had more space than we could use: two huge living rooms with high ceilings and French windows leading to a garden with bushes of raspberries and blackberries. One room we painted in terracotta, with the decorated rose for the central lamp picked out in white. We sanded the floor, and my father came up to put in bookshelves along the walls.

In the winter, though, the house was very cold, with the wind lashing under the front door. I remember standing in a coat to take phone calls. I often spoke to Andrew Crozier in Eltham, where he lived with his mother. He was some fifteen years younger than I was, and strikingly beautiful, with huge dark eyes. I found him wildly attractive. He never said a great deal in postgraduate seminars at Essex, but when he did speak it was always to say something unexpected. On long-haul drives back to Cambridge from Colchester, I took him with me, usually putting him up in a spare room of our Trumpington house. That is where I listened with him to a recording of Olson reading at Berkeley.

Andrew was the first person I showed my Tsvetaeva translations, and when he said that he "liked the way they moved", I sent off lyrics 1, 6 and 8 of 'Poem of the End' to *Grosseteste Review*, edited by the previously mentioned Tim Longville – a large, bearded man who I am told has long since abandoned poetry for farming. I don't know the circulation of his magazine then, but I doubt if it was much above a hundred.

And then my life changed unexpectedly. A few weeks after those first translations appeared in *Grosseteste Review*, an editor from OUP and an editor from Penguin wrote to me – independently – to ask if I had considered doing a book of her work. I had not, but I accepted the chance eagerly. Angela was willing to make literal versions of 'Poem of the End', 'Verses to Blok' and many others. This was very time-consuming for her, and she had her own creative life to pursue, so she involved her friend Professor Valentina Coe to make a version of 'Poem of the Mountain'. Meanwhile, I translated 'Attempt at Jealousy' from the prose crib at the foot of a Penguin anthology of Russian verse, and brought a version of it to a new friend, Masha Enzensberger, recently separated from her husband, the poet Hans Magnus, and at that time teaching Russian language at Essex. We sat for hours in the Essex student bar talking about married life and discussing Tsvetaeva's magnificent power to transcend the ignoble emotion of jealousy. Masha's mother was the Russian poet Margarita Aliger, a central member of the nomenklatura.

Masha had a white-skinned Slav beauty, with high cheekbones and eyes greeny-grey like the Baltic sea. She resembled her father, Alexander Fadeyev, the distinguished novelist, rather than her gentle, brown-eyed mother. He had been Aliger's lover during the Second World War; however, he had also been the Secretary of the Writers' Union under Stalin, and remained a controversial figure, as I shall discuss later on. Masha had Russian literature in her blood. This was the version I produced with her help.

An Attempt at Jealousy

How is your life with the other one,
    simpler, isn't it? One   stroke of the oar
then a long coastline, and soon
    even the memory of me

will be a floating island
    (in the sky, not on the waters):
spirits, spirits, you will be
    sisters, and never lovers.

How is your life with an ordinary
    woman?   without godhead?
Now that your sovereign has
    been deposed (and you have stepped down).

How is your life? Are you fussing?
    flinching? How   do you get up?
The tax of deathless vulgarity
    can you cope with it, poor man?

"Scenes and hysterics   I've had
    enough! I'll rent my own house."
How is your life with the other one
    now, you that I chose for my own?

More to your taste, more delicious
    is it, your food? Don't moan if you sicken.
How is your life with an *image*
    you, who walked on Sinai?

How is your life with a stranger
    from this world? Can you (be frank)

love her? Or do you   feel shame
   like Zeus' reins on your forehead?

How is your life? Are you
   healthy? How do you   sing?
How do you deal with the pain
   of an undying conscience, poor man?

How is your life with a piece of market
   stuff, at a steep price.
After Carrara marble,
   how is your life with the dust of

plaster now? (God was hewn from
   stone, but he is smashed to bits.)
How do you live with one of a
   thousand women   after Lilith?

Sated with newness, are you?
   Now you are grown cold to magic,
how is your life with an
   earthly woman, without a sixth

sense? Tell me: are you happy?
   Not? In a shallow pit How is
your life, my love? Is it as
   hard as mine with another man?

A few years later, when I wrote a talk for the BBC about Tsvetaeva's life, Masha read the poems for me in Russian, but would not allow her own name to appear in the *Radio Times*. The Thaw had been tentative and might well be brief. (It was.) Tsvetaeva, as an émigrée, was only gingerly rehabilitated – mainly through the journalist Ilya Ehrenberg's enthusiasm for her work. Since

Masha needed to be able to return to the Soviet Union, she was wise to be cautious. She read the poems with great passion, however. My English versions were, I think, read by Frances Horovitz.

After the broadcast I had a letter from Anna Kallin, who was living with Princess Salomea Halpern in a flat in Chelsea. She invited me to tea. The Princess was Osip Mandelstam's "Solominka", part of the inner circle of St Petersburg's literary café The Stray Dog and a close friend of Akhmatova. Salomea's celebrated beauty was still easy to make out. The china was exquisite; there were Russian cakes, but I ate nothing. Their words were so kind I felt I had been given a blessing. *Brushed by history.*

CHAPTER 7

History Lessons

History is not often so benevolent. In June 1967 another war between Israel and the Arab States began to look inevitable. The prospect distressed me. I remember watching Colonel Nasser on TV proudly rejecting diplomatic pleas to reopen the Suez canal to Israeli shipping. He remained adamant. Every time TV showed a map, the situation looked more hopeless. Young Israeli soldiers were being called up – most of the army is made up of conscripts. They looked plucky and tough, but the odds were against them. Uneasy memories of Wajda's films surfaced. I feared any war would be as brutal and one-sided as the doomed uprising of the Warsaw ghetto.

Israel was not an unpopular country in those days. In Great Britain the Left had no great love for the autocratic Arab regimes around them. The Israelis still remained within the strip of land the United Nations had allocated to them. Images of the camps remained vivid in the minds of most of my generation. Still, there was no question of any intervention by well-wishers.

Arnold and I were driving back from his lab as the first news began to come in on the car radio of a pre-emptive strike by the Israeli Air Force. We pulled off the road to listen incredulously. Nasser's air force had been destroyed on the runway. Was that possible?

And why were we so overjoyed? I was not exactly a Zionist, but I felt the country of so many desperate survivors must continue to exist. I had visited Israel in the year following my broken engagement, and remembered travelling there from Marseilles, in an old boat without air conditioning which took seven days to cross the Mediterranean. The cabins were so hot most of us preferred to sleep on deck. The English students were far more seriously committed than I was – younger too, and very energetic: on deck there was lively dancing, in circles, rather like Greek dancing. Songs too. The boat's first stop was to pick up a group of Moroccan emigrants – students for the most part – who were leaving for Israel. Most spoke French and had family in France, but preferred to go to Israel.

When we arrived, we were given a strenuous tour on buses, to look at Masada, the Dead Sea and the Golan Heights. Then we were taken to our allotted kibbutz to work in the fields. Gesher HaZiv is now a flourishing kibbutz in the north of Israel, but in the early Fifties we were only offered tents without so much as a mosquito net. Our task was to cut bananas. We had to get up at 4 a.m. to do so, since the heat in the middle of the day was unbearable. We were warned about spiders which might bite us.

What amazed me was the idealism of the Israeli spirit. Tough as the *sabra* (cactus) after which they were named, boys and girls alike shared work in the fields and took their turn in the kitchens. Both sexes did National Service and were admirably fit and fearless. I admired the way they carried themselves, as if their self-reliance gave them a stance quite different from the Jews of the Diaspora.

I found the Israeli belief in what they were doing and their willingness to sacrifice themselves to it admirable, but soon found I could not emulate their vigour. My arms ached as I laboured in the fields. After a couple of weeks, I began to run a high temperature, perhaps a consequence of an allergy to mosquito bites. If I had ever considered emigration to Israel, the physical demands of kibbutz life decided me against it. In any case there was always the question of language. Miraculous as it was that the Hebrew of the Bible had been revived as everyday speech, I knew I could never write poetry in it, even if I learnt to speak it. I retreated to Jerusalem, sold off silver trinkets I had bought earlier, and there met again a young doctor from the boat who was spending some months as an intern in the Hadassah hospital. I flew home without much regret, but a little ashamed of being an indoor, sedentary creature.

* * *

I can't remember when I first heard Yehudah Amichai read – probably in London at Poetry International twenty years later. He is Israel's greatest poet, one of that amazing generation who shattered traditional forms and used the materials of daily life and the language of the streets. His poetry is wry, matter-of-fact and without rhetoric, the voice of a man who was both amused by the world and pained by it in equal measure. He writes in Hebrew, a language few speak outside Israel – "torn from its sleep in the Bible" – as he put it. Fortunately, he read his poems in English, using the splendid translations made for him by Ted Hughes and Assia Gutman.

Yehuda and his family were forced to leave Germany for Israel when the Nazis began to take over, and his poetry shifts between his sense of displacement, the biblical past and his new secular culture; he changed his German name for a resonant Hebrew one: Amichai means "My people lives". He fought for the British in the Second World War. But he also worked for Haganah in 1948, and fought in all Israel's subsequent wars, though he didn't like soldiering and he never forgot the murderous cost of war.

> The bereaved father
> has grown very thin :
> he has lost the weight of his son.

He transmutes the pain of loss into lyrics of great tenderness.

Arnold and I met him in Jerusalem on our first visit together to Israel, not long after the Six Day War. Amichai was then in his forties, short and compact, with a shrug I thought peculiarly Israeli – that is to say, less weary than an Eastern European shrug, but acknowledging equally the desperate unpredictability of events.

I am, of course, well aware that the outcome the Israelis saw as a miraculous deliverance in 1967 was experienced by Palestinians as a *naqba* (disaster), and I am familiar with Israeli revisionist scholarship – indeed, I spent a month in Bellagio, where I was staying thanks to a Rockefeller Foundation Fellowship to complete my novel *Dark Inheritance*, with Benny Morris, one of the earliest documentary historians. Nevertheless, on that first visit Arnold and I met a people genuinely astonished by their victory. We met Amichai at the house of Arieh Sachs, our friend from Cambridge days, once equally close to Tony Ward, the Obscene Potter and Francis Crick. Arieh happened to be holding a party on the night we arrived. He was by this time a well-known theatre director.

The party resembled no party I have been to, before or since – rather like I imagine a symposium in ancient Greece. Any topic raised was taken seriously, mocked or explored with the same energy. There were other poets – T. Carmi and Dan Pagis among them – and Professor M.L. Rosenthal from New York. They were all in a state of preternatural alertness. Tables were covered with fruit, salads and many kinds of fish in great abundance. Nobody left until it was morning, and we took a taxi back to the American Colony hotel. I am not sure I have ever seen Arnold so much in his element, until perhaps the Darwin lectures at LSE in the last years of his life.

We saw Amichai many times after that. Once, with Ted Hughes, after a reading, as we made for a well-known fish restaurant walking down Regent Street. I remember Amichai's little skip of pleasure as he looked around and registered where he was. "In Regent Street *b layla* (at night)," he sang out. London streetlights in winter were wonderfully exotic to him, and he was determined to eat lobster, which is a forbidden dish in Jerusalem.

On another occasion he and I arrived in Oxford to read together at one of the colleges in a downpour of rain. There were no taxis at the station, and we had to walk towards the appointed hall, which was embarrassingly empty. The organizers fussed over us, apologetically, as a few gallant people took their seats, but Yehudah seemed mainly amused, and I remember he whispered to me con-spiratorially: "*We cleared the streets!*"

Two decades later, Arnold and I took two of the children to meet him in Jerusalem. It had been a disappointing trip up to that point. The seas around Eilat had been much colder than we expected, and I fear snorkelling had been the main attraction of the visit for the boys. The high point of the holiday so far had been a day riding on camels through the desert alongside the pink hills of Jordan. Neither Joel nor Martin were much interested in the country itself, while in Jerusalem the first Intifada was beginning to make the Old City an unwise place to shop.

Arnold, too, was morose. Several of the friends we had made in Israel had died. We were staying in a beautiful apartment in Mishkenot Sha'ananim, a guesthouse for visiting artists which overlooks the spectacular Valley of Cedron, but not many people were in residence alongside us, and he took no pleasure in the beauty of the view.

Fortunately, Yehudah and his wife Hana were living in their newly refurbished house on Malki Street, a short walk away. Amichai answered the telephone with a terrible cold, but invited us for a meal anyway. As we walked along towards him, I remembered his poem about the impermanence of all buildings in Jerusalem, where the "stones of the mountains roll down at night towards the stones of newly built houses"

> Like wolves coming to howl at the dogs
> Who have become the slaves of men.

Jerusalem is a city with a terrible history of being razed to the ground and then rebuilt, only to be torn down again. Something of that knowledge was infecting us.

Hana had spread a Levantine plethora of exotic dishes on the table, and we ate as we talked. Suddenly, perhaps out of boredom, Martin asked Yehudah whether he did not feel a little guilty about the occupation of Arab land. (Yemin Moshe is, in fact, well inside the green line allocated by the United Nations vote in 1947, which recognized the right of the Jews to a sovereign state.)

Yehudah did not take that defensive tack, however.

"I feel absolutely unapologetic," he said. "I was driven out of Germany, and I bought this house years ago. It didn't belong to an Arab even then."

Suddenly the whole conversation took fire, and both children came to life. They liked him. They argued with him, but they also laughed with him.

He was always Israel's best ambassador.

The last time I saw him was in London, a few months after we moved from Cambridge to Chalcot Gardens, NW3. He had just come from Egypt, where he had been awarded a major literary prize, but I thought he seemed uncharacteristically glum. When I asked why, he said simply, "They hate us."

I wish I could ask him how he felt about the Arab Spring.

CHAPTER 8

The Brighton Year 1967–68

If Arnold began to feel at the periphery of my emotional life as poetry began to occupy so much of the centre I could not blame him. The timing of our lives in any case had been out of sync for some time. I got up early to take the children to their different schools; he got home late, preferring to work in the laboratory in the evenings when it was quiet. Sometimes he continued experiments long into the night, ignoring all other commitments, or else he brought work home and fell asleep in a chair. If he came home early, he liked to read the children stories at bedtime – *Huckleberry Finn* and *Great Expectations* – while I was grateful to have a little free time in our library.

A naturally gregarious man, he sometimes joined me when young poets arrived to visit me there. He questioned them, at first amiably enough, but with growing exasperation when their replies were perfunctory. I once tried to explain that they liked conversations to grow spontaneously and were uneasy under cross-examination. He particularly disliked the desultory drift of such exchanges, and when the visitors had gone, his wrath often turned on me.

We had been married ten years, and that was when I wrote 'Marriage', which opens:

> Is there ever a new beginning when every
> word has its ten years' weight, can there be
> what you call conversation between us?

The poem ends tenderly, for I still loved him, and I showed him the whole five verses before I published it. He read it without comment, only objecting to lines in the fourth stanza, which I could not remove, because they seemed to me true.

> We have taken our shape from the
> damage we do one another, gently as
> bodies moving together at night, we amend
> our gestures, softly we hold our places:
> in the alien school morning in the
> small stones of your eyes I know how
> you want to be rid of us, you were
> never a family man, your virtue is
> lost, even alikeness deceived us
> love, our spirits sprawl together
> and both at last are distorted.

He insisted he was a family man, even though he preferred to avoid the "alien school morning". He was unmoved by the tenderness of the last verse, which concludes: "It hurts to think of dying when we close."

Arnold was a man of many paradoxes. He remained as untidy in appearance as ever, but he could not tolerate the least sloppiness of thought. He loved the stories he told the children, but when he did join us for meals he only wanted to debate and discuss ideas with them, rather than exchange anecdotes.

And for all his acuity, he did not make decisions easily.

When Professor Asher Korner – the husband of my Newnham friend Shirley – invited Arnold to become Reader in Biochemistry at the newly formed University of Sussex, Arnold hesitated, not because we would be leaving our Trumpington house or moving the children's schools, but because he had never taught in a university and had trained as a physical chemist rather than a biochemist. He had no appetite for titles. Or position. He was to show the same reluctance to take up the post of Head of the Immunology Department in the ARC after the death of Dr Gilman in 1970.

And when he did take Gilman's job, he decided not to move into the huge office of his predecessor. Instead, he converted that room into a periodicals library, preferring to work at the bench alongside his fellow scientists.

He was passionate about research, not recognition. He had already worked on pioneering studies of antibody structure and been among the first to use electron microscopy, with Ed Munn, to make images of individual molecules. His photographs of the molecular structure of immunoglobulins which first appeared in *Nature* were widely used and remain on the web today. He was always a fount of new ideas, though his absent-mindedness in mundane matters was legendary.

If I urged him to make the move to the University of Sussex thoughtlessly, I hardly had my own interests in mind. (Getting to Colchester from Sussex is a long drive and an awkward train journey.) I think what was decisive for him was the offer from the ARC to hold his job open for him if Sussex did not work out.

So we went down to look into the housing situation. Most academic staff chose to live in Lewes, where the University was based, and there were large, comfortable houses. Arnold and I, however, were more attracted to the raffish centre of Brighton, with its dodgy-looking boarding houses and tempting shops in the Lanes. Once a hoods' town, Brighton had gone up in the world, and successful actors now bought the white buildings facing the sea.

We fell in love at once with a tall Georgian house in a crescent around communal gardens. This was owned by an antique dealer who had covered the walls with paintings and filled her huge living room with period furniture. It was only a few steps from the Brighton Pavilion, just where the Lewes Road began, and we made an offer for it at the asking price. Then we returned to Cambridge and put Trumpington on the market. We found buyers almost immediately.

The decision was made. I began to investigate schools. However, just as we were about to exchange contracts on our house in

Trumpington, there was an unexpected hitch. Our purchaser's solicitor belatedly discovered there was planning permission to build a bypass which would run through the room we had made into a library. It was, our solicitor pointed out – a little defensively, since it had surely been his responsibility to uncover that threat when we bought the house – very unlikely the council would be able to afford to widen a road which would destroy so many expensive landmarks – the Coach and Horses pub across the road for one. (Indeed, fifty years later, there is still no bypass.) Our alarmed purchasers nevertheless refused to exchange contracts. The obvious solution was to rent out the Trumpington house and raise a bridging loan so we could still buy Park Crescent. This proved remarkably easy.

Arnold went off to a conference in Japan, and I set about packing books and clothes with the help of a loyal young village girl so I could move down with the children on completion. As I remember it, I played tracks from the Beatles' *Sgt Pepper's Lonely Hearts Club Band* again and again. Their refrain "Love is all you need" reassured me whenever I allowed the thought of our new financial commitments to surface.

Once the children and I were in Park Crescent, I began to look forward to sharing Arnold's delight when he joined us. He came back fired by an enthusiasm for Japanese culture – with two satin jackets, one red and one black, which I wear to this day – but rather later than expected, since he had not been able to resist a visit to Bangkok. I was not resentful of the delay. We were very permissive to one another's explorations.

But I *was* dismayed that he was less pleased with the house than I had hoped. As he walked round the huge private gardens that the Crescent enclosed, he observed, as if for the first time, that No. 46 – our house – was on the north-facing side of the Crescent and had much less sunshine. Moreover, there remained a great number of unsorted boxes and broken furniture in the room next to the kitchen. And the living room which ran from tall Georgian windows at the front to tall windows onto communal gardens at the back was empty except for our grand piano and a single Chesterfield. The woman who had sold the house to us had removed most of the carpeting and all the paintings, which had disguised the peeling walls that ran from the ground floor to the top of the house. Arnold observed gloomily that the money we had been lent to improve the property would not stretch even to the necessary repairs.

The houses along Park Crescent now change hands for two and half million, so if we had managed to hold on to No. 46 we should have done rather well for an investment of £7,500. But a shadow fell on my heart as we considered the new financial realities. Interest rates on our bridging loan had risen to eight per cent. If I had any thoughts of abandoning my Colchester job, I put them out of my mind.

Term had not yet begun. In the afternoons I sometimes took the two older children to run on the pebbly beach, finding treasures of coloured stone or sea-smooth bottle glass, popping bladderwrack and paddling in the waves. Or we rushed along the wooden pier with the sharp wind on our faces and the sky as brown as snow slush. An au-pair girl looked after them in the mornings. Arnold began to devote himself to revising the standard biochemistry he would have to explain once term began. I sat in my new study at the level of the tree tops working on an odd piece of writing, somewhere between prose and poetry.

I was discovering what different creatures my children were. I have a photograph of two of them, taken when they were not yet at school, with Martin in a toy wheelbarrow looking mischievous and Adam sturdily pushing him. It catches something of their characters. Adam learnt to play the piano from a talented American, and soon read music easily. Martin refused to sight-read, but could play any tune by ear. Adam was physically strong – Martin delicate, and his nickname at school was "Fingers". I imagined this was because he could make origami boats, but he tells me it was given to him by a PE teacher in his primary school in Grantchester Meadows, Cambridge – not chosen with particular affection, but because the teacher liked Martin to play the piano while the class did exercises. Adam read books and wrote poetry. Both of them had my own large eyes, and I suppose resembled me, in different moods. Joel was still a baby in Brighton. All three played together amicably.

Friends came to visit, including Michael Dempsey, who had taken over Hutchinson's New Authors imprint soon after coming down from Cambridge. He had already picked out Barry MacSweeney and published his first book, *The Boy from the Green Cabaret Tells of His Mother* before he was twenty-one. Barry came from the north-east and had been tutored by Basil Bunting before Michael launched him as a 1960s counter-culture personality, soon mentioned in *Vogue* and nominated for Oxford University's Chair of Poetry. He was unimpressed by this public success. It wasn't really what he wanted. Writing MacSweeney's obituary when Barry died, aged only fifty-one, Andrew Crozier (by that time a professor at Sussex) wrote in the *Guardian*: "His notion of the artist was formed around a myth of exemplary failure and belated recognition: Rimbaud was an early model for this; others included Chatterton, Shelley, Van Gogh, Jim Morrison."

Dempsey had read three pieces of my new prose writing, probably published in *Grosseteste Review*, and declared them to be the beginning of a novel. Moreover, he bought an option on that novel without seeing any outline of the way it might develop. Michael liked to back a hunch. He enjoyed taking risks, his blue eyes sparkling with amusement. Everything came to Michael easily: laughter, success, sex. He became a close friend, visiting us in Brighton, and later in Basel when we were there on a sabbatical.

We had other visitors. Robert Duncan, for instance, the San Francisco poet, who stayed with us for a weekend and gave a reading in our living room to a crowd of poets including a network of Prynne's followers, who willingly sat on the bare floor boards to hear him. There were also local poets such as Lee Harwood, whom I met again recently at the Swedenborg Hall in London, seemingly unchanged after forty years.

Duncan's reading was a great success. He was an exhausting guest, however. A dapper, handsome figure, he spoke continuously from the moment he arrived –sometimes wittily, sometimes informatively – never pausing for reply or comment. Not that there was much I wanted to say. His continuous flow of words emptied my head. I admired the poems, but I recall nothing of his conversation, I suppose because I was never part of it.

I think it was through Dempsey I learnt about Bill Butler. Bill ran the Unicorn Bookshop, which sold periodicals from small poetry presses and complete runs of City Lights Pocket Books and *Evergreen Review*. For a time, before coming to Brighton, he had managed Better Books in Charing Cross Road alongside Barry Miles. He went on to publish Mike Moorcock in the 1970s. But in this particular year he was in trouble with a local magistrate. Arnold and I went to meet him one evening after he had shut up shop. We rang his door bell, and a window went up on the floor above. We gave our names, and he dropped the key to the front door down to us.

"Don't worry about the dog," he said. "He only bites policemen."

The dog was standing just behind the door as we entered and was as fearsome an Alsatian as any I have seen. It gave a far from welcoming growl as we approached the stairs. Arnold stopped and spoke to the great beast gently, almost as if it were one of the rabbits in his lab. Then Bill appeared at the top of the stairs and ushered us upwards. Perhaps the dog was some kind of test.

We had brought a bottle of scotch by way of introduction, and as he opened it he filled us in on his story. He was being prosecuted for selling obscene books. These included Ginsberg's *Howl*, J.G. Ballard's pamphlet *Why I Want to Fuck Ronald Reagan* and the anonymous *Story of O*, which I had not then read. Did I teach at a university, and would I be prepared to go into the witness box and say that these books were literature? I agreed in principle, adding cautiously that I would have to see the books first. He told me he would send a box of them round to us in the morning. Then Bill

– or was it his partner? – read us an outrageous poem about the policeman who was masterminding the prosecution.

Of course it was already a cause célèbre. Another bookseller, Larry Wallrich, had published a large collection of poems and prose to raise funds for Butler's defence. Contributors included Michael Hamburger, Thom Gunn, Allen Ginsberg and Lawrence Ferlinghetti. Professor Eric Mottram from King's College London had offered to speak in Bill's defence at the trial.

"Are you sure you really want to do this?" Arnold asked as we walked back towards the Lewes Road.

Bill's trial did not take place until August 1968, and perhaps anxiety for his fate was a little overshadowed by more public crises. The day after it opened, the Soviet Union invaded Czechoslovakia to crush Dubček's Prague Spring. Nevertheless, a whole string of witnesses arrived in Brighton to speak for the literary merit of the books in question: a very pretty lady in a blue hat from Penguin, as I remember, and George Macbeth, then literary panjandrum at the BBC, who said he was thinking of making a radio programme from J.G. Ballard's pamphlet. Eric Mottram, at his most cheerily professorial, declared several of the books would form part of his course. We all had a very good boozy lunch. However, the magistrate was implacable, and the verdict went against Bill. He had to pay legal costs and a huge fine; his shop was closed down. I am not sure he ever recovered from the defeat.

* * *

Our own lives had changed as our first companionable summer faded and the academic year began. After my first week back at Essex, I realized it was going to be simply impossible to commute twice weekly as I had planned. Two students – Alastair and Gina Wisker – offered me a spare room in their cottage on the quay in a little village close by, and I accepted gratefully, with a little bleakness in my heart at the distance from the children and some anxiety about Arnold as he had to tackle his new university life alone.

By the end of his first term in Brighton, Arnold was beginning to find that writing his lectures in biochemistry took up most of the week. What he loved best was research, but this was a new university: lab assistants had to be shared, and ordering new equipment was not as simple as it had been in ARC. Also, he missed his familiar lab assistant.

Meanwhile, the Vietnam War, which had escalated under Lyndon B. Johnson, produced a flood of young Americans who had burnt their draft cards and left America for Europe. At Essex, we were all agreed the war was madness. Some declared all wars were madness. (I had my reservations about that, however, since I recalled bitterly what happened to people who had no army to put up a fight.)

In 1968, Essex students marched on the offices of Albert Sloman, the Vice Chancellor, flaunting placards complaining of America's military ruthlessness, while clamouring for the right to revise their own syllabus. It was a violent, frightening demonstration. Dorn, in jeans and an open-necked shirt, marched with the students, who naturally adored him. My own loyalties were split. Davie, a decent, neatly suited liberal, was mocked by the students and found the violence and hatred directed towards Albert Sloman abhorrent. The whole demonstration was fascist, and I recognized as much even as I shivered in the excitement of it. I have never marched for any cause since. And I guess the incidents must have played some part in Donald's decision to move to the States.

* * *

This unfocused but absorbing life was abruptly knocked off course by a series of events which I cannot now be sure to put in the right order. I think Arnold's wish to return to Cambridge was the first, and it took me by surprise. Perhaps it shouldn't have done: he had been muttering for some time about the chores of clearing sinks of dead rabbits. He had also complained that teaching biochemistry to undergraduate level involved so much work that he no longer had time to do research. I was unsympathetic to this at first, until he asked me to imagine what it would be like to teach Russian to the same level. Put like that, I could not deny the problem. However, I was dismayed by the awkwardness of telling my friends, the Korners. And the children – or at least Adam – was far happier at his new school than he had been at the Perse, and with his friend Kevin had won a place at Varndean, the best state secondary school in the Brighton area.

The next two surprises belong to the same morning. I came down to collect post and found, among the bills, a letter from Faber and Faber inviting me to be part of their series *Poetry Introduction 1*. In those days, it seemed an invitation to enter a charmed circle. I was told later that Ted Hughes had pulled my poems out of a slush pile – and whether that is true or not, he was certainly responsible for suggesting to his sister Olwyn she should act as my agent. I rushed up the four flights of stairs to our bedroom, where I imagined Arnold still lay asleep, wanting to share this astonishing piece of good fortune.

I found our au-pair girl in his bed. It could hardly have been the first time, either: they were so casually cuddled together.

I remember most clearly sitting on the edge of the bed feeling pale and a little faint as the girl rushed from the room. I was ashamed at the physical intensity of the pain. Adultery in the late Sixties was regarded permissively. I had been completely tolerant of my friends' extra-marital affairs. And I was not altogether innocent myself. But this betrayal went far beyond a sexual act. It went to the heart of our life together – all the worse, somehow, since I was after all in the house, not away, not going about my own business, but entirely available. I sat down, finding it hard to breathe, trying to work out my response. I was not yet forty, and was convinced I could look after myself and the three children financially. In many ways I felt I had been doing exactly that for a long while. So I offered to leave, at once, taking the children with me. Arnold was astonished I could even contemplate such an action.

"If it had happened out of the house," he reasoned with me, "I would have had to really like the girl."

I listened, not much convinced by his arguments, but silenced by a wave of shock which changed my whole body chemistry. And I stayed on. Suspicion now came readily, however. I remember an occasion a month or so later, when I had left my keys at home and returned from Essex a day before I was expected. No one answered the door bell. This was surprising, since the children were at home. Eventually, I had to call the police, who had some difficulty breaking in through the shuttered windows. (One of them said: "It's like Fort Knox.") Woken by the banging, Arnold came down the stairs to let me in. Nothing was wrong. What should be wrong? I did not attempt to explain my feverish imaginings.

A little before the Fort Knox episode, a phone call from Professor Edwards, Chairman of the Department of Comparative Literature, brought an invitation to take on a lectureship at the University of Essex. It was my first experience of numbness in the face of good news. I accepted at once, but without the least pleasure, an offer which would have made me euphoric only a few weeks earlier. The only activity which now released me from the sick brooding knot in my chest was the strange prose that went into the novel I was writing for Dempsey, which I now called *The Circle*.

Some time during the second term of our Brighton year Arnold changed his mind about wanting to return to Cambridge. The floors in the Brighton house were now sanded, our home was beautiful. Moreover, he had discovered an excellent lab assistant, as devoted as his assistant in Babraham had been. But it was too late by then. His successor had already been appointed. So it was we returned to Cambridge, and after a few months sold Trumpington and were able to buy No. 27 Park Parade. Before then, I had handed *The Circle* to Dempsey, and I waited to hear what he thought of it. He telephoned me within days, to say he loved it.

"I'll tell you where you've broken new ground," he told me. "It's with the children."

As I looked through *The Circle* again in 2010, when the novel was longlisted for the "lost" Man Booker prize, I saw with a pang how sharply I had entered their loneliness and their courage, and wondered how I had the obstinacy to continue on the course I had chosen. There was Martin at eight, thinly disguised as "Michael", shivering over a blower heater, looking for a matching sock, and Alan, a part of Adam, trying to hurry his brother up, with his good nature fraying. Other memories rose as I read on: of Martin with his tin of worms and beetles gathered from the garden, or Adam waiting tensely for a school friend, late for tea.

But, most troubling of all, is the potent image of the freak snow-storm, seen from my second-floor study as I worked on, oblivious of any danger. Buses failed and cars had to be abandoned under drifts – by the time I woke up to the situation, the phone lines were dead. It was nearly two miles to the school. Would they try to walk home? Could they?

Even now I can remember my desperation as I ran uphill through the deep snow looking for them, almost in tears as I passed families laughing together. There was no sign of my children. When I reached the school I found a cleaner, who told me yes, they had set off, with the younger one crying because he had no gloves. I was in despair as I tried to call the police from a phone box. Then a dumpy woman in tin spectacles tapped the glass, and I opened the door to tell her the phone was dead. But she had guessed who I was. Like an angel, she had taken the boys in and given them chocolate cake for tea. My tears were of relief and guilt equally – and I gave both emotions to my central figure, Lena.

* * *

The whole family was on holiday in Brittany when *The Circle* came out. I had determined not to give any thought to its reception. It was a cheerful holiday: we clambered over rocks, risked the tides of Mont-Saint-Michel, ate crêpes and laughed as we tried to assemble our new tent in the rain. In a little village we watched a small travelling circus. Two clowns – who resembled Beckett's tramps – yelled to one another: "*Prosper, tu as besoin de moi*?" Arnold and I recognized one another in them, and were once again very close.

On the day we planned to go back to England I let myself telephone Michael Dempsey, who took a reverse-charge call at Hutchinson. Had there been any press at all, I wondered, my voice as casual as I could make it. But indeed there had been a great many column inches. I had enjoyed something of a success across the board. Gleefully, he read me the reviews.

When I showed Arnold the manuscript of *The Circle* as I finished it, he had seemed quite indifferent. I imagine he thought it would have a circulation no larger than the poems. The punctuation was so eccentric – I've always regretted that. However, Judith Burnley at Penguin bought it and it came out in paperback in 1973.

Thereafter, the novel came to haunt Arnold in unexpected ways. He once told me unhappily that a spiteful lab assistant gave a copy to every new arrival in the department. He began to say: "It's the kind of novel people write when they are leaving, isn't it?" I didn't remind him how he had persuaded me not to leave. I felt guilty, simultaneously, as women often do, both for writing the novel and for staying on. In the event, *The Circle* rescued me, but I can see it damaged him.

CHAPTER 9

Metropolis

We rented a house in Grantchester Meadows until we could move into Park Parade, and it was there I received an unexpected call from Olwyn Hughes. She thought I might need an agent. Since I had not yet finished my second novel, or indeed my Tsvetaeva translations for OUP, I did not really see that I did, but she had a dark, amused voice, and I liked the sound of her. When I pointed out that I had nothing at the moment to sell, she suggested that she come and talk to me in Cambridge anyway. As I mentioned before, she later told me that it was Ted's idea that she should look after me. I asked her to wait until we had moved into Park Parade.

By the time we met, the pretty upper living room was more or less in order, even though builders were at work knocking through walls on the ground floor to make a large kitchen. From the upstairs bay-window seat, hanging over Jesus Green, you could see long willows trailing into the river Cam, a pub on the corner where we often had Sunday lunch, red tennis courts and lines of poplars stretching across Jesus Green to Ferry Path. No. 27 had once served as digs for Jesus College undergraduates, though the landlady took in other lodgers during the summer months. (Many years later I discovered from Anne Stevenson that Elizabeth Bishop had once rented a room there.) We were just round the corner from our old niche in Portugal Place, a minute's walk from Trinity Street, the new Heffers bookshop and Market Square. It felt like home at once. I was to spend nearly twenty years there – some of the happiest and some of the most wretched of my life.

Olwyn Hughes was an impressive figure: handsome, with a big-boned body and straight hair cut fashionably to turn up at the cheek when she leant forward. She dressed with style. I remember a magnificent leather coat and a huge handbag closed with a metal clasp, not commonplace in those days. Diffidently, I brought her a few unfinished Tsvetaeva translations and a chapter from *The Amberstone Exit*.

She read everything with great intensity, smoking continuously the while. Then she suggested some of the translations should go right away to *Modern Poetry in Translation*, founded a few years earlier by her brother Ted and Daniel Weissbort. Would I be interested in writing about Marina Tsvetaeva for the BBC? Indeed I was, and very soon did. I took Olwyn's address – she was living in Arkwright Road, Hampstead, in those days – and so it was she became not only my agent, but a close friend.

By an odd quirk of happenstance, even as I returned to Cambridge I had put a foot on the path to a metropolitan world. When I went to London, usually to give a poetry reading, I always called on Dempsey first, but soon I began to leave Cambridge a little earlier to include Olwyn on the same visit. I remember she took me in a taxi to a hotel somewhere in Kensington where I met Jean Rhys. She must have been in her seventies then, since I recall *Wide Sargasso Sea*, her prequel to *Jane Eyre*, had been recently republished, but her face still had the bones of a remarkably beautiful woman, however deeply cut the lines on it. Her eyes were a dark, credulous blue.

I loved her books about the *demi-monde* in Twenties' Paris, where she easily found men eager to take her to bed and two to marry her – one a crook who went to jail. Her crisp short novels came straight out of her own life. Ford Madox Ford helped her place them, and Francis Wyndham had rediscovered her, more recently. I have always admired writing unclogged with description – and books which rely on dialogue.

Her own conversation that evening was desultory: she seemed withdrawn. Olwyn explained afterwards this was because there were no interesting men at the drinks party. I can't remember now who else was there (perhaps Diana Athill?), but I do remember Jean looking through the hotel window at a crescent moon and starting back in superstitious horror. She asked me in a low voice whether it was a new moon, which would be unlucky. It was certainly a very thin sliver, and I guessed it probably was a new moon, but I lied to her anyway, and she nodded, though as her eyes looked into mine I knew I had not reassured her.

We were all drinking quite heavily, and the rest of the evening has blurred, but as soon as I was back in Cambridge I read every one of her books again. She was too distinct a voice to be taken as an influence, but I recognized in myself the insecurities she explored so pitilessly in her heroines.

Through Olwyn, I met a network of friends who have lasted to this day – Ruth Fainlight and Alan Sillitoe among them. I met Ruth first over a lunch in Mon Repos, a restaurant on St Martin's Lane. Olwyn thought we had much in common. Perhaps we do. Now we are older, we are sometimes confused as women poets who are both Jewish in origin. We joke about that, but neither of us is quite at ease with the blunder. We are such very different creatures.

Ruth trained as an artist and has a passion for painting, exotic legends and anthropology. Not for nothing did she call one of her most important collections *Sybils*. The influence of Robert Graves, with whom she and Alan made friends in Mallorca, is pervasive. He has never been a major influence on me, especially not *The White Goddess*, which possessed a whole generation of Cambridge undergraduates, including Ted Hughes. I found the whole fascination with magic and myth dangerous nonsense. For all my academic credentials, Ruth's disinterested intellectual curiosity ranges more widely than mine. I like to read books which relate to whatever I am working on, and I am more interested in geography and history than the rituals of alien tribes.

We were both unusual in the literary world in having long marriages, but the dynamics of those relationships were dissimilar. (Or so I imagine – Ruth has not written about her marriage nor confided in me.) Certainly, we led very different lives. Her initial decision to run off with Alan Sillitoe, live abroad and become writers *side*

by side was admirably reckless. But once Alan had his wild success with *Saturday Night and Sunday Morning*, she had no need
to work for money. I certainly did. Arnold and I became a family
much sooner than was sensible. It was always part of our marital
arrangements that I worked to keep the family afloat. When there
were financial pressures, I was the one who took on extra work,
not Arnold. It was down to me to see the bank manager and write
all the difficult letters. In return, I did not expect to look after the
minutiae of domestic responsibilities, which were generally dealt
with by paid helpers.

Ruth has sometimes explained that she saw herself in the same
situation as her friend Sylvia Plath: a woman poet married to a
far more famous male writer, and for that very reason taken less
seriously. Only the other day she told me I was lucky to have had
a husband working in a completely different field. I am dubious
about that, but perhaps there were gains in not having her ready
entry into the literary world.

Ruth had other problems, however – among them her brother
Harry. I had already met Harry Fainlight on several occasions at
Better Books, usually with Andrew Crozier. Harry read English at
Cambridge and spent some time in New York as a protégé of Allen
Ginsberg. His poetry is infused by an erotic lyricism, sometimes
explicitly homoerotic. When I met his mother at a poetry reading
in Hove during our Brighton year, she asked anxiously if Harry was
eating. I remembered the thin, ill-dressed boy who had blundered
into a pub with us and tried to reassure her, though I feared he
did not eat. A decade after I met Ruth, Harry visited me in Park
Parade, on his way south from a mental hospital in Scotland. Both
Ted Hughes and Stephen Spender had written to urge his release,
and I too felt indignant at the diagnosis of schizophrenia.

At first, drinking coffee in our long boat of a kitchen, Harry
spoke vividly about American poetry, but even as I listened, his
inner demons began to show themselves: he began to explain the
codes in the car number plates parked outside our house, which

he thought were directed at him. As he responded with hostility to my attempts to challenge his interpretation, his vehemence began to frighten me – I had three children playing upstairs. When Arnold rang from the lab, I asked him to come home urgently. Once Arnold was there, I noticed, Harry reverted to his former style of conversation. Later, Arnold drove him round to two friends who had been instrumental in having Harry released, and I wondered if something in me had changed his demeanour.

Harry died, far too young, in a field close to the cottage he had chosen to live in, somewhere in the West Country. He was "a true and faithful poet", as Ruth described him in her preface to a book of his collected poems she edited after his death. He does not deserve to be forgotten.

* * *

Everybody loved Alan Sillitoe. He was decent without being priggish, always ready to mock pretension, unimpressed by status. His indifference to his image in the media was profound and genuine. After winning the Hawthornden in 1960 for *Saturday Night and Sunday Morning*, he never allowed his publishers to enter his books for literary prizes. He was a wiry man, with an impish face and a generosity of spirit which made him ready to help younger writers. His modest demeanour was misleading. He understood what good writing was, and knew himself to be one of the finest writers of his generation.

Although he made his reputation alongside the so-called Angry Young Men, he had little in common with them. He was an autodidact who had formed his literary ambitions not in a university or even a grammar school, but through reading the great classics of European literature on a sickbed. Far from disdaining the world beyond this English island, he had an encyclopedic knowledge of its geography and a particular passion for its history. He lent me a remarkable book about the shtetls of Belarus the week before he died.

Alan has written with unnerving honesty about his violent, illiterate father, and the way the family had to move house with all their property in a handcart to escape creditors. Unlike Orwell, say, who investigated a world he found largely repellent, Sillitoe understood amoral rebels like Arthur Seaton in *Saturday Night and Sunday Morning*, because he had been one of them, leaving school at fourteen to work in the Raleigh bicycle factory before enlisting in the RAF. He was in any case profoundly sympathetic to the pursuit of pleasure in a world of puritanical monotony.

With his small RAF pension – a consequence of TB, caught in Malaya during the war – he and Ruth lived in Morocco, the south of France and most importantly Mallorca, which is where they made a close friendship with Robert Graves and his family. *Saturday Night and Sunday Morning* was his first novel to be accepted, but he had written six others before it. Rather like D.H. Lawrence, another working-class son of Nottingham, Alan relished making a home wherever his wanderings took him. Both he and Ruth delighted in local markets and had a practical resourcefulness, which balanced their daily writing lives.

Something in Alan's childhood, or perhaps in the jungles of Malaya, had made him fearless.

Soviet Russia fêted him as a genius of the working class, but he did not succumb to the flattery as so many left-wing writers did. When invited in 1968 to address a congress of the Soviet Writers' Union, with Brezhnev present, he dared to condemn the cruel abuses of human rights they had carelessly allowed him to observe. Thereafter, he campaigned on behalf of all political prisoners in Eastern Europe, and especially individual Jews – such as Ida Nudel – who were subject to an old-fashioned Russian anti-Semitism if they tried to emigrate to Israel. Indeed, Alan remained unfashionably loyal to the beleaguered State of Israel, even in the last decade, when more conventional liberal sympathies have switched to the Palestinians.

Early in our friendship, he and Ruth had a big house in Wittersham, Kent, and invited Arnold and I with our three children to stay with them. I remember Alan pottering about the immense garden, tying up beans, with a hat on the back of his head. I think of him now in shirtsleeves and a leather waistcoat, gleefully poring over a map of Eastern Europe. There were some eccentricities in his study – for instance, the wireless equipment which enabled him to listen in Morse, a relic of his years as a wireless operator in the RAF – but he kept his immense library of books in perfect order.

* * *

Olwyn sometimes took me to literary occasions she was attending – I remember particularly one at New Zealand House which seemed immensely glamorous at the time, with a constant flow of Martinis. Usually, though, I was happy to sit and gossip in her flat. On one memorable occasion, her brother Ted was sitting in the sunshine of her bay window, a huge presence against the bright light. It must, I think, have been 1969, in the aftermath of Assia Wevill's suicide, but I knew nothing of that then.

Assia had killed herself with her four-year-old daughter Shura earlier that year. A beautiful woman, half German, half Jewish by birth, she had grown up in Israel after her family had to flee the Nazis. Since then, she had been married three times, and was with her third husband, David Wevill, when they rented Ted and Sylvia Plath's flat in Chalcot Square, before the Hughes left London for Devon. The revelation of her affair with Ted, which led to the break-up of his marriage to Sylvia, has now been written about in some detail. I knew Assia only as a ghost, but Ruth and Alan knew her well, and Ruth spoke of her wistfully. The Polish-born film director Mira Hamermesh, whom I met around the same time, had known Assia as a crisply dressed teenager in Israel, and both admired and pitied her. She once described her to me as "driftwood" – sharing, as Mira herself did, the trauma of losing her first language, German, and having to move from Hebrew into English to express her own being. Assia was as fragmented and vulnerable as Plath, but without Plath's genius.

As I said, I knew nothing of that tragedy when I first met Ted in Olwyn's Arkwright Road flat. I think on that occasion we talked about Marina Tsvetaeva, but I can't be sure. He was fascinated by all the great poets of Eastern Europe, with whom he felt an instinctive sympathy. He had already set up a remarkable festival to honour them, alongside other poets writing in foreign languages. People think of Ted as quintessentially English. But fishing for that pike in its pool "as deep as England" was only a part of him. He looked outside Larkin's England to find his true affinities, and was drawn to the poetry of the Yugoslav Vasko Popa, the Pole Zbigniew Herbert and, especially, Yehudah Amichai, whom he translated brilliantly with Assia's help. Those translations have never been bettered: they have the authentic voice of Amichai in them.

Through Olwyn and Ted I also met János Pilinszky, a Hungarian who had witnessed the horrors of a Nazi concentration camp over the fence from his own prisoner-of-war hut and never recovered from that experience. All of the poets Ted admired were survivors, and Ted shared some of their preoccupations. This is a poem of mine from *Cities* which recalls my meeting Pilinszky in Budapest:

> In the messy flat of János Pilinszky,
> his most loved records lie
> without sleeves, horizontal
> on his bookshelves. See,
>
> his parchment face is bloodless,
> lit like a lamp from within,
> his bones fine, his lips
> shrewdly curved, humorous.

In his poetry, men are harnessed
to a cart, or watch an execution.
A tin cup tips over in the straw.
He lives in the guilt of witness,

still wanting to write
but as if he remained silent.
His companions at night:
Alyosha – or Stavrogin.

He longs for the Lord,
to bury him in his embrace
but *the old are alone*, he says,
and believe in nothing.

* * *

It was not through Olwyn, however, but through Michael Dempsey that I first met Emma Tennant. Michael had clearly been bowled over by her style and presence, and they were already lovers. She was, I think, at work on her first SF novel, *The Time of the Crack* (later republished as *The Crack*), a knowing satire on London in the early Seventies. At that time, she had two homes, one in Cheyne Walk in Chelsea and the other in Wiltshire, in the grounds beside her celebrated uncle Stephen's great house.

Emma wrote me a letter after my novel *The Amberstone Exit* came out in 1972, and with casual generosity invited me and my whole family for a weekend in the country at New Year. Dempsey came too. Emma and I drank a great deal and talked about feminism and families, her interest in the Gothic, and a possible new magazine. We walked around the misty grounds of her uncle's house – an alarming experience, which went into a key poem of my second collection, *The Celebrants*. Below is the third lyric in a sequence of poems which gave the book its title:

in it, I reject the temptations of the dark, magical knowledge Ted was so eager to explore and to which Emma was instinctively drawn. I set the poem in the wintry woods we walked through that weekend.

> Trees, under wet trees, I am beckoned down to a river
> that runs into land through a sink of sedge and rushes,
> white trench gas, between roots galled with witches fungus
> cut stumps, where bodies of bald dogs stir at the crunch of my feet.
>
> The mud and black leaves are frozen these last hours of the
> year, I follow this sloping path downwards, like a lost sleeper, in
> fear of finding the faces, and hearing the voices, of those
> who came this way   by the black stub alder   and under
>
> in frost against spindle shrubs, or wych elm in tangles of
> twigs, and who swim in the smoke on the stream and beneath
> the rotting bridge, and float head-high in the dark evergreen
> yews, and hang waiting in that poisonous foliage.

I remember that Martin went off with her son the next day to shoot at plates, and how carefully Emma showed him the way to break his gun open so there would be no nasty accidents. I think Adam and Joel played chess. Perhaps Arnold talked to Michael – I can't remember. Emma's presence was so powerful. I was as fascinated as Michael by her bold laughing face and her energy. When we arrived back in Cambridge, she phoned to invite me to meet her for lunch when she returned to London, and thereafter she became at once the most challenging and the most supportive of my new friends. For many years we met every week.

I did not quite grasp that she was part of an aristocratic family, a daughter of Baron Glenconner and half-sister of Colin Tennant, who owned Mustique, a Caribbean island, and who had once been gossiped about as a possible fiancé for Princess Margaret. I saw her only as a member of the literary bohemia I had always wanted to join. She was witty – often at her own expense – and loved writers. When I first visited her house in Cheyne Walk, she was giving a dinner party for Jerzy Kosiński, whose novel *The Painted Bird* told the story of an orphan Jewish boy surviving peasant bestiality in war-time Poland. It did not purport to be autobiography. Indeed, the casual betrayals and fortuitous escapes resembled anecdotally the early life of Roman Polanski.

* * *

I can't quite remember when David Leitch came back into our lives. He had visited us intermittently, even when we lived in Babraham, once arriving in a low-slung sports car with a fair-haired beauty from *The Times* who had recently been part of the Queen's entourage on a royal visit to Africa. I remember asking stupidly how much you could ever hope to see of life in Africa on such a tour, and she quietly put me in my place with her remark: "You see everything there is to see. Only, at its best."

I examined David's car with open envy, observing the while that it was not fitted with seat belts. He chuckled and replied with judicious calm: "The salesman pointed out that if you have an accident in a car like this what you want is to be thrown clear."

Shortly after that visit he went off to live in Paris as a columnist for the *New Statesman*. He moved into a flat in the Marais with Jill Neville, a stunningly good-looking Australian writer, and we lost touch with him for a few years. I don't remember when he acquired the reputation of an alcoholic. During the war in Vietnam, he had been one of the first journalists to parachute into Khe Sanh, and always drank before the jump. When I read his memoir *God Stand up for Bastards*, I began to realize the source of much deeper disturbances. We still had rapport, his charm was undiminished.

But he was changed. He was quite open about a period spent in the Charter Nightingale Hospital for rehab.

I knew little of his family background, except that he had been brought up respectably in Pinner, Middlesex (since 1965 Harrow), and had been to a good school. In his third year at Cambridge, while his father was dying of cancer, David returned most weekends to visit him. He seemed very fond of him, though I don't think he spoke much of his mother. I had no idea that he was adopted, though he already knew as much when we were living in Portugal Place. When his father died, he left David a letter from his birth mother, but no clues about her whereabouts.

The style of his adoption was certainly unconventional. A woman called Truda put an advertisement in the *Daily Express* which offered a baby nine days old for sale and proposed a meeting in the Russell Hotel, WC1. After the financial transaction was concluded, his adoptive parents took the baby home to Pinner and Truda promised to stay in touch with them. She did not. A letter came offering excuses, but soon letters from the Leitch family began to be returned, unopened, because Truda had moved on. Indeed, she disappeared from David's life altogether. Part of his reason for writing *God Stand up for Bastards* – completed in Paris in 1972 – was to flush her out, as he put it. Rather surprisingly, as the sequel, *Family Secrets,* reveals, he succeeded in doing just that.

He and Jill had by then moved back to London and bought a two-storey flat in Little Venice facing the canal. Jill began to be offered jobs on every newspaper in town. David wrote an excellent book with Bruce Page and Phillip Knightley about the defection of the Cambridge spies Philby and Burgess, but he began to drink more heavily, and I heard he lost a job he liked after hitting his boss. Whatever the strains between them, he and Jill let me hold large parties in their grand flat as my novels began to come out.

How did I have the freedom to explore such a beguiling world? At the beginning of this period I was still slogging back and forward to Colchester by car. I wrecked that car through sheer exhaustion, miraculously without injury, one morning of blinding sunlight. We only had third-party insurance however, and I had to switch to the slow diesel train across the fen. I wrote as I went, and had many ideas for other books, so I was not altogether sorry.

Some time after the publication of *The Amberstone Exit,* I was approached by another publisher, who offered me a great deal more money than Hutchinson ever had for one of these projects. I thanked her and – without the least idea of making commercial use of the situation, which I saw as a quandary rather than an opportunity – I phoned Tony Whittome, who had taken over Dempsey's job. Tony sounded more agitated than pleased by the news, and cautioned me to do nothing until he had taken the problem to Charles Clarke, then Managing Director of Hutchinson. He came back more quickly than I expected and offered to pay my university salary for three years in return for a novel a year. I was delighted. Three years of freedom to write with a publisher guaranteed. How could I refuse?

In a way it was a Devil's bargain. My feet had never been very securely on the academic ladder, and I had still not written up my PhD thesis, so I was not likely to find another lectureship if I resigned. I had no hesitation, however, and so it was I tasted a temporary freedom.

* * *

There was another factor.

Some time in 1972 the ARC gave Arnold a sabbatical year. He chose to go to Basel, where Andrew Kelus, an old friend from post-doctoral days in Cambridge, was then living on a comfortable salary paid by Hoffmann-La Roche. Andrew was a charming Pole who had spent the War as a child in Nazi Warsaw and was a friend of Andrzej Wajda. He liked to wear expensive clothes, often in browns and yellows, which gave him a teddy-bear appearance. An extravagant man, he liked posh restaurants and good hotels.

And his Swiss salary enabled him to enjoy many such pleasures, including homosexual adventures, which had been dangerous for him in England in the Fifties and Sixties.

The Immunological Institute he worked in, though financed by Hoffman-La Roche, was entirely independent of pharmaceutical pressures. The head of the Institute was Niels Jerne, a Dane, soon to be a Nobel Prize winner for his work on monoclonal antibodies. A man of immense culture, Jerne had a home in Provence and a beautiful wife. Something of the elegance of his chateau went into my description of Alex Mendez's palatial home in my novel *The Children of the Rose*.

In the summer vacation, the children and I went to join Arnold in Basel. We took a flat on Dufourstrasse, the same street as the Kunstmuseum, which had some very good Paul Klee and Kurt Schwitters. Other Cambridge scientists on visits to Basel preferred to live in the suburbs, where the houses had huge swimming pools. Our children enjoyed going to swim in those pools, but Arnold always craved centrality.

Some evenings the whole family went to eat at the Rheinkeller, a splendid restaurant niched into one side of the cleft that divides the town of Basel from the slope leading up to the Münster. Kelus wanted to introduce us to the fleshpots of the city. In the Rheinkeller we ate *Schnecken* (snails) – carefully tended, I was assured, which I devoured with relish, though after a while I decided what I was really enjoying was the garlic butter. And I wouldn't eat them now.

Scientists from all over the world who visited the Hoffman-La Roche Institute were mainly drawn by the seemingly bottomless resources which allowed them to order whatever equipment they fancied. To English scientists, the salaries were astronomical. Gerry Edelman, however, with whom Arnold had chaired a meeting a few years earlier in New York, asked Arnold what on earth he was doing in such a backwater. Edelman already had his sights set on a Nobel Prize.

I was still in touch with Michael Dempsey, though he had moved on from Hutchinson and was soon to become the road manager of a pop group. He wanted to visit us. Since we had no spare room, Andrew Kelus put him up in his smart modern house, where he was living with his latest boyfriend. They all got on well.

Michael drove us up the wine routes in a hired car to try the local white wines of Alsace and to visit Grünewald's Isenheim altar piece. On the same trip, we went to see Holbein's greeny-blue image of the coffined Christ, which so horrified Dostoevsky that he almost lost his faith in the Resurrection.

Some time in late summer, we visited Niels Jerne in his chateau in Provence. We had driven first to stay with our old friend Tony Ward, who was spending August at the family home of his wife Nicole in the small hamlet of Mas-en-Cruyes. We were put up in the barn with our three children, and Tony visited us daily with wine, thrush pâté and other delicacies. Nicole's father took Arnold off to visit his laboratory in Marseilles, but we saw very little of the rest of the Jouve family, who perhaps disapproved of us.

Tony and his son Gil came with us to see Jerne, who received all of us with great hospitality. After a rich French dinner, we sat talking and drinking cognac. It was very gratifying, after spending a week secluded in a barn as if we were gypsies. Some time during this conversation, Jerne remarked that the whole world would have been much improved if Napoleon had managed to conquer Russia. I was too much influenced by Tolstoy's *War and Peace* to agree, but Jerne's hypothesis was plausible enough. Geography and climate were against such an imperialist dream, but if Napoleon had managed to impose his will on the immense Russian land mass, sixty per cent of Russians who were still serfs would have enjoyed an astonishing emancipation, and Jews might have been released from the Pale. I am not quite sure why Tony and I quarrelled so angrily over this, but we did – and he set off back to Mas-en-Cruyes, a little red in the face with brandy and fury, so that I feared for his safety. Fortunately, he was fine.

We came home from Basel with enough money to pay off the second mortgage we had taken on from Caius College. Joel won a full scholarship to the Perse at ten. Adam made it quite clear that he preferred the Sixth Form college on Hills Road to the Senior Perse, and Martin was settled in an excellent village college at Comberton. Our monthly outgoings suddenly looked manageable.

CHAPTER 10

Bananas

Bananas was a literary periodical set up by Emma Tennant in 1975, with the aim of introducing the liveliest writing of the day to as wide an audience as possible. She was an adventurous editor. Unlike most other literary magazines, which were decorous even when far from glossy, this was designed by Julian Rothenstein to have the appearance of a racy underground newspaper. And Emma rapidly attracted an amazing roster of distinguished writers. She was not so much an entrepreneur as a muse.

Among her contributors were poets as varied as Jenny Joseph and Peter Redgrove, Frances Horovitz and Ted Hughes, and there were stories by J.G. Ballard and Beryl Bainbridge. Angela Carter, already a much-admired novelist, was part of the inner circle. Indeed, something of her macabre inventiveness rubbed off on Emma's *Hotel de Dream* and my own *The Ecstasy of Dr Miriam Garner*. Emma turned an amused eye on the absurdities of English snobberies, letting one dream leak into another. My academic heroine witnesses her former lover raping a drugged girl, and is transported on a wave of sexual pleasure from contemporary Cambridge into Moorish Spain.

Angela was a clever and unusually pretty woman. For all her seeming Englishness, she had lived a crucial year in Japan, where she had, as she put it, "come to terms with her own sexuality" – indeed, she owned Japanese comics of perverse eroticism. The relish she took in fairy tales often had a sexual component. In the Seventies, she was living with a large and gentle man much younger than she was, with whom she had a child.

Although Angela sparkled in her writing, she sometimes stammered to get out her thoughts in speech. When Arnold was present at Emma's table, he liked to challenge Angela about feminism, and was inclined afterwards to dismiss her ideas as merely fashionable. I knew she was a completely independent thinker. When he began to read her *The Sadeian Woman*, he lifted his head penitently and remarked: "I wronged her: Angela is an intellectual." To me, Angela was mainly a shrewd and generous friend.

As I look back on the excitements of this period when I had so much time to write and went so often to London, I do see I was leading a very selfish life. That I brought Arnold into it whenever I could hardly conceals the fact that I was no longer devoting much energy to furthering his happiness. It seemed to me he no longer needed such devotion. He was head of a good department of immunology, he had a fellowship at Gonville and Caius and dined there most evenings with new friends – the composer Robin Holloway a subtle and unusual spirit among them. John Casey, an English don with alarmingly right-wing opinions, sometimes invited both of us to his parties. On one spectacular occasion there was a ritual book-burning – one young man burned his own thesis – and Arnold argued with another Casey protégé who thought the law should never be changed to make racist remarks illegal. (Arnold, who would have made an excellent lawyer, soon demolished his belief in the legal sanctity accorded to freedom of speech in common law).

Since he now had a privileged world of his own which he seemed to be navigating with ease, I was more irritated than sympathetic when he spoke of low spirits. Indeed, on a bus trip to Norwich, with the Cambridge Opera Goers to see *Così fan tutte,* I remember meeting his complaints with the words: "It's my turn now!"

It was not a remark he allowed me to forget. He had no reason to envy me, but if I had enquired more closely into his situation, I would have made out reasons for his unhappiness. Some of his new appointments in the lab, made generously, had worked out badly. Even though his own research was going well, he felt lonely there. Our elder sons had left home – Adam for university, Martin

Elaine in Delphi in 2012

Elaine at the age of five

Elaine at the age of twelve

Isidore Cooklin,
Elaine's father

Fay Compton,
Elaine's mother

Arnold Feinstein,
Elaine's husband

Adam Feinstein,
Elaine's first son

Martin Feinstein,
Elaine's second son

Joel Feinstein,
Elaine's third son

Rosie Boycott and David Leitch cutting the cake
at their wedding, with Tony Ward (far right)

Elaine with Ted Hughes and students
at an Arvon course at Totleigh Barton

David Leitch

Jill Neville

Elaine with Carol Ann Duffy

Elaine with Odile Crick
in Mexico, 1985

Joseph Brodsky

Fay Weldon

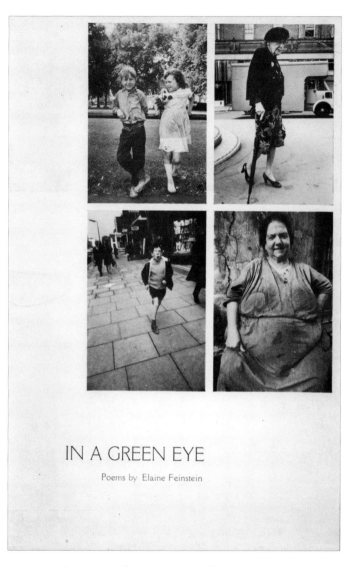

IN A GREEN EYE

Poems by Elaine Feinstein

Front cover of *In a Green Eye*, Elaine Feinstein's
first published book of poems (Goliard Press, 1966)

The 2002 Carcanet edition of Elaine Feinstein's
Collected Poems and Translations

for the Royal College of Music. Everyone in the family seemed to be enjoying what they were doing more than he did.

One of the novels I was reviewing then for *The Times* – Sylvia Tennenbaum's *Rachel, the Rabbi's Wife* – portrays a woman who makes wonderful patterns of coloured wool which earn her fame and fortune; her husband has a series of affairs in response. Arnold read the book with unusual attention, remarking at the end that Ms Tennenbaum was a more intelligent novelist than I was. "She understands."

However, our domestic bickering was never about my unlooked-for success. On the contrary. It seemed to me he was fascinated only by the literary success I had *not* achieved: as a dramatist, for instance, before I wrote plays, or as a biographer before I wrote biographies. All these genres demanded qualities I simply did not possess, he warned me. I half-believed him, but I attempted them anyway.

Fortunately, I continued to have a loving relationship with the children. They were good-natured and affectionate, and knew I would have crossed England to help any of them if they needed it. Domestic order, however, was neglected, even though we now had a good deal of domestic help. "The trouble is no one is in charge of it," Arnold liked to point out.

In contrast, Emma was magnificently in control of her own ménage. Her affair with Michael Dempsey had ended, but she had had a child with him, and one of her reasons for moving from Cheyne Walk to Notting Hill was to have enough space to offer a live-in nanny a flat on the top floor. She bought a huge house in Elgin Crescent, which she furnished with great style. She had a genuine fine-art eye for colour and a flair for choosing fabrics – I remember startlingly beautiful curtains in her upstairs living room, with little squares as colourful as a Paul Klee – and she made decisions quickly and calmly. She ran *Bananas* in the same spirit.

She launched each issue with a large party. I think of her standing at the door, usually laughing, to welcome her guests. She laughed whatever situation she was in. It was not so much that she found life funny – more a kind of recklessness in the face of risk. And *Bananas* was not so much a financial gamble, as a more or less certain financial loss.

The usual party nibbles were home-cooked by a cheerful, round-faced Italian woman, who immediately took to Arnold because he always displayed such delight in her food. He came to all Emma's parties and was usually among the last to leave. The guests included Jonathan Miller – then publicly nostalgic for science, which made Arnold an interesting party companion – J.G. Ballard, from whom Emma had drawn an account of his life in a Japanese prison camp which grew into *Empire of the Sun*, and Bruce Chatwin, then seeming still little more than a radiant boy. He knew of me, to my surprise, through Simon Karlinsky – whose book had led me to Tsvetaeva a few years earlier. Karlinsky had spoken warmly of my translations on Chatwin's visit to California, and Chatwin had a passion for Russian poetry: he wrote an intriguing piece for *Bananas* about Mandelstam's *Journey to Armenia*, and felt that great poet's sharp eye over his shoulder when he wrote his own book about Patagonia.

Emma admired Ted Hughes as the greatest poet of his generation. She included him not only as a poet, but as the author of that disturbingly violent short story, 'The Head'. She had already accepted the story, I think, when we set off as fellow tutors for a five-day stint at Arvon in Totleigh Barton, which is close by Ted and Carol's home at Court Green, North Tawton, the house he had bought with Sylvia Plath. It was not Emma's usual habit to take on the tuition of creative writing for a modest fee.

CHAPTER 11

Marina's Gifts

Although I was by now publishing all my poetry and novels with Hutchinson under the friendly eye of Tony Whittome, Olwyn remained a close friend and continued to fix other deals for me, the most spectacular of which was selling the US rights to a biography of Marina Tsvetaeva which I had not yet begun to write. Olwyn introduced me to Fran McCullough – then, I think, at Dial Press, though later at Harper and Row. Fran was immediately taken with the shape of Tsvetaeva's story as I told it to her. She offered, quite casually, 15,000 dollars, and I accepted, equally calmly, though it was then almost the equivalent of the sum we had paid for the Brighton house.

I remember my heart sank a little even as I did so. It was a project I was far from certain I was capable of pushing through. It would be a formidably difficult task. The manuscripts of letters and journals would be in Russian, and many would be handwritten. I should have to visit Russia – certainly not a tourist destination in those days – and meet the Committee for Marina Tsvetaeva's Memory in Moscow. I knew my Russian would be nowhere near adequate. Then, in 1973, Yevgeny Yevtushenko arrived at our door – a visit I could not but regard as a gift from Marina to spur me on. It was a meeting which came about not, as so often, in London and arranged by Olwyn, but in Cambridge, and through George Steiner.

George had then been world-famous for almost a quarter of a century. I read all his books as they came out and admired the intoxicating rhetoric which brought so many students to hear his lectures: one-off occasions for the most part, since he worked as Professor of Comparative Literature in Geneva in term time. I remember writing for *The Times* – I reviewed novels every three weeks in those days – admiring his novel *The Portage to San Cristobal of A.H.* Sometimes George took me to lunch at a pleasant salad bar on King's Parade. I remember the occasions vividly. At those lunches, I discovered he was not only an unforgettable lecturer, he was also one of the best and most intimate gossips in the world.

One day in October 1973, Yevgeny Yevtushenko was having lunch with George in Churchill College and, since Yevtushenko was always eager to introduce Marina Tsvetaeva's poetry to English readers, he mentioned how, in a recent tour of USA, he had included a few of her poems among his own to bring her greater attention. George asked which translation he used, and when he discovered that he always used mine, he gave him my telephone number. Yevtushenko telephoned that same evening.

He arrived at 10 p.m. with his new wife Jan – a graduate of Girton he had met in Moscow – and they stayed until the morning. When he heard I had been commissioned to write a biography of Tsvetaeva, he was very excited. He had read the letters to her Czech friend Anna Teskovà, which describe the family poverty in Paris, the horse meat they ate and how she had to beg for a dress to wear when she gave readings. He described his own visit to Yelabuga – the icy Tartar village on the river Kama where Tsvetaeva had taken her own life in 1941 – and how he had found the very nail from which she hanged herself, and was appalled to see how *low* it was. He gave me a poem he had written for her after that visit – we had an old fashioned reel-to-reel tape recorder out by then – he knew it by heart, as all Russians know their own poetry, and recited it readily into the machine. He was eager to write an introduction to my still-unwritten book. And, most importantly, he invited me to Moscow and promised to look after me there.

We talked until the light began to change, drinking whatever spirits we had. What strikes me now, looking back, is that while he expressed horror at Stalin's crimes, he seemed genuinely to believe that Lenin had been idealistic and wise. The left in the West held fast to the same story of course – but was he, *could* he be as self-deceiving as we were? When I read Orlando Figes's *A People's Tragedy* a few years ago, I was dismayed to read of Lenin's cruel orders, the kind of routine prison tortures he set in place. In the Seventies, we only blamed Stalin and his minions for the Terror. We preferred to think socialism had been a true hope at its inception.

Just before breakfast, Yevtushenko pronounced himself hungry. One of my sons, who had come in to listen, offered to unfreeze a steak from the freezer and fry it for him.

"I like it bloody," Yevtushenko told him, with a grin.

When he had eaten the steak, he added, "You are a *completely* Russian family" – a term of great praise which we had hardly earned. Then, unaffected by the night without sleep and a good deal of whisky, he and Jan both set off into the school morning sunlight without a blink.

"Come to Moscow," he told us again. "I will look after you."

* * *

He was not the only friend to offer help and encouragement. Sometime after I left the University of Essex, Masha Enzensberger had been appointed a Fellow of King's College, Cambridge, to write a thesis on the cultural life of the Soviet Union in the Twenties and Thirties, with particular reference to film. I think she was also translating essays of Eisenstein. Her spirits, which had been at a low ebb while she was living in Battersea and commuting to Colchester, were given something of a lift. She had splendid rooms in College, and hoped to find new companionship. To this end, she began to hold dinner parties in her rooms, with Russian mushrooms, caviar, champagne and other delicacies brought back from Moscow. She ran those dinners like a Georgian *tamada* (master of ceremonies), tapping a glass to command attention and insisting all present should make a toast.

However, she was disappointed to find very few people returned her hospitality. They were too busy or financially pressed to make such lavish feasts. Only at the end of three years, when her fellow-ship came to an end, was she suddenly overwhelmed by invitations. She told me this with something between amusement and bitter-ness. "They can invite me safely now. I'm leaving, and won't make unreasonable demands."

We saw a good deal of her the while. When I explained, rather anxiously, my contract to write Tsvetaeva's biography, she was delighted and threw herself into the problem. It turned out that Masha's mother, the poet Margarita Aliger, was on the very com-mittee set up to establish Tsvetaeva's reputation and would be happy to help me. Simon Franklin, then only one year postgradu-ate, and Jana Howlett, perhaps already a Fellow of Jesus College, began to translate some of the material I was gathering. Andrew Kelus sent me Xeroxes of manuscripts Tsvetaeva had lodged with the University of Basel before she returned to Russia.

There were other contacts surprisingly close at hand: for instance, Vera Traill, who had known Tsvetaeva well in Paris. Vera's second husband, Pyotr Suvchinsky, had been one of the founders of the Eurasian Movement along with Tsvetaeva's own husband, Sergei Efron. This initially idealistic organization helped in the repatria-tion of Russians who needed visas to return to the Soviet Union, but soon became an ideal front organization for NKVD, the Russian secret police. Vera's English sounding surname was that of her third husband, who had died in the war.

By another fortunate coincidence – these seemed to follow me through all the early stages of this commitment – Vera Traill was actually living in Cambridge, and at that moment was in Addenbrooke's Hospital being treated for burns. She linked me into a whole network of Russian émigrés who had lived in Paris in the Twenties and Thirties – although Masha felt she must warn me that Vera had worked for some years as a Soviet spy. Intrigued rather than shocked by this, I set off to visit her – with a bottle of red wine, as Masha instructed me, rather than flowers.

Vera was the daughter of the wealthy industrialist Alexander Guchkov, who had been an important member of the Duma before the Revolution. Vera's own sympathies had always been with the Bolsheviks. Her whole life had been filled with drama: she had been part of the Civil War in Spain, lived in France under Nazi occupation and made her escape from a German prisoner-of-war camp once the German invasion of Russia made her an enemy alien.

I found her sitting up in bed in a public ward. I could not guess her age, but she was a beautiful woman. Her bold face resembled Marlene Dietrich's, though she wore no make-up and her dressing gown was woolly and entirely functional. She had an assured English voice, with just a slight rasp on the Russian R. She also had a remarkably precise and occasionally indelicate memory for detail.

When I asked her about Tsvetaeva, she shrugged. "Of course she was one of the greatest poets of the century." After her second cup of wine, however, she began to speak more readily, confessing she had always preferred Seryozha (as Sergei was usually known), who – she thought – was absurdly faithful. "There was another woman he might have gone off with," Vera murmured to me. "A Swiss heiress whom he liked, but he could not leave Marina Ivanovna, because she was a great poet."

I noticed she seemed to dislike much reference to genius. For instance, she found the way Tsvetaeva spoke the name of Pasternak unseemly. She mimed the tone of voice. "Of course Pasternak was a great poet, but all this *awe* and *reverence*…"

A pause in my questioning gave her a chance to plunge into a story about an encounter with T.S. Eliot when she first came to London as a beautiful young woman, accustomed to arousing desire in famous men. She made no bones about offering herself to him explicitly, and took some pleasure in imitating the panic in his rejection of her. As she told the story, it seemed to cast a sad light on Eliot rather than herself.

Vera's admiration for Tsvetaeva's poetry was genuine enough, but she professed astonishment that she could neglect her person and her flat as she did. She found the stench repellent, and described with aristocratic disgust the layers of grease in her kitchen. I suppressed my indignation. She was speaking of a time in Tsvetaeva's life when only her unusual stamina kept the family going at all. Seryozha had a recurrence of tuberculosis and could find no job. His Czech pension had been discontinued when he left Prague. The family had to be fed on the pittance Tsvetaeva earned by writing for émigré journals or begged from rich friends. With more humane concern, Vera disliked Tsvetaeva's exploitation of her daughter, Alya, as a domestic skivvy, to give herself time to write.

I know now that she and Tsvetaeva had shared lovers. Prince Svyatopolk-Mirsky, for instance, the distinguished literary critic, had taken Tsvetaeva to London in the spring of 1926. Vera reported, a little spitefully, that Tsvetaeva had appeared unexpectedly in his bed, and that he been taken aback by her boyish beauty when undressed. Vera added slyly that he had not found the experience satisfying. Mirsky fell deeply in love with Vera, however, and took her with him when his conversion to Communism led him to return to the Soviet Union. Only a few years ago I discovered that Konstantin Rodzevich, Tsvetaeva's great passion in Prague, had been Vera's lover too.

After that first encounter, Vera and I met frequently. I visited her in her small flat across Jesus Green and garnered much material I initially treated with suspicion, though most has since turned out to be true. She lived alone in those days, longing for a visit from her estranged son. Characteristically, she was not overly impressed when Solzhenitsyn came to see her, to enquire into her memories of her father's study.

CHAPTER 12

Russia

Arnold and I flew into Sheremetyevo airport in December 1975, amazed at runways which remained completely clear beside huge walls of snow. Once inside the terminal we could see Yevtushenko, dressed in green velvet, even to his cap. We were ushered briskly through the customs, where Zhenya, as people used to call him, presented me with winter roses. He had a car waiting to take us to our tourist hotel on what was then Ulitsa Gorkova. He brought us to the hotel reception to help us check in.

I have never forgotten the stir of incredulous excitement in the girls behind the counter as he appeared. Poetry has a sexual charge in Russia. Only Paul McCartney or John Lennon could have elicited the same response in England. This was Brezhnev's Russia, and the brief Thaw was over, but poetry readings could fill football stadiums.

There was a note waiting for us as we collected the key: Simon Franklin, still only a precocious young man, was in the same hotel with Natasha, his lovely wife to be. He had come to Moscow to marry her. He was experiencing more than the usual difficulties in arranging to do so, since he had fallen in love with the daughter of a KGB officer of some seniority, who was not best pleased that his own position should be put in jeopardy by a family connection to Britain. Many obstacles had been put in their way, but by now it was only a question of a train to Voronezh and all would be well. I guessed that Zhenya must have helped smooth their path. An hour later, we went to see Simon and Natasha in their room, ready to celebrate lavishly with Georgian champagne.

The following afternoon, Masha's mother had invited us, along with others concerned in preserving Tsvetaeva's memory to her flat in Lavrushinsky Lane. Ilya Ehrenburg, a leading Soviet journalist, had served on the same committee for many years. A key figure in promoting Tsvetaeva's poetry during the Thaw, he wrote articles about her poetry in *Novy Mir,* and there was a whole chapter about their friendship in his autobiography. Sadly, he had died in 1967. Marina's daughter, Alya, a loyal Communist, after her return from fifteen years in the Gulag, had also been working alongside Aliger through the Sixties. Unfortunately, she too had died of a heart attack only months before my arrival in Moscow. A great loss, though I had in fact been rather nervous about meeting her. She was likely, I had been warned, to ask me: "Have you read every single word my mother wrote?"

Aliger had taken some trouble to gather several other people who might be helpful to me, including Viktoria Schweitzer, who had been working on a biography of Tsvetaeva for twenty years, and Pavel Antokolsky, who remembered Tsvetaeva as a friend from Moscow in the Civil War years, when Tsvetaeva had been in love with him.

Masha led us across the burning cold of Red Square towards St Basil's and over a bridge on the Moskva river towards Aliger's elegant apartment in a house for distinguished writers, close by the Tretyakov Gallery. Both Ehrenburg and Pasternak had lived there once.

Aliger was a small, brown-eyed woman in her sixties, then highly respected as a poet. Yevtushenko had dedicated a poem to her just before I arrived in Moscow, called 'Poet in a Market'. This describes her going to buy honey for her elder daughter, who was then very ill. He saw in Aliger's frail figure "standing among the cabbages and the lard", unrecognized by other shoppers, someone who carried

> The pure light and pride
> of both a Jewish woman
> and a Russian poet.

Masha disliked the poem, because she found it unflattering to her mother as a woman. I wondered if she was also displeased by the emphasis on Aliger's Jewishness. In early photographs, Aliger looks a little like Anne Frank, alert and eager, with large eyes and a rather pointed nose. As I mentioned before, Masha's father, Alexander Fadeyev, was an excellent novelist, though not well known in the UK. His most celebrated novel, *The Young Guard*, is about fighting behind German lines. However, he held the post of General Secretary of the Writer's Union from 1939 to 1953 – that is to say, he was there when Akhmatova was forced out of the Union by Andrei Zhdanov's decree, there too on the Night of the Murdered Poets, when the great Yiddish poet Peretz Markish was killed, and all through Stalin's anti-Semitic purges which followed. Inevitably, there is speculation about which writers died at a stroke of Fadeyev's pen. Understandably, Masha liked to mention those he saved.

Aliger and Fadeyev never married – he already had a wife – but he does seem to have been the love of her life. They parted soon after the end of the war. Fadeyev took his own life in 1956, the year when Khrushchev exposed the enormity of Stalin's murderous regime. His suicide may, however, have been more to do with his alcoholism than his sense of guilt.

When Aliger came to stay with me in Cambridge, a few years later, she had taken some trouble to improve her English and was able tell me how, in spite of all the hardships of the Second World War, she had probably been happiest then, "because it was when all our people were on the same side – and we were fighting a common enemy." It is also of course the time when she was closest to Fadeyev.

It was Aliger who gave me the address of Konstantin Rodzevich, the lover at the heart of Tsvetaeva's great sequence of lyrics 'Poem of the End', written in Prague.

* * *

When I met Rodzevich in Paris, a few months after Aliger's visit, I expected to find him old. Instead, he was an attractive, well-dressed man in late middle age, his eyes still alive with sexual curiosity. He told me that his wife was so jealous of him that he could only agree to meet me when he was sure she would be out. I imagine she had good cause to be suspicious, but I didn't quite believe him when he told me that she was particularly jealous of Tsvetaeva. I would have been glad to think so. It was very important to Tsvetaeva to feel Rodzevich had been as passionately involved with her as she was with him. I strongly doubted this, before questioning him in Paris. To my surprise, he talked of his love as *un grand amour*. In his tiny, meticulously neat flat, he kept a locked drawer full of memorabilia of their relationship: photographs of Marina in her twenties and a vivid painting of her he had made himself.

I remained sceptical, but then I was suspicious of him for other reasons. He had fought in the Red Army in the Civil War, but told the émigrés in Prague that he had been part of the White Army, a well-judged subterfuge which did not suggest he was particularly trustworthy. I also remembered Tsvetaeva's sad words: "I know I will be the most important person in my friends' memoirs" – even as she reflected that she never counted much as a woman with men around her. If it was *un grand amour*, why had he ended their affair, I could not help asking. He told me it was because of the great affection he felt for Seryozha.

Rodzevich had two other secrets, however, which I have only recently discovered. I knew he was an enthusiastic member of the Eurasian Movement along with Seryozha, who drew a salary from it. I knew Seryozha had become an agent for the Soviet government in an attempt to secure a visa to return to Russia. What I had not realized was that Rodzevich, too, was working as a Soviet agent, though he did not attract the attention of the French police as Seryozha did. Nor did I guess then that he was Vera Traill's lover. That last is evident in an intimate and long-running exchange of letters discussed in Irma Kudrova's *The Death of a Poet* (2004) and throws new light on Vera's irritable dismissal of Tsvetaeva's feminine charms.

About one thing Rodzevich was accurate enough: Tsvetaeva's involvement with a man he thought of as a friend drove Seryozha to the point of leaving her. When he suggested separation to Tsvetaeva, however, she was distraught, as Seryozha wrote to his sisters in Moscow: "For two weeks she was in a state bordering on madness. Finally she informed me that she was unable to separate from me, since (without me) she was unable to enjoy a moment's peace."

In the years since Vera's death I have filled in some aspects of her life she did not reveal. She had certainly told me that when she visited Yezhov – Stalin's sadistic dwarf who ran the NKVD – he warned her to leave Russia immediately or he could not help her. But why did she visit Yezhov? And why would he have wanted to protect her? Valentina Polukhina, a friend of Joseph Brodsky, described her contemptuously as a "knocker" – or, as we might say, an informer. Presumably, she was reporting to him. But did they have any other kind of relationship?

* * *

Russia is a brutal country, and my ancestors were certainly eager to leave it. Why have I linked my own creative life to its poetry?

Just last week I had a rather charming letter from a young man who attended that Arvon course at Totleigh Barton long ago with myself and Emma Tennant. He remembered Ted and Carol at the birthday party I had arranged for myself, and how Yevtushenko came down from London to join us. Zhenya was very late, lost in the Devon lanes, and I was beginning to wonder if Ted and Carol would leave before he arrived. But not so: he arrived bearing a case of champagne, as I remember, and was energetic beyond anything in the students' experience.

The next day we went across to Ted and Carol's house in North Tawton. It was not the first time Arnold and I had visited Court

Green. Once, on a holiday with the children in Devon a few years earlier, our tent had flooded and we had arrived wet, bedraggled and desperate for a hot bath. Court Green was a large timbered house with white-painted walls and dark beams, and bowls of attractive stones on window ledges. The atmosphere was calm and relaxing. Carol was a graceful woman and warmly hospitable. Nevertheless, I was aware of another kind of electricity, partly engendered by Emma's presence and Ted's undisguised interest in her, but not only because of that. (In fact, Emma returned to London after the briefest social visit and several days before the course we were both supposed to be teaching came to an end.)

All through lunch, Yevtushenko was trying to cajole Ted into making a trip to Russia as a guest of the Writers' Union, while another visitor at the table sat bristling with silent hostility. He was Leonard Baskin, the American painter and sculptor who had brought out several of Ted's books on his Gehenna Press. He was also responsible for many of Ted's most striking covers. Baskin's own obsession with the ferocity of birds of prey may have been one of the triggers for Hughes's *Crow*.

When Zhenya and Jan left for London, Ted asked me how, as a Jew, I could countenance visiting Russia. Did I not know that Jews who applied for an exit visa to join family in Israel lost their jobs immediately, and sometimes their homes?

Indeed, I knew a good deal about *refuseniks* through my friend, the poet Emanuel Litvinoff, who was one of the leading spirits campaigning for Jews to be allowed to leave Russia. I also understood that anti-Semitism in Russia was, and indeed still is, pervasive. That is exactly why Yevtushenko's poem *Babi Yar* was such a brave declaration of human compassion. And the line in that poem about not having a drop of Jewish blood in his veins was not self-protective. Written by a Jew, the poem would have sounded like a whine, rather than an angry shout for justice.

On my very first visit to Russia, I was given the address of a group of *refuseniks* who would be grateful for a visit. I thought initially that might not be a great plan, since I should need other entry visas in future years, and I would of course be watched – but, as it happened, a personal promise took me to visit them anyway.

Michael Frayn, whom I have known casually for many years, asked me to call on his translator, Nyella, who was in some kind of trouble which she refused to discuss on the phone. I had taken her number and address and promised to call on her. But once in Moscow it proved impossible to reach her. As soon as Nyella heard an English voice on the telephone, she hung up.

When I explained this to Masha, she suggested I ring from her mother's flat, rather than the hotel, and let her explain the situation. On our last night in Russia, I did just that, and arranged a taxi to take us there. It was only as I was giving the address to the taxi driver that I recognized we were travelling towards exactly the house of *refuseniks* I had hesitated to visit.

The flat was out in the suburbs, on Prospekt Vernadskovo, a neighbourhood not diligently cleared like central Moscow. On each side of the street there were brownish piles of frozen snow almost as high as a three-storey building. Passageways were cut in that wall at intervals so people could reach their houses – that is, if you knew where your house *was*. We were looking for Dom 99, but the numbering of Russian streets follows no obvious order. Several times the taxi driver stopped and yelled through to ask if 99 were close by. It could hardly have been a more public search. He got out and went through the wall of snow several times, only to come back shaking his head. It was getting late: my thoughts began to turn to our morning plane.

Suddenly, a large, bear-like figure, dressed in fur, appeared in the centre of the road and flagged us down. He identified himself as Volodya, the partner of Frayn's translator. We got out into knee-high snow, bearing our gift of vodka from a *beriozka* (a hard-currency shop), paid the taxi and followed him into a block of flats, or perhaps bedsitters.

Nyella welcomed us effusively, though she was still a little suspicious. She asked me to tell her the names of Frayn's children, which I was unable to do. I did not even know the name of his first wife. But then she poured out her story. She had lost her job as a translator at a publishing house and had been waiting a long time for an exit visa to be processed. She had been forced to give up her flat in central Moscow. Her tiny room was warm enough, however, and soon people from other parts of the building began to pile in to join us. We were made welcome with more vodka, tins of sardines and black bread. Many sat on bare floorboards, between the sticks of chairs.

All were *refuseniks*. Their poverty was obvious, but they were far from gloomy. One was the nephew of Naum Gabo. A young musician who had studied at the conservatoire explained to me why he was so desperate to leave Russia. Did I know about the quota system? For Moscow University a Jew now had to have ten per cent higher marks than an ethnic Russian. Luckily he had a musical talent, but he had wanted to be a mathematician. I know now there would be many such as he on the pavements of Tel Aviv when the floodgates opened. I hope he found his way once he was there.

I remember a fair-haired boy with almost invisible eyebrows. He was astonished to hear I was Jewish, though with my black hair and dark eyes I looked far more so than he did. I suppose each country recognizes its outsiders in different ways.

We did not leave until it was almost time to collect our hastily packed suitcases from the hotel. As we left, Volodya insisted on making us a present of two black wooden carvings, both of priests – a large one for Michael Frayn and a smaller version for me.

A few months after delivering this carving to Frayn, I met him at a small drinks party, and he gave me news of Volodya, who was not, it seems, Jewish. He had separated from Nyella, and was now in the West. He was said to be living on the proceeds of icon smuggling.

* * *

Some of these events I reported to Ted and Baskin in Court Green as the October evening drew in – and Ted gave my account some thought.

"Yes. For you it is different. Your purpose is to find out about Tsvetaeva. If I went, it would be a kind of declaration of support. It would be used by the regime."

In the event, Ted never visited Moscow, but back in London the Hughes family found Yevtushenko an entertaining companion. Olwyn, particularly, was charmed, and liked to make dinners for him. She did not respond to Joseph Brodsky in the same way.

Meanwhile, Arnold and Baskin had taken to one another as if recognizing long-lost kin. Being Jews of much the same generation, they shared the same vocabulary and the same sense of humour. I remember one particular exchange. Arnold admired Käthe Kollwitz and, indeed, we had recently bought one of her etchings from a Cambridge gallery. He mentioned his regret that she lived so easily under the Nazis.

Baskin exploded indignantly: "You are full of shit!"

For some reason that rude reply delighted Arnold.

Baskin continued: "The Nazis took all her work out of museums because she was a socialist and a pacifist, the Gestapo threatened her with a concentration camp. She lost her youngest son Peter in World War One and her grandson in World War Two."

Arnold, always docile in the presence of someone who seemed to know more than he did, listened intently as Baskin talked about the pitiless self-portraits, her understanding of human evil and what he had learnt from her as an artist himself. As we left, Baskin gave us two or three of his magnificently illustrated books, including his Haggadah.

Unfortunately, the friendship between Arnold and Baskin did not endure – and it came to an end through me. Baskin had offered to draw a cover for my book *Some Unease and Angels: Selected Poems*, and I was in Court Green to make suggestions. More exactly, I watched him at work. As he was drawing a flat-faced woman with small mean eyes, he began to ask me questions about an affair he guessed Ted was having in London.

"Ask Ted," I replied guardedly.

"You know all about it. Don't you? Who is it? Has Olwyn arranged it?"

I was astonished.

"Why Olwyn?"

"She likes to involve herself. That witch! What does she do for Ted?"

"A good deal," I insisted. "Arranges fees, works hard to promote him. Edits the Rainbow Press…"

"You think Ted *needs* her?" he growled incredulously.

I was relieved to find myself on safer territory as I began to defend Olwyn's professional commitment to her brother. I knew about the affair, of course. Ted was open about it as he moved around London literary parties. Arnold and I once had breakfast with him and his pretty Australian girlfriend in her Notting Hill flat. Moreover, I knew there was not one woman, but two. My friend Emma was one of them.

Baskin was very dissatisfied with my replies. The anger I had seen in him on our first meeting now returned. The line drawing for my cover now looked a little surly – I suppose I was lucky it wasn't a bird's head.

When I left Court Green, Baskin brushed aside my invitation to visit us in Cambridge. That upset me a little. Ted could look after himself, and Olwyn too, but Arnold had been looking forward to a visit from Baskin. The friendship was important to him. And I had screwed up the opportunity. Ironically, Olwyn and Baskin remained good friends, partly because I never disclosed what Baskin had been saying about her.

* * *

Towards the end of our first visit to Moscow, Yevtushenko collected us from the hotel and suggested we lunch at his flat rather than a restaurant. He took us accordingly to shop at the Georgian market. There, he bought a huge lump of beef, fresh vegetables from southern Russia, a string of exotic mushrooms as a present for me and other delicacies. Since Moscow shops were markedly lacking in goods, I was puzzled. Was this a perk for the *nomenklatura*, like the special *beriozki* which sold books of poetry you could only buy as a foreigner? Not exactly. It seemed that Georgian *kolkhozniks* were allowed to drive north to sell their goods: it was a little island of private enterprise.

Zhenya lived in one of the Stakhanovite blocks of flats originally intended to reward the hardest-working among the proletariat, now more commonly given to notables. The interior spaces were bare white and freshly painted, and I was very impressed by the steel-and-wood solidity of the lifts. He laughed when I praised them and told me a story about Pablo Neruda, who had left his apartment to go to a party and returned about an hour later. "Not a good party then?" Zhenya asked, surprised to see him back so soon.

"What party?" Neruda responded. "I have spent the last hour in your lift."

The flat was barely furnished, with none of the rich textures of Aliger's flat – indeed it would have been too bare if it had not been for the paintings on the walls. There was a magnificent blue-period Picasso, and I stood in front of this for some time before asking him how he came by it. Smiling, he told the following story.

On a visit to Paris in the early days of his celebrity, he had been invited to meet Picasso in his studio. The painter was delighted with the lively, uninhibited young Russian and took him round his atelier before offering to give him any of the paintings he liked. Yevtushenko walked around trying to decide, but none of the new paintings attracted him. To Picasso's astonishment, he admitted the problem.

Picasso was not in the least offended. "Until this moment I never really believed that story of Dostoevsky's about Nastasya Filippovna throwing a hundred thousand roubles in the fire. But now I see it is possible for a mad Russian."

We laughed at his story, though I pointed out that it in no way accounted for the Picasso on his wall.

"Ah," he continued. "The following day I went round to meet Fernand Léger's widow and told her the same story, maybe a little troubled by it. She beamed at me – I suppose she felt that Picasso had stolen much of the glory that belonged to Léger. "You are right," she told me. "Everything Picasso does now is shit.""

Yevtushenko agreed politely, but then became aware of a painting hanging behind her of a woman at her ironing board.

"But *that* I do like," he exclaimed.

She followed his finger.

"*Like* it? You can *have* it," she said – and there and then made to take it from the wall.

Yevtushenko hurried to help her and took the gift away happily.

* * *

It was through Zhenya I met his former wife Bella Akhmadulina in 1975. She was Queen of Moscow then, admired equally for her flamboyant beauty, her dazzling poetry and her readiness to court trouble with Soviet authorities. All Akhmadulina knew of me was that I was an English poet who had translated Marina Tsvetaeva. She trusted me for that reason alone with memorable stories and several unpublished poems which I later translated for the BBC.

Zhenya brought me to the grand apartment she shared with her third husband, Boris Messerer, the stage designer for the Bolshoi Theatre. She had come to prominence in the Sixties alongside Yevtushenko, whom she married when they both graduated from the Gorki Institute of Literature.

I remember her kitchen had a long oak table on which stood little pewter saucepans filled with chicken livers and walnuts. Bella herself was standing by the huge stove, her presence surprisingly that of a mischievous child. I wondered if she had prepared the complicated dish herself. Yevtushenko muttered glumly that she had never cooked while she was married to him.

Certainly, her poems do not suggest domesticity. In many, the poet behaves gleefully, in ways that invite the contempt of more conventional people. In 'Fever' she writes of being possessed by such a violent shaking her doctor cannot examine her. At the centre of her 'Fairy Tale for Rain,' her heroine visits the home of wealthy Party apparatchiks. All day she has been pursued by Rain, a tender spirit, which seems to represent the human imagination. When she arrives at the party, she is soaked through, and her hostess and the other respectable guests urge her closer to the fire to dry out. She hears in their voices the tones of those who would once have pushed her to be burned as a witch. In another powerful lyric, she gives the name of Yelabuga – the little town on the River Kama where Marina Tsvetaeva took her own life – to a supernatural monster which she threatens to destroy, even as the hideous creature turns one yellow eye towards herself. The political implications of all these poems were easy to make out.

We met again in Paris a few years later. She was dining with a group of émigré writers in a restaurant near the Bastille. I remember red spiky sea urchins, piled high on ice, waiting to be cracked open like chestnuts. Bella was the guest of the editors of *Kontinent*, a right-wing Russian-language literary magazine. Was it dangerous for her to be eating with them, I wondered silently. It would, of course, have been noted; but she was always quite reckless.

Still, it was no place for conversation between us. It was she who offered to show me the ladies' room downstairs, and I followed, a little woozily. All I can remember of what we said on that occasion is my banal question: "Do you feel a poetic talent is a dangerous gift?" Generously, she made sense of it in her own way. She thought most talent condemns whoever has it to some kind of danger, and added: "So when young people come to me for advice I tell them if you are able *not* to write, then stop! The only valid reason for writing is the total inability to live without doing so."

As I think of her fearless behaviour, it occurs to me that she must have had what the Russians call "a roof". The novelist Andrei Kurkov explained the term to me when I visited him in Kiev some thirty years later: it means some form of protection. Surely it cannot have been only her beauty and her popularity that kept her safe? But perhaps so. She had always shown great courage. She wrote in support of Boris Pasternak in 1959, and was briefly expelled from the Writers' Union for doing so. She published an open letter supporting Andrei Sakharov in his internal exile. Four years after our first encounter she was involved in a major confrontation with Soviet authorities. Together with Vasily Aksyonov and other members of the Writers' Union, she published in *Metropol* alongside several "unofficial" writers, insisting that if anything was censored the magazine would be published abroad. As a result of this threat, many writers were thrown out of the Union. Inna Lisnianskaya, a lovely poet, now much heaped with Russian state prizes, resigned in protest and was prevented from publishing for nearly thirty years. Akhmadulina was rebuked, certainly, but went otherwise unpunished.

Much as Bella admired Anna Akhmatova, she did not like the reverence the great poet commanded, and her own contacts with her had often been prickly. Akhmatova was suspicious of the reading circuit on which the new poets liked to perform, and may, I suppose, have been a little jealous of their youth and celebrity. Some of Ahmatova's remarks about Andrei Voznesensky are particularly spiky. Nevertheless, Bella readily acknowledged her debt to Akhmatova

She told me that one day the two women were invited to the same reception, and Bella offered Akhmatova a lift in her car. Akhmatova accepted, grandly, and they set off. Bella's car was old, but she was surprised when it coughed and came to a standstill in central

Moscow. Bella tried everything she could to ignite the engine, flooding the sparking plugs in the process, while Akhmatova sat with her usual composure waiting. At length, a friend of Bella's drew up and offered to drive them to wherever they were going. Akhmadulina was delighted, but Akhmatova stepped out of the car and shook her head, saying proudly: "I never make the same mistake twice."

I remember the relish with which Bella told the story and the impudence in her voice as she repeated those words of dismissal. They completely failed to describe the shape of Akhmatova's life.

Sadly, as the years went on, Bella's health deteriorated. On 29th November 2010, she died aged seventy-three in the writers' village of Peredelkino, just outside Moscow.

* * *

A couple of years after the fall of the Berlin Wall I booked a trip to St Petersburg in preparation for my biography of Akhmatova, which I was not to complete for nearly a decade. By this time, Arnold had formed the habit of travelling with me. However, just before we were due to leave, a group of hardline Communists toppled Gorbachev while he was on holiday in the Crimea. For a few days everything looked very uncertain. Tanks moved into the centre of Moscow on the orders of military commanders who had been planning a coup.

Russians had never been as enthusiastic about Gorbachev as the West. "Lots of *glasnost* (freedom of speech) under Gorbachev," one friend remarked, "not much *perestroika* (reconstruction)." In the New Russia there was still very little food in the shops, many people had lost their savings, and pensions had little purchasing power. Still, they had no wish to put themselves back under the control of the army.

A line of women, holding hands, blocked the tanks from approaching the Russian White House, in the hope that the soldiers would not fire upon women who might well be their own mothers. My friend Masha was among those women, and she described it as among the most exciting moments of her life. Then Boris Yeltsin stood on a tank and harangued the soldiers – a dramatic gesture which could well have been a foolhardy one, but no shots were fired. He and his supporters then took over the White House, the parliament of a country in transition.

By the time we reached Moscow a week or so later, the situation was calmer, and Yeltsin was seemingly in control. All the same, the restlessness in the streets was palpable. On an impulse we telephoned to see if Yevtushenko was at home, and caught him just as he was about to drive down to his dacha. He invited us to go with him and meet his new young wife. He was in an unusual state of excitement himself, since he had been on the balcony of the White House with Yeltsin at the time of the failed coup.

He admitted the decision had been taken impulsively. He had been taking his daily run in the Peredelkino woods when a neighbour caught up with him and asked if he was going to support Yeltsin. Yevtushenko had not yet decided, but when his neighbour said he was off to do so, he made up his mind. He was clearly proud of the decision.

When we reached his dacha – much smaller than the Pasternak family dacha, we observed – his wife was waiting for him. She was delicately pretty, much younger than Jan, and far younger than Zhenya. She was not literary, we gathered, but a practising doctor. And she was clearly furious. Her greeting to us was so perfunctory we began to wonder if we should have come at all.

Yevtushenko told us more about "the life behind the balcony" and Yeltsin as heroic victor, until she could stand it no longer. She had been silent up till that moment, but her English was perfectly adequate to her anger. She pointed at her husband.

"Children have their teddy bears. *He has his Revolution*!"

Zhenya looked completely subdued by this. I guessed he had wanted her to be impressed by his courage, while she saw the risk he had taken as vanity. And they both understood there could easily have been another outcome.

CHAPTER 13

Family Travels

Russia was not, in fact, our first encounter with the Eastern Bloc. Some time in 1972 we decided to visit Poland, primarily to visit Arnold's cousin, Hanna Krall, a remarkably original writer who had made her name initially as a journalist on *Polityka*. She had interviewed Marek Edelman, one of the leaders of the uprising in the Warsaw Ghetto, who had escaped through the sewers as the Germans destroyed the area. Edelman then joined the Polish Resistance and always refused to leave Poland for Israel, even when it became possible, because he would not allow Hitler's murderous hatred to define him. He felt he was a Pole, and was determined to stay in Poland.

Hanna, a small child during the war, had been hidden by clients of her mother's beauty salon. It took some courage for them to do so. She would have been spotted as Jewish at once on the streets of Warsaw, because she had large brown eyes and dark hair. "It was only women," Hanna assured us – in Arnold's brother's house in Clapham, where we first met her – "who were willing to take the risk." And it was certainly a substantial risk: the bodies of those who dared defy Gestapo orders by hiding a Jew could be seen hanging in the main streets of the city. The men, Hanna said, insisted on moving her on. All together, more than forty families played a part in saving her life – and she, like Edelman, was determined to think of herself as primarily Polish.

Her stories made use of Jewish themes, nonetheless, often taking off from an interview with someone who has a story to tell. I remember one, translated by the film director Mira Hamermesh, in which the horror of the camps became a backcloth to a tale of female devotion. In it, a lovely and resourceful woman dedicates her life to saving that of her husband, who is imprisoned in a Nazi Camp. To transfer him to the comparative safety of slave labour, she sleeps with men who have influence and works at menial jobs to buy him what he needs to survive. At the end of the war he is freed, but the camps have destroyed whatever gratitude he felt. He meets his exhausted wife with indifference and soon goes off with a younger woman.

Hanna's – and Arnold's – family, apart from her mother who had blond hair and blue eyes, had been gassed at Majdanek by the Nazis. She knew the precise location of the gas chamber, and insisted that Arnold write down the details so that he could stand in the very spot where his relatives had stood together for the last time. She also gave him the exact address of the flat on the town square in Lublin where their grandmother's family once lived.

We set off by train in July – with a car, camping equipment and the three children – to take our summer holidays driving through Poland towards the Tatra mountains, and then across Czechoslovakia. We had arranged the visas and booked the tickets to take our car on the train when we heard that Hanna wouldn't be there at the same time. A visa – I think for the USA – had just come through, and she was not going to miss the opportunity.

This was disappointing, but we decided to go anyway. Arnold knew scientists in Warsaw who had promised to find accommoda-tion and look after us; there was a Writers' Union I could contact, and Andrew Kelus had given us an introduction to the Actors' Club in Warsaw and Wajda's theatre in Krakow. It would be fine.

And we were curious. In those days, among Jews of my parents' generation, there was a shiver of horror and hostility to the very idea of such a trip. Rumours abounded about the complicity of the Poles in German massacres. It was said that whole families had been turned over to the Gestapo for two bags of sugar, and there were tales of villages where Germans were able to leave their murderous work to the Poles themselves. Even the Polish Resistance was said to be indifferent to the fate of the Jews when they made their gallant stand in the Warsaw Ghetto. That ambiguous, lovely poem of Czesław Miłosz, 'Campo dei Fiori', describes fairground music and a turning carousel close by the ghetto as the Germans set fire to it. We knew about Kielce too, where survivors of the camp had been killed by former neighbours when they returned to their old homes after the war ended.

We decided to ignore these anxieties. With the car on the train and the children lying on bunks in our own carriage, we rattled across Europe. In those days of the Cold War, the line between East and West Germany was the most ferocious border. We reached it with all the children asleep, to be woken by the rasp of German voices reminiscent of wartime films. It was a frightening reminder of how things once were. The East Germans examined our passports with particular attention. Arnold answered their questions: his school German was much better than mine.

Arriving in Poznań with our car safely off the train was a relief, though Poland looked grimly shabby and there were few cars along the road to Warsaw. There we found a café and phoned the University. From then on, we were in the hands of a minder. He sat in the back with the children, directing us first to our summer-camp hostelry in the outskirts. This was not prepossessing: all around were heaps of sand and narrow concrete cylinders. Below, a few women and small boys were banging carpets on a line.

"You will like the Old Town," our minder promised reassuringly, seeing the dismay on our faces.

"I thought the centre of Warsaw was reduced to rubble?" Arnold said.

"So it was. But we had maps and photos. We built it again to the last niche for candles."

The Old Town square was a sad fairy tale. There were postillions in snuff-coloured livery: horses and carriages waiting for non-existent tourists. Yet here all the façades were repainted, the frescos restored, all the doors made of oak, the doorknobs gilded. Our minder's plan was to take us to the Palace of Culture, where there was, he promised, a good restaurant. The Palace was a present from Stalin – a similar gift was made to all the capital cities of the Eastern Bloc – and a hideous example of bombastic grandeur. Seeing our reaction, our minder told us a Polish joke: "Where must you sit to see the loveliest view in Warsaw? The answer is: inside the Soviet Palace of Culture. It is the only place in Warsaw you can't see the building." He was right about the restaurant, however.

We found more to entertain us in the Actors' Club, which had a kind of dusty splendour, with nineteenth-century cartoons on green baize walls, deep armchairs and button-back couches in worn brown leather. The chandeliers were elegant in shape, though they badly needed a wash: their glass resembled salt. It was rather like an ill-preserved piece of Vienna. Everyone drank vodka, at our expense I imagine, and voices arose around us, first in halting English, then in German. If I needed to argue, I used French. One argument turned on the heroic madness of the Poles – which had led their cavalry to gallop uselessly at tanks as the Germans invaded – and whether it was a national asset. We did not demur. Our friend Kelus claimed that very quality had made it possible for him to take a knife away from a would-be mugger on the New York subway.

*　*　*

We decided to make our pilgrimage to Arnold's grandparents house in Lublin first, surprised to find it was to the east of Warsaw, since we had been told it was a handsome town in yellow stucco, a relic of what had once been the Habsburg Empire.

The house was on the main square, and impressive, though it had probably always been divided into flats. Arnold's family were called Zimmerman, and we tried that name on the tenants from the first floor, who answered the door – in those days, there was no question of reparations or claims on property, so they let us in hospitably enough. It was light and airy, with Georgian-style windows and a large stove covered with blue and yellow tiles at the centre of the building. This heated the rooms on all four sides in winter.

Since we had no minder to interpret for us now, conversation was only possible in German, which the tenants spoke rather well. Did they remember the Zimmermans? we wondered. It was more than a quarter of a century ago. They remembered them as pleasant elderly people. They knew what had happened to them, and were sorry. We thought of that, as we travelled towards Majdanek, with Hanna Krall's instructions in Arnold's wallet. I wondered if we should put our children through what might well be a traumatic experience, but there was little left to see in that camp. No glass cases of shoes, suitcases or spectacles, which we were later to find in Auschwitz – no small shoes in the mud, as in Birkenau. Only claustrophobic concrete buildings, not much bigger than bunkers on the south coast of England left standing after the war.

* * *

We drove away through suburbs of matchbox-shaped new apartment buildings, finished in brown, cream and green. There were no lights on the roads once the sun went down, and no cat's-eyes that make Western highways easy to negotiate. Quite soon we had to pull out sharply to overtake a horse-drawn cart loaded with grass. The horse looked round slowly at us as we passed.

"There's no one driving it," the children called out, amazed.

"Yes, there is. Look – in the back, asleep on the grass."

As the evening darkened, there were peasants straggling five abreast across the road – and once, when we had to stop, a group of villagers, all very drunk, gathered around the car. I was a little afraid of them, and I remember Arnold advising the boys to roll up their windows. The villagers had narrow faces; when their mouths opened we could see ugly black stumps of teeth in them. One youngster began to fiddle with our windscreen wipers – we had been told in London that these had some commercial value on the black market – but when Arnold tooted the horn the fellow stopped. Another villager fell drunkenly under the front bumper, but a friend dragged him to safety. Another toot and the crowd parted altogether, and we made our escape into forest darkness, barely penetrated by the car's full headlights.

An unknown animal ran across their beam, and one of the children wondered about wild boars. Wild boar had been a great delicacy on the menu at the Palace of Culture, and we were told there were many in the local forests. Indeed, when we saw signs in Polish warning us against something, we thought we recognized the same word that had been on the menu. (We were wildly wrong: in fact, the signs were forbidding us to light fires.)

Krakow, when we reached it, welcomed us with its yellow-stone arches, and we could see it was a beautiful city. The trumpeter in the Rynek, the central square, still played every hour. We were, however, too exhausted to register the beauty of the ancient buildings. The children, I think, were asleep. I don't remember how we contacted our next minder – this time from the Writers' Union – only that we shared him with the Chilean novelist José Donoso and his handsome wife, whose features resembled those of an Inca princess. He had substantial royalties in *zloty* which he was unable to take out of the country. Sadly, there was nothing he could find to buy that he wanted.

He was then living as an exile in Spain. He was a wry, humorous man, intrigued by our three children and the way they amused themselves. He was much more indignant about our Krakow minders than we were. His own was designated as a Spanish interpreter. I remember José saying: "He even follows me into the lavatory. And I wouldn't mind, but he refuses to translate the graffiti. Why? Do you suppose there are listening devices in there?"

We became quite close to Donoso, and a few years later, I think in 1978, I met him again in Madrid. His wife had by this time returned to Chile, but he was in two minds about joining her.

Franco was dead, and he liked Spain. Allende had been replaced by Pinochet in 1973, and he loathed Pinochet, but it was not the reason he gave for his hesitation about returning to Chile. He told me he was in flight from an image of himself he could never lose in a Chilean context.

Donoso came from one of the oldest families in Chile, and was brought up in the wealthy part of Santiago. He seemed ashamed of that, positively disliking the way everyone he knew was related to one another. He told me his only relationship with his fellow countrymen had been a master-servant one. He had watched women who brought him up and slept with him as a young man becoming prematurely decrepit. He mused about their fate as an emblem of exploitation. Not that he was a communist, or even altogether a socialist. "I don't like causes," he insisted, "but Allende was at least an honourable option."

Though he backed away from political allegiance, he thought Latin American novelists had a rare opportunity to confront their governments. He was one of a group of writers, alongside García Márquez and Vargas Llosa, whose "magical realist" writing had reached an audience worldwide. I was personally most attached to his novel, *The Obscene Bird of Night*, because it includes an image of three chess-playing children which he confessed was based on our own children as he observed them in Krakow.

At some point I wondered idly whether he and his wife did not find their separation painful, and he looked a little evasive. I could see that displacement, even loneliness, suited him. I know now he was homosexual: his papers at Iowa made this clear after his death.

When he came to visit us in Cambridge, we walked him round the city and wondered if he had perhaps considered living there. His English was flawless, but he found the city too cosy. I think it was in Cambridge he told me that when he left Chile for the first time at eighteen he chose to work as a shepherd in Patagonia. His job was to look for sick sheep before their eyes could be eaten by seagulls.

"A good cure for squeamishness," he remarked.

* * *

I made use of some notes on our Polish travels in my fourth novel, *Children of the Rose*, but the novel is suffused with a profound melancholy which did not characterize our trip at the time. It sometimes seems to me that writers create their own future when they invent stories. Perhaps in writing about a separated couple, I had intuited problems I preferred not to acknowledge. Reading it recently, I was struck by the vivid loneliness felt by the central woman. It must have come from an inner world I was deliberately concealing from myself.

But I did not feel lonely then, in 1973, as we put up our tent in open fields, with the children eating *Bratwurst* and laughing.

We drove across the Tatra Mountains into Czechoslovakia, where I planned to visit Miroslav Holub in Prague. I had met him at a poetry festival in London, and Arnold knew him as a fellow immunologist. Whatever vision we had once had of Czech life – from films like Jiří Menzel's *Closely Watched Trains* perhaps – had to be modified at the border. We were very efficiently examined – not only our passports, but also our luggage.

Czechoslovakia had been invaded by troops of the Eastern bloc sent in to put down Dubček's Velvet Revolution a few years previously. We became conscious that in leaving Poland we were leaving a country made comfortable by laxity, if not actual corruption. Even ordinary friendliness was missing on the Czech side of the border. It would have been helpful if someone had at least warned us, as we set off finally along the main road to the West, that signposts to Prague were rare, and that there were few garages along the way.

There were several crises as we tried to choose the correct route – almost out of petrol, we found several bifurcated signs, indicating two roads of seemingly equal importance going towards villages unnamed on our map. Never a mention of Prague. When we arrived at last, the children were very hungry, and we parked between two Tatra cars and looked for a restaurant. We found somewhere we could buy rolls filled with *Bratwurst* and mustard, and felt rather better.

When we came out, two policemen were waiting for us, who smiled, indicated our car and asked for two hundred crowns in cash. We pointed to the two cars on either side of our own indignantly. Their smiles broadened. Those were cars used by state officials, who had quite different rules. Arnold asked them what would happen if we refused to pay?

"Two hundred crowns here," they explained. "Or two thousand at the border."

I cannot remember where we stayed in Prague, or much about our time there, except that East Germans seemed to have bought all the tickets for the opera house in which Mozart's *Don Giovanni* had been first staged – Arnold by sheer persistence found us a box we couldn't really afford – and then we set off to meet the irrepressible J. Stertzl.

Arnold knew Stertzl as the head of a distinguished immunology department in Prague. A barrel-chested, tough-faced man, he was known to drink heavily, and one of our friends from Basel days, Ivan Lefkowitz, another Czech, assured us that there was nothing Stertzl liked more than to drink through the night with a visiting scientist and sit in the front row early the next morning to confound the hapless speaker with his own energy. When Arnold rang him at the lab, he had some trouble getting through, but when he did, Stertzl invited him to give a talk on his latest work. Before that, however, he would like the whole family to eat with him.

We were taken to an outdoor café in the woods with a group of scientists, all speaking English, the international language of science. Stertzl ordered food for everyone before explaining that he had just been fired. It was the reason the switchboard had some trouble finding him.

"This man," he pointed to one of his colleagues, "was put in my place last week."

Everyone nodded. He was evidently not joking.

"Since then – I don't know why – it has become very difficult to get supplies of the reagents we need. This man," Stertzl continued, pointing to his successor, "must be in trouble with the authorities."

Everyone laughed at that, but the new head looked embarrassed.

Stertzl continued: "I am not sure whether he ever trained as a scientist."

The man looked even more uncomfortable, and said he had not.

"He knows his function," said Stertzl drily. "And I'm sure he does his job well. But that's why they let me hang around. Someone has to ask questions of our guests."

"So you will sit in on my lecture?" Arnold asked.

Stertzl grinned and ordered more beer. "Naturally."

I am not sure how we came to be discussing Holub a little while later. Probably I expressed my admiration for poems I had heard him read.

This diverted Stertzl from his scientific enquiries.

"Miroslav is in trouble," he told me. "He has been in trouble a long time, of course. You must know his poetry is unpublished here in Czechoslovakia – and to publish abroad is not regarded as patriotic."

"He travels abroad quite a lot."

"Yes. That may stop. He has written a letter in the press this week renouncing all contact with the West."

"Why would he do that?" I asked.

"In return for the possibility of publishing in Prague. He is a poet. He wants to see his words in his own language."

I said incautiously: "I was hoping to see him."

Stertzl stared at me, his expression unreadable. "When he has just renounced all contact with the West? That would not be kind."

Arnold and I discussed what we should do as we walked back to the car with the children, who were rather sleepy and bored. Stertzl's advice made sense. The children slept through the opera, and the following day, without any attempt to contact Holub, we set off for home.

A letter from Miroslav was waiting for us in Park Parade when we returned. He had heard of our presence in Prague and was sorry not to see us.

"In times of difficulty you need to see your friends," he wrote.

We were distressed to have interpreted the situation so poorly. Fortunately, there were many other occasions, notably over breakfast in Park Parade during a Cambridge Poetry Festival. I found him charming but also inscrutable, cautious, ironic – essentially hidden.

I only really saw him happy and relaxed on a visit to Prague, after the Soviet Empire had collapsed many years later. Our accommodation then was organized by Ivan Lefkowitz, but Holub took charge of much of our entertainment. He was a friend of Jiří Menzel and took us to meet him at work on a theatre production, explaining that Menzel rarely directed films now: he disliked the post-Communist demand for instant profitability. Holub had been more fortunate: he was now the President of the Writers' Union which had once bullied him.

Later in the day, he took us to a newly restored art-deco café, where we had coffee, and after that to a rotating restaurant built on a former Jewish cemetery, where his wife joined us for dinner. Holub spoke without reserve of Jewish relatives he had never mentioned before. Both of them seemed relaxed, unburdened by the past. It was a shock to hear from Ivan only a few weeks after our return that he had died of a heart attack.

CHAPTER 14

Grief

The dynamics of my own domestic life changed dramatically with the death of my mother. I had not thought of her as ill – or at least had not for the twenty-five years since her surgery for colon cancer. I spoke to her by phone most weeks, and one day she confessed she had not been feeling well. I was more disturbed by this than her words warranted, and phoned again a few days later to ask if she felt any better.

"Not yet, dear," she replied.

There was an unfamiliar tone in her voice: enfeebled, though stoical. I said I would drive across to see her that weekend, but she hesitated, because it was 1973 and shops were lit by candles, petrol stations often closed. She was concerned we would not be able to get back to Cambridge. I certainly did not want to be stuck in Leicester, but my father came on the line and insisted there would be no problem: he was sure one of his nephews would know where to find petrol. We decided to risk it.

My father had cooked for us, while my mother lay in bed, resting. Her doctor had been to see her and declared she was fine, Dad told us. She didn't look fine to me. She was pale, and not particularly appreciative of my father's efforts. I could see he was enjoying his new role, but he had to keep coming in and asking for instructions. He was preparing chicken soup, chopped liver and roast brisket, which we gobbled up in a rather late lunch.

Some time in the middle of the afternoon I went in to see how my mother was doing, and found her trying to reach the potty that was under the bed. It was a huge effort for her, and she fell back, quite suddenly, looking exhausted. I called for my father, who padded in, making reassuring affectionate noises. She did not respond. He called her name again and again with mounting agitation. "She always replies to me. However bad she feels."

Then Arnold came in behind me, and said softly, "Why don't you take your father into the next room? It'll give your mother a better chance. I'll phone the doctor."

If he guessed my mother was dead, he did not say so. I led my father into the living room and held his hand until the doctor came. He went in to examine my mother very briefly. Then he astonished my father with the terrible news.

Dad was transfixed with incredulity, then wild tears. I had never seen him cry before. The doctor said – rather uncomfortably – there would have to be a post-mortem, since he had found nothing to suggest she was seriously ill on his last visit. I can't remember how long it was before men came to take away her body, or even when we were told the outcome of their investigations. It is all a blank in my memory. The death certificate declares she suffered a heart attack.

My father was not listening to the trolleys coming to take her body away. "We never had a chance to say goodbye," he repeated miserably

The doctor wrote out a prescription for him – and left two Diazepam, which I later gave him with a cup of tea. I washed up and put the food away in the fridge, too stunned to weep.

The telephone numbers I now needed were listed in a blue leather book, in my mother's scrupulously neat writing. As I set about making my calls, numbness took over my whole being. Everyone's voice seemed to come from a long way away. I received commiserations without feeling any pain. Frank was genuinely upset, I could hear – Maurice was just out of hospital himself, and too frail even to come to the phone. Her sister Annie was dead, of course, and Jo too. But my mother had many friends. When I had done all I could, I sat on the hall chair silently.

My cousin Gerald came round to help arrange the funeral. The children were old enough to be sad and a little bewildered. She had been a kind grandmother. I remember Adam was alarmed to hear that he was expected to say Kaddish for her at the funeral. He had been Bar Mitzvah two years earlier and indeed had to learn his portion twice, since his teacher initially picked the wrong bit, but he had little familiarity with the Hebrew script.

After the funeral, my father was pale and quiet. I began to wonder how he would cope on his own, and saw he could not. So it was I brought him back to Park Parade, where he immediately decided we needed a new bathroom and, once he had picked a bedroom on the first floor, arranged to put down a fitted carpet. But I had a hunch things were not going to be as easy as they seemed initially.

The most obvious problem was the question of my father's need to observe the dietary laws. I did not keep a kosher home, and as far as I knew there was no kosher butcher in Cambridge. Louise Mestel, a friend married to a traditionally observant mathematician, explained that a butcher brought kosher meat from Luton once a week. Arnold did not much like the idea, but I pointed out there would be other goodies, almost forgotten, as rewards: chopped liver, *chrane* (horseradish with beetroot) and cheese with paprika.

My instinct that all would not go well, however, soon proved sound. The fear of turning into my mother, which had hovered about me all through my adolescence, now became a palpable threat. His old indulgent self had been buttressed by my mother's constant attention. And I could not provide her level of companionship.

Dad had been – as he expressed it – my mother's "only chick", and he now found himself with four rivals. Arnold, a Fellow of Gonville and Caius College, already had the habit of dining there quite often in the evenings (they had a very grand kitchen) and now rarely joined the family for supper. Nevertheless, a certain animosity grew up between Dad and Arnold. My father disliked Arnold's whole way of life, particularly the hours he kept. And he was very worried about the girls who came to see my sons.

My father saw my permissiveness towards them as neglect, and could not understand why the children offered no help in domestic chores. He thought I should organize them to help me run the household. It might indeed have been good for them, but I liked them to relax over tea after school, and then play music or do their homework without interference.

All of them were intelligent, and I was proud of them. There was little sibling rivalry. Adam had a natural gift for languages and loved to play Chopin. He was an excellent chess player. Joel, now at the Senior Perse, was already uncannily good at maths.

Martin, with his mischievous grin and huge eyes, was enjoying life at Comberton Village College. He had many friends, and girls liked him. He was already a gifted performer. I remember one hot speech day, when he was still at primary school near our rented house in Grantchester Meadows. There were welcoming speeches. Dutiful parents. An unenthusiastic choir performed madrigals to polite applause. Martin came on, his black hair tousled, holding a guitar. He had been asked to sing a folk song, and so he did, but he gave it an unexpected rock rhythm. The audience, which had been on the verge of dozing off up to that moment, visibly revived and, rather to his surprise, clapped delightedly.

A little after that, he set up a gig at a local pub, where he played jazz piano for £5. At Comberton Village College, where he began to take an interest in academic subjects for the first time, he learnt to sight-read on the flute and soon could do so more rapidly than anyone else in the family. He made friends with Martin Taylor – now one of the most celebrated jazz guitarists in the country – and I sometimes drove him to Harlow so they could play music together. Martin, my son that is, decided he too wanted to be a professional musician and began to practise hard to get into the Royal College of Music.

My father jeered at his sudden dedication: "What, do you expect to make a living out of that little *pipka*?"

I found my father's gibe unforgivable. In fact, that is exactly what Martin has done, although he excelled in the sciences too, and liked to have long conversations into the night with Arnold, who counted him as a natural ally against my dreamy, inconsequential world.

* * *

I could see Cambridge was an awkward town for my father. He joined the golf club, but found little matiness there. He was just an old buffer with an unremarkable handicap of about eighteen by then. (Adam sometimes walked round with him as a caddy.) As for cards, I knew no one in those days who played poker.

Always enterprising, he decided to join a university course of Modern Hebrew for beginners, and Adam helped him good-naturedly with the exercises, explaining the strange syntax, which he was learning himself as he went along, both of them sitting against a radiator in the kitchen.

One day I took my father, without much hope of rousing his interest, round the Fitzwilliam Museum and was surprised to see him strangely excited by a Corot, which showed a river with trees reflected in it. He went out the next day to buy brushes, paints and an easel, which he set up by the Cam. He was irritated to discover how difficult it was to paint reflections in the river and decided to take a painting course at what was then the Cambridge Technical College and is now Anglia Ruskin University. All this was admirable: other problems, however, did not admit of easy solutions.

"Eggs," he would say mournfully, over lunch. "I'll turn into a chicken if I have any more eggs."

He called up the stairs when I was trying to write, wanting me to come out in the country for tea. And sometimes we quarrelled fiercely.

"What do you do for me? Cook my meals? I could get as much from a boarding house."

Some of his efforts to enter the household helpfully had real pathos. He decided to learn to cook himself, particularly Yiddish dishes I did not attempt to provide: I remember a bread pudding taken from my mother's book of favourite recipes. The taste of cinnamon and sugar brought tears to my eyes, and I'm still hurt to remember him with a tea towel round his waist, his face lined with the thyroid deficiency which dried his skin, turning up a white tired face to me and looking for my approval. How could I have been so niggardly with my demonstrations of love, so possessed with my need to finish a book?

Several times he made a bid to escape. He would get into his white Morris Minor and set off with pyjamas and a clean shirt in a suitcase. But much about the time when my anger died down and turned into anxiety, he would phone and say "I'm on the way to Bournemouth, don't worry" or "I'll be back after the weekend".

One day, chattering over a gin-and-tonic in David Leitch's flat, I rang home to say I would not be back till seven.

"Not before then?" My father sounded very disappointed. "I've got something to show you."

He had finished a painting he liked, and was framing it as a present.

"I'll get the next train," I agreed, and set off to Liverpool Street.

He had his heart attack before I got home. Martin found him with blue lips, huddled up in the kitchen, and telephoned a doctor. When I arrived in a taxi, all three – Dad, Martin and the doctor – were still waiting for an ambulance, and my own heart went cold as I looked at my father.

He seemed surprisingly unemotional. He had been ill a few months earlier, and then he had called me Elainski or Elainela and held my hand all the way to the hospital. No pet names as we reached Addenbrooke's A&E this time. And there was an unexpected hiccup. No one could find his files. Nurses shuffled papers and rang other departments. I reminded them that he had been to see a thyroid specialist only a few weeks earlier. Dad made no attempt to chivvy them as he usually would.

"Elaine. Is it all ending?" he asked me, his brown eyes looking deeply into my own as I stood at his bedside.

"Nonsense, you're as tough as old boots," I told him, with a confidence I was far from feeling. And later I regretted that jauntiness bitterly. He was offering me a chance to give him a loving goodbye, and I did not take it.

Still, when the nurse came back to check his name, he exploded energetically, "Get the spelling right!" – so that I wondered if, after all, I was exaggerating the danger.

About midnight, he was wheeled off to a ward, loudly berating the porter, and sounding almost his usual self. But he was not. At 2 a.m., the hospital phoned to say he had suffered a second heart attack and was dead.

It was not my first loss, but this one I felt with painful intensity, blaming myself for everything I had not done, or said, or even felt. After the funeral, I let myself sink into a black misery, from which no one could rouse me. I found it a struggle to write my three-weekly reviews for the *Times*, and I could not even approach the novel I had been trying to finish through the eighteen months he had lived with us.

When I visited Tony and Nicole Ward in Paris, I wept over their dinner table as I remembered the little folk song he used to sing to me when I was a child:

> Eile lulah lulah lulah bye-bye:
> Do you want the stars to play with?
> Or the moon to run away with?
> They'll come if you don't cry.

The extravagance of such love was gone for ever. In my grief, no one could reach me. What saved me, in time, was a poem, the only poem I wrote that terrible year. I don't remember giving any readings – and if I did, I could not have read it aloud then. But later, when it was out in the world, I realized I was speaking for many people, not just myself, and it was a turning point for me to know I could do that.

Dad

Your old hat hurts me, and those black
   fat raisins you liked to press into
my palm from your soft heavy hand:
   I see you staggering back up the path
with sacks of potatoes from some local farm,
   fresh eggs, flowers. Every day I grieve

for your great heart broken and you gone.
   You loved to watch the trees. This year
you did not see their Spring.
   The sky was freezing over the fen
as on that somewhere secretly appointed day
   you beached: cold, white-faced, shivering.

What happened, old bull, my loyal
   hoarse-voiced warrior? The hammer
blow that stopped you in your track
   and brought you to a hospital monitor
could not destroy your courage
   to the end you were
uncowed and unconcerned with pleasing anyone.

I think of you now once again safely
   at my mother's side, the earth as
chosen as a bed, and feel most sorrow for
   all that was gentle in
my childhood buried there
   already forfeit, now forever lost.

CHAPTER 15

Exile

In my early days of writing poetry, I remember the group who published in the *English Intelligencer* were much taken by the culture of nomads, who were thought pure because they could not accumulate unnecessary *things*, and so were spiritually indifferent to a consumer society. I remember once saying to Prynne that every time we moved house I felt closer to the nomadic way of life, and suggested that Jews were natural nomads without being tent-dwellers. In my own family history, we had learnt to pack up and go many times. But no, he insisted, we were *exiles*, a quite different matter. I was quietly mutinous. Britain was my home. Exiles know where home is, even when they can't go back to it. A number of poets I particularly admire were exiles of this kind.

Joseph Brodsky, for instance, was deported to the West very much against his will. I met him first in a London pub in 1972, in the company of my old Cambridge friend Peter Papaloizou. I had not seen much of Peter since he went down. He had published poems as an undergraduate, but had moved away from English Literature after his degree – he took a First – to write a PhD in Anthropology based on his old Greek Cypriot village. He was involved for a time in making films. By 1972, he had returned to the academic world, and later went on to become a professor at LSE. He came back into my life on this occasion, because he had read Donald Davie's review of my translations of Tsvetaeva in the *Sunday Times*. I don't know how he came to meet Brodsky, who was already famous and had been since his trial in 1964.

His life had an unusual shape for a Soviet poet. He had walked out of school at fifteen and lived on casual work while writing poems which his friends typed out and shared. Akhmatova recognized him early as a poet of genius. Many of his poems were known by heart, but he was not published in official journals and he wasn't a member of the Writers' Union. He lived without a fixed job, and so was prosecuted as a "social parasite".

His trial aroused international interest, in part because of his idiosyncratic answers to the court, which were recorded in short-hand by Frida Vigdorova and soon read with fascination all over Russia and far beyond its borders.

The most celebrated section of the interrogation concerned his right to call himself a poet, and has been published many times. He was asked for his specialist qualification.

"Poet. Poet translator," he replied.

"But who put you on the list of poets?"

"No one. Who put me on the list of human beings?"

"And did you study for this?"

"For what?"

"For being a poet. Did you take a course in Higher Education?"

"I don't think it comes from education."

"Where does it come from then – poetry?"

"I think it comes from God."

The court gasped at such a reckless answer and, unsurprisingly, the judge remanded him in custody for psychiatric examination before a second hearing. The Soviet Union vehemently denied the existence of God. After his time in a psychiatric ward, the court handed down a sentence of hard labour in the far north.

In the bleak, frozen world of Arkhangelskoye he comforted himself with the thought that he belonged to the Russian language, that he was still a Russian poet. He made little of the physical hardships when two poet friends came to visit him in 1965, pointing out that at least he was able to listen to the BBC there. Deported into the West, however, he looked surly and bored. The separation from Russia depressed him far more than hard labour. Certainly, he looked older than his thirty years: a powerful man with large shoulders and a huge forehead.

I had brought him a hardback copy of my Tsvetaeva translations, and told him how very much I admired his own poems in
their earliest translations – made by Alan Myers – particularly the
'Elegy for John Donne'. Brodsky nodded and began to look through
my book while speaking aloud the Russian lines he remembered.
Tsvetaeva's poetry was one of his deepest loves. It was not a comfortable experience, and Peter soon began to look as uneasy as I
felt. Brodsky's English was fluent, but I guessed he would find it
impossible to hear the delicate shifts and decisions that shaped my
versions. At one point he read a line and burst out laughing and
gave me back my copy.

"You don't rhyme," he said simply.

Three years later, we met on a televised translation forum in
Cambridge dedicated to Osip Mandelstam. It was the day after the
official festival programme ended. There were notable figures on
the platform with Brodsky – Professor Henry Gifford, I remember,
among them – but they deferred to Joseph, and he soon seized the
centre of the conversation. The audience liked the authority and
assurance of what he said. So did I, until he instructed the audience that there could be NO true poetry which did not rhyme. At
this point I put up a hand, and Nigel Williams, who was making
the programme, sent a microphone up to me.

I did not challenge what he said about Russian poetry, naturally,
but I suggested that Milton, Wordsworth and T.S. Eliot had some
claim to be considered true poets. Incautiously, I added that rhyme
was difficult for any English poet who wanted to preserve natural
word order. He responded with a story about a visitor to New
York asking a taxi driver how to get to Carnegie Hall and being
told: "Practice, practice, practice." I was incandescent. Was he
suggesting English poets needed to try harder?

Afterwards, in the bar, I discovered a number of the poets who
were still in Cambridge for the Festival – including Miroslav
Holub and Vasko Popa, both well acquainted with European
Modernism – who readily agreed with me, since they did not

use rhyme in their own languages. Brodsky did not like that and moved away from the discussion. That evening, he did not turn up for a party given in his honour at the house of George and Zara Steiner.

Our relationship had a bad start, but it changed when Joseph became a visiting Fellow of Clare Hall in Autumn 1977. He was wretchedly lonely there. Octavio Paz, with all his charm, felt isolated in Cambridge. And Clare Hall is not an old college with a formal hall and distinguished resident Fellows, which Joseph might have enjoyed. Most Fellows are only visiting. During the time he was there, he often came round to our house in Park Parade for a meal. He liked to watch football on television with Joel, who was much the same age as his own boy, left behind in Russia. He spoke of his unhappiness at leaving his parents behind – he was their only child – and feared he would never be allowed to see them again. It was impossible to mistake his homesickness.

He was reluctant then, I remember, to think of himself as a Jew. He still felt the stigma of what it meant to be Jewish in Russia. His father had lost his position in the Navy because of it. And the word *Yevrei* (Jew) still pierced him like a knife. (In contrast, the colloquial *Zhidi* (Yids) felt almost friendly.) When he spoke of God, it was a Christian God. I tried to explain that for me so many of the psalms and so much wisdom writing feeds the New Testament that I see it as a continuous tradition.

He was always an obstinate man. I remember on an early visit to Cambridge he developed a pain in his chest, but would only agree to go into hospital when Arnold arranged a particularly pretty doctor to assure him no one would force him to stop smoking.

When we met a few years later in New York, he was much happier. He had been given a MacArthur "Genius" Award which made him financially independent for five years. We sat in his small, rather dark flat in the Village; I could see he had found his place in New York, where his abruptness and his habit of dominating every conversation did not appear rude, as they had in England. He was no longer lonely: he had good friends, including the brilliant essayist Susan Sontag and Bob Silvers of the *New York Review of Books*. Both of them must have had some hand in giving Joseph the centrality he now enjoyed, and perhaps in editing the essays in *Less than One*, which reached a far wider audience than his poetry. I can hear his true voice in that prose – without his omnipresent "Waal" of course – and his account of Tsvetaeva's poem for Rainer Maria Rilke, 'New Year's Greetings', is among the greatest close readings of the century. It led me to that resonant, difficult poem, though I only took the risk of translating it a couple of years ago for my enlarged book of Tsvetaeva translations, *Bride of Ice*.

We were living in Chalcot Gardens in 1987, when Masha Enzensberger telephoned one morning to tell me Joseph had been awarded the Nobel Prize. The poetry world was pleased by it – for the most part, and for the time being. There was, however, a rising murmur against Joseph as he began to dispense with his translators. First, he began to translate the poetry himself, and then to write his own poems directly in English. For all his command of spoken English, he could not truly *hear* how English sounds on the page, still less respond to the lyricism of American free verse, which he actively disliked – and his ingenious, colloquial rhyme endings stopped his lines and ran against the very sinews of the language.

I happened to be with him in New York when he first heard that he would need a bypass operation. It was a far riskier operation then than it would be now, and though he agreed to allow it, without question he felt he was looking Death in the face. He drove me to the airport, talking, as if to himself, about his chances and without the least show of defiance. I remember too that he lent me a marvellous book by Henry Roth, *Call It Sleep*, a heartbreaking American novel about life in Polish Galicia.

Valentina Polukhina, who has dedicated much of her life to Joseph and his work, told me that he refused to have a third bypass operation, but I know nothing of his reasons. I don't know what choices he was offered, or what the prognosis was. He had a young, very pretty wife by then. It may be there was little that could be done to prolong his life for more than a few months.

I wrote a poem in my novel *The Russian Jerusalem*, which invents a meeting between Brodsky and Tsvetaeva in that next world which so many Russians continue to believe in, even after seventy years of enforced atheism.

Joseph and Marina

Europe below us, water and stone,
falling like Venice into the sea. A young
man with ginger hair stands alone,

on Pushkin's parapet, with shoulders
like a footballer, his forehead slant.
"What are the things you remember

Joseph?" Tsvetaeva whispers tenderly.
"Your words, Marina." "But from your own life?"
"Just now I thought of sliding happily

over the snow to school as a little boy,
my head already filled with Russian poetry,
my fists ready for a playground battle.

When did I first learn I was Jewish scum?
It was long before my wife
refused the name of Brodsky to my son.

Well, in America, my new homeland,
my books, my bedsheets and an unchained door
bewildered those who could not understand

I only cared for poetry and talk.
So I was rude, almost a boor, perhaps
that's why they liked me in New York.

Here with only a candle for company, I wonder
how it was I took their honours as easily
as I picked Chinese dumplings from a trolley."

CHAPTER 16

Nezlin's Stamp

Some risks Arnold could take without a moment's hesitation. Fear did not come easily to him. I saw as much on our first hitch-hiking trip abroad together, when Adam was a year old and being looked after by my parents. On our way back towards the Channel ports, we accepted a lift from a man driving through Europe to make an illicit visit to his mother in Belgium. He spoke quite openly of his work as a smuggler, then operating out of Tangiers, but nonetheless wanted by the Belgian police. When he discovered we were a few pounds short of our fare across the Channel, he insisted on lending us the money.

My own instinct was to make some excuse and get out of the car, but Arnold wrote out our address and telephone number and promised to repay the money as soon as next month's pay came in. I was suspicious of the man, and rather sulky when Arnold accepted his offer of a good meal in Liège, which meant diverting our journey. I was desperate to get back to Adam. Still, we were both hungry, and he promised us a good restaurant. Our only payment seemed to be a willingness to listen to his story.

The next day we took a train to Calais – a luxury – where we were able to buy a ticket and return to London by ferry in remarkably good nick. The man had made no attempt to ship us off as white slaves to some African trader, as I feared, though Arnold laughed at my suspicions. He had a human intelligence I probably lacked, and I trusted it in the matter of Nezlin's stamp.

Roald Nezlin is, or rather was, a distinguished Moscow immunologist, whose career in Soviet times cannot have been helped by having a father who was one of the Jewish doctors imprisoned for his supposed part in the trumped-up plot to kill Stalin. In spite of this, Nezlin had earned an international reputation, and was well known to immunologists working in Cambridge.

On our first visit to Moscow together, Arnold naturally wanted to meet him, but found it impossible. All Nezlin's visits from foreigners were at that time blocked by the KGB. Arnold was allowed to visit the lab, however, and there came across someone he had recently made friends with at a conference. Since this scientist was allowed to have visitors, Arnold managed to make surreptitious contact with Nezlin; in return, the other scientist received reagents of which Nezlin had a surplus. A friendship more familial than scientific was struck up, and later that evening we dined at the facilitating scientist's flat.

The following year we travelled to Budapest at the invitation of Peter Z. It was my first stay in the Gellért Hotel, a romantic if shabby grand hotel from the old Habsburg past, as I wrote in *Cities*:

...a green

nymph poised in the marble lobby. Beneath the floor
hot springs, blue pools smelling of sulphur;
and an expressionless country girl waiting stolidly
to pummel hotel guests in muddy water.
This city always beckoned stories from me.

Z. was our host, and as he collected government pocket money for Arnold from the lobby I remember marvelling at the profusion of hotel staff, all seemingly willing to hang up our clothes and eager to take away any left about – not simply for cleaning, but to repair them or sew on a missing button if it should be necessary.

Looking through his conference booklet, Arnold noticed Nezlin's name among the delegates. He thought this might mean that Nezlin was now allowed out to the West, but Z. soon disabused us. "Hungary is a kind of halfway house," he explained. "The border into it is porous from the East but he won't have an exit visa to the West."

At dinner, Nezlin and Arnold struck up an easy rapport nevertheless.

Though I have often written about Budapest, I have never told the story of Roald Nezlin and his valuable stamp. Some time in our week at the Gellért, Nezlin asked Arnold if he would take that stamp back to London for him, not to deliver it anywhere, simply to hold on to it until he could get to London as he planned. Arnold agreed to take it through customs and tucked it into the inner pocket of his suit. Nezlin looked quietly satisfied, and Arnold told me about it late that night in bed.

I was not as sanguine about carrying it through customs as he was. I remembered how once, coming back from Russia, Masha Enzensberger had asked me to take a suitcase of books through Russian customs for her. Masha waited in the departure area so she could step forward and claim them if I were challenged. They were very valuable, old Slavonic books, which she sold when she returned to England and could live on for some considerable time. But Masha had protection in the shape of her mother Aliger (and perhaps as Fadeyev's daughter). We had no such protection in Hungary.

Arnold could see no danger in it. Who would look inside his jacket? We packed up carefully on the last day, and Z. took us by car to the airport in good time. As we reached the airport, I watched Arnold put his hand into the inner pocket of his suit. His face, often as impassive as a poker player's, suddenly registered dismay. I guessed at once that the envelope containing the stamp was not there.

He spoke to Z. urgently.

"I have to go back to the hotel. I have forgotten something."

Z.'s eyes were blue as ice.

"You will miss your flight. And it is not necessary."

"Yes, it is," Arnold insisted.

Z. smiled. "Please don't worry. I will see what you have lost is kept safely."

There was a pause.

"And returned to its owner?"

"Naturally," said Z., looking rather hurt.

On the plane we were uneasy. Had Z. stolen the stamp to protect Arnold? Or for himself? He had not had the air of a Soviet "minder", but perhaps that had been his role.

It was not to be the last we saw of Nezlin, though we had moved to London before we had the opportunity to discover what had happened to the stamp. After 1989, Nezlin was able to make his way to Israel and was there offered a chair in the prestigious Weizmann Institute in the Negev. From that position, he was given a sabbatical in Oxford, and telephoned us in London to ask if we could meet him at Victoria bus station. We were glad to do so. He and his wife were not where they said they would be, but Arnold rooted them out, and we brought them home to our flat in Chalcot Gardens. Nezlin looked brown and fit, and had brought me a present of a bilingual edition of Akhmatova's poetry.

I remember asking about his father, who had been in the Gulag.

His face lit up at once. His father had outlived not only Stalin, but the whole Soviet Empire. Even more unlikely, he had made his way to Israel in his late eighties with great excitement.

"And the stamp?" Arnold asked.

Yes, Z. had returned the stamp. Probably he had observed the original handover, Nezlin suggested. As to which hotel minion had stolen it from Arnold's jacket, perhaps while we slept, Nezlin had no clue.

"There are always so many willing hands," he said.

CHAPTER 17

Rewards and Explosions

Some time in 1980, Arnold was invited by a Swedish collaborator to receive an honorary MD from the University of Linköping for his work on the structure of IgM. It was to be a highly formal ceremony: the King of Sweden would place a gold ring on his finger. I was altogether more delighted than he was about the honour. He had been in low spirits for some time, and I hoped a new landscape would revive him as it often did. Several notable figures in the Swedish arts world were also to be honoured, and would be given laurel crowns. Arnold quipped that he would prefer a laurel crown to a gold ring any day. I think it was not altogether a joke.

The ceremony took place in a large church. As I looked down over the proceedings, my excitement was rather like the pleasure I took in prizes given to my children, or applause at one of my son's concerts: an intense, vicarious maternal thrill.

The next day our host read us poems by Tomas Tranströmer, first in Swedish and then in English translation. I was delighted with his rendering, and in return he thanked me for two books of my own poems I had given him the evening before. He had arranged for me to travel to Stockholm the following day so I could meet a few poet friends, while he showed Arnold the laboratory. Arnold smiled wryly. I guessed he might have preferred a visit to Stockholm, a city where the sea rolls deeply into the town and the air is alive with salt.

That 1980–81 was to be a year of triumph for the family – I felt confident. Joel had taken a fourth-term entry to Trinity College and won a major scholarship to read Mathematics. Martin had won the Concerto Prize at the Royal College and a scholarship to study the flute under Karlheinz Zöller, first flute of the Berlin Philharmonic. Adam had embarked on an adventure in Spain, and had found himself a job as a journalist there. For Arnold, too, success seemed to be confirmed when he was invited to apply for the Chair of Immunology at Hammersmith Hospital. The chair was one of the most distinguished in the country – John H. Humphrey's chair – and attached to a great research institution. Professor Mark Pepys had suggested Arnold apply, but he was strangely reluctant to do so. He told me that he had not published enough, that he could not bear to expose how little he had done – in a word, he felt he was simply not up to it. Since he had just been given a gold ring by the King of Sweden, I thought this could not be the case. And he had come to dislike working in Babraham, hadn't he?

And not only Babraham. For some time he had begun to complain about the provinciality of Cambridge itself and his wish to live in London. This chair would give us an ideal opportunity to do so in some style. I could enjoy my London friendships, and there would be the whole variety of exhibitions, concerts and plays that Arnold craved. There seemed to be nothing to outweigh all these obvious advantages. Nevertheless, Arnold sat for some days in the upstairs living room looking at the application form, deeply pondering. He always found forms difficult. I remembered filling out his application form for that first MRC grant which brought him to Cambridge. So I suggested he make a list of his most important papers on a separate sheet of paper, and my secretary completed the form for him, just a couple of days before the closing date. To be sure of its arrival, I took the form in its envelope to Senate House and handed it in myself.

He was summoned for an interview as I had hoped, though it seemed unfortunate this would take place two days after I had a plane ticket to Toronto Harbourfront Literary Festival. We both had some misgivings about that, but I flew off anyway, quietly optimistic. Arnold was always far more impressive in person than on paper. I remember Yevtushenko describing him as "a juicy man"

– not quite the right English word perhaps, but assuredly catching something of his rich presence.

The morning of the interview, I was walking round Toronto Zoo with Miroslav Holub. We were both in a state of mild unease for very different reasons. Holub's old friend, Josef Škvorecký, a Czech novelist who wrote brilliantly about jazz, was living in Toronto as an exile, and had bought me lunch on the day after my arrival. He particularly wanted to meet his friend Holub, and hoped to arrange it by chance in the hotel lobby. Miroslav was steely in his refusal to let me organize any such meeting. His eyelids concealed what he was thinking, but I guessed he was afraid of being watched – and perhaps he was right to be anxious. I did not press him to explain. I was wondering how the interview was going in London.

When we came back to the hotel from the Zoo, a telegram was waiting for me saying simply "I have the Hammersmith Chair". Overjoyed, I rushed up to my room to phone home. Arnold sounded over-the-top happy, but a little incoherent, rather like an excited child. "I got all my clothes ready myself," he told me proudly. "Bathed, shaved and got a train to London without *anyone's* help." I think I felt a frisson of alarm at what lay behind that assertion, but mainly I was delighted things had gone so well.

However, by the time I returned from Toronto he had already begun to question the wisdom of the move. When I came through the door of Park Parade, back from Toronto, I expected him to be still euphoric. He was not. He looked morose, and greeted me without particular enthusiasm.

"Is something wrong?" I asked

"I have to write a twenty-thousand-word grant application for them," he said.

He could not have sounded more appalled if the obstacle had been the ascent of Everest.

Maybe, if he could have produced the words, however tentatively, I might have been able to trim and shape them under his direction.

He had written several papers with collaborators using this method, talking through the ideas, then severely critical until the prose was accurate and elegant. It was, after all, the way we had long ago written film criticism for *Cambridge Review*. On this occasion, he found it impossible even to begin. He sat upstairs looking out over Jesus Green watching the girls playing tennis, worrying over whether he was making the right decision. When Adam and Martin came home for a break he begged their advice. Was it a sensible move? Should he take the chair? We went to look at houses in London, but found nothing without problems. Olwyn, who had moved to a house on Lensfield Road in Cambridge suggested he consult the I Ching. In his desperation, he may even have tried to do so, unlikely though it seems.

Perhaps I might have been more inclined to examine the very real financial incentives if I had not been taken ill. A few years earlier, in 1975, the same year I gave up cigarettes completely, I developed asthma. It was seasonal, probably related to my child-hood hay fever, but far more terrifying. It set in early that year. At night, I had to prop myself up on pillows, wheezing, fighting for breath, afraid of sleep. Our GP gave me a Ventolin inhaler, and I puffed. But the relief was short. My face became haggard with fatigue, and my weight dropped below eight stone for the first time since adolescence. During the day I was listless, while Arnold tried to discuss his decision. He continued to change his mind several times a day. I could no longer follow his arguments, and cannot now remember what there was to hold him in Cambridge other than the absence of any need to write twenty thousand words.

Looking back, I think I might have called in help from Mark Pepys, who writes easily and well – but I am not sure if Arnold would have allowed me to do so even if I had suggested it. He seemed to feel the task had been set as a kind of *test*, which he was failing. My guess, brooding over it now – and having spoken about it to Joel – is that Arnold had come to feel his success at the interview had been a kind of confidence trick, and feared if he asked Mark for help, this would be exposed. Silly, really. They were appointing a brilliant scientist – a thinker, not a writer of good copy.

Meanwhile, 1981 was one of the great years of the Cambridge Poetry Festival. I read on the evening of Friday 5th June with George Barker, W.S. Graham and Elizabeth Smart. Both Graham and Elizabeth Smart were very nervous. The acoustics were terrible at the Corn Exchange. I watched Elizabeth choosing and rejecting poems frenetically. George Barker was completely serene, and he reassured her – she was his former wife – "Don't fuss so. They've only come to see how we *look*." Most people recall Barker's sharp tongue, but I witnessed a good deal of kindness.

A few days ago I met George's widow Elspeth, still looking rather beautiful, at a party given by Michael Schmidt, and we recalled both that Cambridge Festival evening and a meeting in Tuscany when I was staying in Gaiole in Chianti with Donald Hope. About W.S. Graham, a remarkable poet, I remember mainly that he kept calling out to his wife in the audience: "Nessie. Nessie. Is it all right?" The poems were very much all right. W.S. Graham was a great poet whom I had somehow missed until then, and read afterwards with enthusiasm.

There were great parties at that festival, and I always set off towards them, though I was too short of breath to stay long. So Arnold usually drove me home early, and then returned to the party himself. He came to life once away from his problem. One evening, I watched him introduce himself as Professor Feinstein, as if already in his chair, to the leading actress of a play we had watched at the ADC. Rather wearily, I saw how easily he flirted with her.

We had arranged to stay a week that summer in Lucca with our whole extended family, including Martin, who was home from Germany for the vacation, and Adam with a new flower-faced

Spanish girlfriend. The house had been found for us by Tony and Nicole Ward. We had only to travel there, hire a car, and enjoy the dry, Italian sunshine.

Looking back, there seems to have been no need to decide anything whatsoever before we left, but Arnold felt it was essential if he were to take any pleasure in the holiday. So instead of battling with the grant application, he began to draft a letter of resignation. At the airport, I watched him put that letter into a post box. Even then, I could have stopped him. He was still hesitating. But I did nothing, exhausted by the long weeks of dilemma. Surely he knew what he was doing?

Wrong again. Almost as soon as we were airborne – and thereafter all the way to Italy – he repented posting that letter. As we flew, he worked out what he could do to correct the mistake. We were flying at the weekend. We would arrive before the letter reached Hammersmith. He would ring on Monday morning and ask the post desk to find the envelope and tear up the contents. That night neither of us slept, as he thought how best to persuade the post desk of his identity.

He made the phone call just after nine o'clock in the morning, British time. I was blearily at his side as he said what he had decided to say. Then he turned to me.

"It's too late. They have already opened the letter. I can't fight them," he said, and put down the phone.

Arnold came to see that moment as the key to his tragedy – and, unquestionably, I was implicated. The rest of our stay in Lucca is a blur. We had hired a very large car – there were six of us – and Arnold was too distressed to be able to drive it safely. So was I. He woke me up several times a night to explain the enormity of the mistake I had allowed him to make. The family was lucky to catch the plane home without a major road accident.

His job as Head of the Immunology Department had been held open for him once again, but this time he was fifty-six, and trapped in a place he now remembered he hated. He remembered too that he would have to retire at sixty, whereas the tenure of a chair ran until sixty-five and could even be extended. This had never been a feature of our earlier considerations. A consultant at Hammersmith had told him that to work there "was like drinking champagne for breakfast every day". He often repeated that sentence, as he sank deeper into depression and the complete breakdown which was to disable him at intervals for the rest of his life. When he came out of his first shock treatment, he was still murmuring "Hammersmith".

CHAPTER 18

Consequences

One morning an invitation dropped on the mat for me to appear at the Adelaide Festival Writers' Week the following March. I accepted without much hesitation on the assumption that everything would surely be better by then.

Not so. The intervening months held new disasters. Arnold fell into a depression so deep he could barely move in the mornings. He had been prescribed monoamine-oxidase inhibitors to help him while he was trying to write the grant application. (Prozac was not yet the drug of choice.) Those little red pills could not be combined with red wine or cheese, and I am not sure he was very careful about that danger. The GP now prescribed tricyclics. After a while he was able to drive off to the university library, where he enjoyed talking to a new group of friends at teatime. I was glad to see him rouse himself to leave the house at all. My own health improved, and I began to make London trips again, mainly to Television Centre, White City. I had written a play for Today – *Breath* – some time in the Seventies, for David Rose, but now I had a television agent, Phil Kelvin, recommended by Fay Weldon, and there seemed to be many possibilities. I wrote a short play for Rosemary Hill, a light-hearted two-hander called *Lunch*, directed by Jon Amiel.

I can't recall exactly when I decided to change book agents. Emma Tennant was always surprised at how little I expected to earn from my novels and – through Emma, I think – I was lucky to find the wonderful Gill Coleridge. Olwyn bore me no ill will, and we remained friends.

I was looking forward to the Australian trip. The Adelaide Festival is a splendid celebration, not only of novels and poems, but of all the arts: David Hare was directing his latest play there; Pina Bausch presented her extraordinary dance troupe. And I would have Fay Weldon as a companion. Some time in the previous decade, Fay and I had been joint editors of an anthology of short stories for PEN. She is a novelist whose presence is as much a tonic as her writing. She has a smile which invites you give up any claim to virtue. For all her sharp eye, she seems to be totally without malice.

In fact, she was amazingly generous, especially with time, that most precious commodity for a woman writer. At the judging lunch for PEN we were delighted to find we had both picked the same story as best; we also spoke of men, domestic issues, the good fortune of having affectionate sons and the accountant we discovered we had in common.

We got to know a good deal more about each other's lives when we travelled towards the Adelaide Festival on the same plane in March. On that twenty-two-hour flight we talked continuously, since I was in a state of shock after narrowly escaping death on the way to the airport. Arnold's driving had always been erratic, especially when he was preoccupied by some contentious issue. With hindsight, I can see that he was indeed so preoccupied, feeling guilty and anxious in ways that were then unknown to me, but he *seemed* to be talking about Australia, his dislike of Australians and his reluctance to join me in Melbourne after the Festival. As we travelled towards the airport, he was so intent on establishing the poverty of Australian culture that he accidentally drove the car halfway across a traffic island. I don't remember being frightened, but as he found it difficult to get the car back onto the road, I began to worry aloud whether I was going to miss my plane. He gave a little smile at that, as his wheel got clear of the flower beds, and it was only as I checked in at the Singapore Airlines desk that I began to wonder what precisely he was smiling at.

I was shaking, and not far from tears, when I finally boarded the plane and took my seat next to Fay. But as I poured out my story to her, it somehow developed a comic shape, and we were both laughing over a gin-and-tonic by the time we were safely in the air. I expected her to be astonished by Arnold's behaviour, but she was not. Only thoughtful. She had guessed instantly, as I had not, that there was another woman in the story. She asked a great many questions about our early life together, and then in return began to tell me something of her own married life with Ron. I gasped at the parallels. When I staggered off the plane in Adelaide, I was transformed into a relatively cheerful woman. How happy we had all been once, when we were young! In Adelaide we were fêted and fed, and put up in a comfortable hotel with a minibar, which Fay and I made some use of when we came back at night to continue our conversation.

In the end, Arnold did not refuse to fly to Australia, as I feared he might. When I collected him from the airport, he seemed glad to see me. He liked the pretty hotel I had found for us to stay in Melbourne after the festival ended. He was exhausted, but we went to bed and made love, though he surprised me by weeping unexpectedly afterwards. The next day we were invited to dinner at Sir Gus Nossal's home. He was an eminent virologist and general patron of science who knew Arnold's work. A refugee from Austria in 1939, he kept a splendid Viennese table with shining silver and a Rosenthal dinner service. He tapped the crystal glasses for toasts in as peremptory a fashion as Masha in King's College. At his command, I described the high points of the festival, but he spent most of the meal talking to Arnold, who seemed to have cheered up.

Our old friend Jill Neville had recently left David Leitch and was now living north of Sydney, deep in the Bush, with their toddler son, and had arranged for us to stay in her brother Richard's flat, which overlooked Rushcutters Bay. (He was no longer editing Oz, but was still living in London.) After a few days, we set off in her car through the Bush, which had an exotic blue tinge which I found peculiarly menacing; Arnold barely noticed. At her home – a large wooden shack – we spoke for hours about her difficulties with David, particularly his verbal cruelty, and the isolation and wilderness that was now curing her unhappiness.

However, the good humour which characterized our Australian adventures evaporated as soon as we were on an aeroplane for home. Arnold thought we should have chosen Bali for our stop-over rather than Singapore – and of course he was right. On this occasion, after buying a few inexpensive presents for the children, we both felt we had exhausted the pleasures of the shopping malls.

Arnold was very keen to see something of the city's night life. Rather as in Russia, he had been told, there was a licensed underworld; Arnold found it on Boogye Street, a destination whispered to him by the clerk at the counter of our hotel, who was astonished to find he planned taking me with him. The street was the place where transsexual prostitutes worked, earning the money for their sex-change operations. Arnold was fascinated by their beauty and their stories.

We boarded the plane for London the next morning. Arnold travelled silently and seemed to be brooding over something he might find in Cambridge. When we arrived home, I rushed to hug the children, but Arnold took the car and drove off immediately to college to collect his post. I wondered about that. What could be so important? He came back looking pale and agitated, dumping a pile of college mail and a single parcel, opened, in the front room.

"I'm exhausted," he said. "I'm going to bed."

I am afraid I did not hesitate long, after he went upstairs, before looking into the opened parcel. There was no letter, just a book about the history of science, inscribed with love and an initial I did not recognize.

I went up the three flights of stairs with the book in my hand. Arnold was lying with his eyes shut in the bed, but he wasn't asleep.

I enquired as neutrally as I could about the initials in the book. He turned to lie on his back, then with his arm behind his head.

"You know," he said.

Did I?

Suddenly, I remembered a large party we had given at Arnold's instigation – at which, he insisted, "there were to be absolutely *no* boring guests". It was rather a good party. In the upstairs living room a small group of people sat talking. Arnold was taking out some of his childhood snaps, including a tinted sepia photograph which had always been my favourite, and was showing them to a pretty girl on the Chesterfield. A historian, I think she said. About thirty I guessed. Very pretty, highly intelligent and a little hostile. When I said I enjoyed reading history, she replied coldly that she had no time to read novels.

Yes, that would be her.

Suddenly I felt very tired, and as I got into bed, I murmured, with one arm around Arnold's warm back: "Don't worry, it's not important."

But I was quite wrong there. It was very important.

Arnold had fallen madly in love, and the girl was already pregnant with his child. I did not yet know that, but almost everyone else in Cambridge knew about the affair. In my novel *Children of the Rose*, written a few years earlier, the closing paragraphs describe how Mendez – into whom I put so much of Arnold's being – spent years trying to find his lost illegitimate child. The longing and the fear of loss which destroyed his abandoned wife in that novel soon came very close to destroying me.

My novel *The Border* was handwritten very fast, as if in one breath, in a lined notebook. I transposed my own pain and my imagination of Arnold's desperate need into 1930s Vienna. Without quite knowing why, I made Inge, the deceived wife, a scientist and Hans, the erring husband, a poet whose reputation was declining. A beautiful girl restores Hans's sense of being relevant. Their stories are told in diaries and letters in the voices of the protagonists, as I tried to enter the inner world of the three people caught up in their own struggle even as the world around them collapsed. Hans and Inge play out the last scenes of their story at Port Bou on the frontier between France and neutral Spain, with a group of other refugees, including the great writer Walter Benjamin. They all find the border is closed.

In the same six weeks in which I wrote the novel, Arnold and I arranged to slip away from Cambridge to Oxford, where we were welcomed as honoured guests by Arnold's collaborators. The Immunology Department in Babraham, however, which had been so kind to Arnold through his illness, baulked at our plan to take a sabbatical in Oxford; there was resentment against any more latitude shown to a missing head of department. As things began to look ugly we returned in shame. We had rented out Park Parade and had to find rooms in Robinson College, where Arnold had been appointed a Founding Fellow a few years earlier.

It was a desperate time for both of us. There were phone calls and conversations of a medical nature to which I did not listen. I remember leaving the flat and going to stand outside on the terrace, looking into the black foliage of the garden, or up at the white moon, listening to the laughter of young students below, and doubting if I would ever be able to laugh again.

I don't remember who found us one of the Peterhouse flats on Trumpington Street. Things were simpler there. I don't know if Arnold went into Babraham or where he went, but he came back at night. Early one morning, the girl rang to tell him he now had another son. Of course he went to see the child as soon as he was dressed.

Who advised Arnold and I to go to a London marriage-guidance counsellor? I can't be sure. I do remember that on the way Arnold told me he was going to move out and join his new family. "Nothing to do with sex," he said, probably out of politeness. "It is a question of *order*." He had always needed order in his life, and he was now going to learn how to have some. He explained this to the marriage-guidance counsellors, too, when we were sitting in front of them: all his troubles had a single source – my lack of organization. I muttered unhappily – for the benefit of the two men who were supposed to be helping us – that to write twenty books demanded *some* organization.

Arnold gave me a pitying smile. "Novels. Poems. Not *scholarship*."

We drove back with Arnold explaining again everything he needed that I wasn't supplying.

Then he moved out.

The man who had recommended the therapists rang up to tell me that they considered me particularly "adequate". He used it as a word of praise. Perhaps it meant I could deal with the situation? I wasn't sure I could. I drank a good deal, and found it difficult to eat. Joel was still at home waiting to go up to Trinity, and he held my hand lovingly. It cannot have been good for him.

I had friends. Jana Howlett, for one, a glamorous creature, a Russianist Fellow of Jesus College, married to a millionaire, whose own marriage was breaking up; Liebe Klug, now a therapist, who warned me not to make the tactical mistake of leaving Park Parade; and Ruth Padel, who offered to help me pack up and escape if I needed to. Ruth was at that time married to Professor Myles Burnyeat, a scholar of Ancient Philosophy, but she had led a rackety life until then, and would in a few years' time return to London and become one of our most adventurous poets.

I wish I could say I behaved with dignity. I did not. One evening, I followed Arnold's car to my rival's house, looked in through the window and knocked on the door. Arnold let me in, dismayed. I looked around to see how this wondrous order manifested itself – pausing to examine her bookshelves to see what she was reading. She came halfway downstairs in a dressing gown after a time, and called to say she was going to bed. I wanted Arnold to come home with me, but of course he did not.

Or not then.

It was the party season. And somewhere in a garden, the composer Alexander Goehr came over to talk to me. He was a worldly man who had been married several times himself. "Things aren't always how they seem," he said, and suggested I should not do anything rash. I already had, however. I had consulted a London solicitor recommended by my Hutchinson editor Tony Whittome.

The man was eager to take on my case, remarking as he did so that there was more to life than "a seventeen-stone depressive". I didn't feel that covered the nature of my loss. When our old Polish friend, Andrew Kelus, at a conference in Cambridge, called to see me, I told him what I planned to do. He seemed delighted at my resolution, which in fact was far from fixed. When he met Arnold at the same conference, Kelus told him he would be receiving divorce papers very shortly. Arnold came back to Park Parade the same night.

I let him in without question, though Joel disapproved, and many friends thought me foolish.

* * *

It was far from a happy ending. How could it be? We were both too bruised where once we had felt casually secure. It was not truly an ending at all, since Arnold continued to visit his son, and when the girl found a job in a town some distance from Cambridge, he visited overnight. The first time he set out to see the child he filled a large suitcase with exotic toys, and I gather the visit went well. Over the months, however, the relationship changed. I don't know what happened – perhaps he quarrelled with his girlfriend. He never discussed it, but eventually I understood there would be no more visits. A sexual relationship, he assured me, was not on offer.

Jealousy, however, was not by then the source of my anxiety. I had come to doubt Arnold's ability to make *any* final choice. When he decided to resign from Sussex and Hammersmith, he had returned to the *familiar* rather than risking the *new* – and we were still living with his regret over those decisions. My friends wondered exactly *why* I was allowing myself to remain in such an ambiguous situation. Would not a clean break be better for both of us? I was stubbornly convinced it would not.

Bernice Rubens, who had once been married to the novelist and wine merchant Rudolf Nassauer, advised me strongly to make a new start, admitting the while, "It hurts for about a year." My TV producer, Rosemary Hill, suggested I come to London and lead a swinging life. Only Maggie Drabble, to whom I had unburdened myself early in the crisis, remarked sagely: "If it is worth it – which it very clearly is, and I don't often say that – just sit tight."

It would have helped if Arnold had been able to tell me what had brought him back to me. He once muttered it was because he was lonely, but he never explained in what way I alleviated this loneliness. But then I could not explain my wish to have him back. I think we had made such a strong attachment early on that neither of us was able to abandon it. Yet, however we might cling together at night, during the day we bickered.

"Circe," he called me many times. "In your arms I died."

I pointed out coldly that whatever happened to his men, Odysseus retained his own form.

* * *

It was the threat of suicide that took Arnold into Fulbourne Mental Hospital. I was not there as he told his story to Professor Roth, but when the doctor questioned me afterwards about our marriage, I gave as accurate an account as I could, too alarmed to hide anything, and he nodded as if I were confirming what he had heard elsewhere. He prescribed talking therapy and ECT if it didn't work.

Arnold did not usually dislike hospitals. He enjoyed the routine and the attention – and, once there, he usually cheered up. There was further reason in this case. On the same ward was the ebullient Malcolm Williamson, Master of the Queen's Music, with whom he was soon fast friends, fascinated by his stories.

Malcolm's problem was a writing block, which had prevented him meeting the deadline for a commission to write a piece for the Proms. He was an Australian, precociously gifted, and recommended for his post by Benjamin Britten. He had a sweet baby smile, dressed like a sailor and had an unusual gift for mimicry.

I remember his imitation of Edith Sitwell, for instance, and marvellously wicked gossip about the Sitwell family. When his partner Simon came to visit, it became clear that it was he who dealt with most of the day-to-day details of their life together and that Malcolm's finances were in total disarray.

Arnold enjoyed this unexpected new friendship, but Malcolm's lament for lost opportunities and the frustration of his early hopes threw him back into his own anguish over the Hammersmith Chair. His very friendly therapist could not reach into this blackness. Even a course of ECT did not ease the pain.

His friend Professor Peter Lachman came up with a solution: a sabbatical in California. Peter had just returned from a year at the Scripps Clinic in La Jolla, and was able to arrange it in a matter of days.

"California," Arnold's therapist said wistfully, when he was told of the plan. He had worked there in the year following a painful divorce.

"You'll come down the stairs of the aeroplane into the sunshine and wonder what on earth was ever worrying you."

CHAPTER 19

California

Glimpses. Surreal glimpses. That is how I remember California, the paradise of the Western world: outdoor pools with Hockney sunlight dazzling on the water – palm trees, red helicopters buzzing overhead – the fizz of a Jacuzzi – white racks of refrigerated food in freezing supermarkets. La Jolla, once chosen mainly by naval families, is an affluent suburb of San Diego. It lies along Pacific cliffs which fall sheer to the beach below. Healthy young people fling themselves on hang-gliders out over the ocean, riding the thermal air gusts without fear. I can conjure the sight of them still.

Along the cliff edge, and along the coast road towards Los Angeles, stand mansions owned by the wealthy – some of them senior scientists from the Scripps and the Salk Institutes. One of these belonged to the widow of Professor Jacob Bronowski, a distinguished mathematician in Cambridge and the author of a book on William Blake, famous even before he was celebrated worldwide as the writer and presenter of the television series *The Ascent of Man*. We knew his daughter – Lisa Jardine – from Cambridge, and were invited to visit them early in our stay. Together, we marvelled at the splendour of the library and the blood-red sunset visible through an immense window of the living room. The experience gave us an exciting look at a Californian life we were quite unable to share.

We found ourselves unexpectedly strapped for cash. Arnold's usual income continued, but was almost halved by the dollar's rise against the pound: in that year the two currencies were close to parity. When this was explained to Richard Lerner, the Director of the Immunology Department, he arranged for the Scripps to top up Arnold's pay. But we were still poor by Californian standards, and La Jolla is expensive, as Raymond Chandler noted thirty years earlier when he was earning Hollywood money.

I was writing a book about Bessie Smith for Emma Tennant's *Lives of Modern Women*, commissioned by Penguin, but we had already spent the signature advance and I was a long way from delivering the manuscript. Worse, the students who were renting our house in Park Parade only paid the rent when they could. It had perhaps been a mistake to let to students, but we had left precipitately, just after term began, and were glad to find any tenants who seemed pleasant.

We had difficulty finding the deposit for a modest flat on Torrey Pines Road. This road, we were told, followed the Californian tectonic-plate fault line, but it also led to the Scripps Institute, where Arnold was to work, and we thought we would take our chance on an earthquake.

"Have you got wheels yet?" asked Richard Lerner.

You can't even post a letter without a car in La Jolla. The distances are immense, and there is little public transport. So we bought an ageing Mazda sports car without air conditioning and parked it rather shamefacedly beside the huge American cars which belonged to other scientists. It would have been completely unsuitable for crossing the desert, but so far we had no plans to explore farther than downtown San Diego. There was no question of a second car, so I drove Arnold into the lab and collected him in the evening.

Arnold always found it hard to settle into a new laboratory, and the shape of south Californian life was quite different from our own. Most of the scientists rose at six, jogged – a habit then uncommon in the UK – and were at their desks by seven. However, there was something of a breakthrough when Ian – a Scot I think – involved him in experiments designed to take place aboard the Space Shuttle. Arnold arranged for frozen tubes of his preparations to be sent from the ARC laboratory to a local airport. I remember driving to pick them up – and even though I had no idea what was to be discovered by sending these tubes into orbit, it was certainly exciting. And suddenly Arnold was part of a team, which he always enjoyed above anything else.

The US edition of my novel *The Border* came out a few weeks after that. To my surprise, it was reviewed with enormous enthusiasm by George Steiner in the *New Yorker*. I gave a copy of the book, which had a stunning Egon Schiele cover, to Richard Lerner. (He had written a good SF novel himself, called *Epidemic*, which he had given me. I've no idea what he made of mine.) And I gave another to Odile Crick when she invited us to dinner in their house up the coast, north of San Diego. I don't know what she thought of it either, but she was very friendly over dinner. Arnold talked mainly with Francis.

Francis was by now working in the new field of neuroscience, exploring the mystery of consciousness. Many of his remarks over dinner were directed against the current orthodoxies of Freudian therapy.

"Dreams," I remember him saying, "are no more than the brain getting rid of its rubbish." He still had his great bray of a laugh, particularly when he said something he knew would be considered outrageous.

I had made some contact with Jerome Rothenberg, through UCSD – the University of California at San Diego – and the conversation turned to the poetry of the Beat Generation. Crick was particularly interested in Michael McClure, who lived in San Francisco – an attractive and confident hero of the counterculture who had written a play called *The Beard*. This had drawn the attention of the same San Francisco Police Department which had tried to ban *Howl* for obscenity. They had more success with *The Beard*. What Crick admired in the play was McClure's understanding of the many attributes human beings share with animals. I imagine he also enjoyed the racy circle of friends around McClure, including glamorous stars of the pop world such as The Doors. After that evening with the Cricks, Arnold seemed almost his old self as we drove south again towards La Jolla.

Meanwhile, my book about Bessie Smith still had to be written. I made contact with the Music Department of UCSD, and they opened their library of books about blues and early jazz to me. While Arnold was at the lab I worked there making notes on early women singers, but determined to shift the book away from musicology towards my own personal take.

As I wrote in the opening chapter:

In her song nothing melts, yields or seduces. Her voice is harsh and coarse, undeterred by everything she knows about touring in tents, street fights and casual sex. She isn't trying to please anyone. The habit of submission, of letting yourself be used, comes too easily to women. In Bessie's voice is a full-hearted rejection of any such foolishness. The strength to do so comes from the big voice itself, with the growl and rasp of a jazz trumpet in it.

Her phrasing is unhurried and subtle. She knows exactly where to place an extra syllable, where to stress a word. And always, under the sadness, lie a sense of freedom and the triumph of her own courageous spirit.

On long-haul drives across country it is Bessie's voice I hear in my ears as I make up my own songs to her music. Her lonely voice opposes a stubborn pride to the ordinary injustice of men.

* * *

I would say that things were beginning to look up, except that Arnold's health now troubled him in unfamiliar ways. Fortunately, we had full insurance from the Scripps, so he was scanned and probed with unusual thoroughness. This felt like a privilege, or would have done if the outcome had been less alarming. One kidney had stopped working altogether, and the other was down to twenty-five per cent of normal function. He was taken directly into hospital. No one had tested for any such possibility in Britain.

Arnold was never alarmed at the thought of surgery, and was rather relieved when a doctor suggested that kidney problems might account for much of his earlier depression. And the operation which removed the dead kidney was successful, but there were other problems, it seemed, and his convalescence was disappointingly slow. I was his only regular visitor. For hours a day he was trapped on his own with time to brood.

I remember one day an early novel of mine – *The Crystal Garden*, I think – came round on a hospital trolley. He was quite impressed by it, and said, unexpectedly: "So *this* is the talent I have been impeding." It was an odd remark: I had no idea he saw himself as standing in my way. The warmth of his approval delighted me, but it was short-lived. In a few days, he was once again ready to analyse our joint mistakes and failures. I usually began to long for our little flat in Torrey Pines Road.

I took to swimming for an hour every day in the communal pool there. The guy in the flat at an angle to ours said he was Oscar Hammerstein III – an unlikely inhabitant of such a downmarket flat, but very charming. One afternoon a week I taught poetry at UCSD, a job found for me by Jerome Rothenberg. I continued to write about Bessie Smith. Otherwise, I spent my days in Arnold's room at the Scripps.

The person who was kindest to me in those grisly weeks was Odile Crick. When she heard I had never even put a foot in Mexico, she collected me in her air-cooled car and drove me not simply to Tijuana on the border, but right down the coast to a hotel where Rita Hayworth had once liked to stay with the Aga Khan. The ballroom was deserted in mid-afternoon, but the food was spicy and plentiful, and she introduced me to margaritas – tequila with lime and salt round the rim of each glass. I have a charming picture of the two of us talking intimately over a table of Mexican dishes.

Perhaps I talked too freely. I remember telling her about Arnold's threat of suicide after Hammersmith, and many other details of our vexed relationship. In talking to her I realized how desperately lonely I had become in California without supportive friends.

In those days, letters and phone calls were the only means of staying in touch. Letters came from Ruth Padel, Tony Whittome and Olwyn Hughes. I spoke to Fay Weldon, Emma Tennant and my sons on the telephone. Martin was still in Hamburg or touring with Ensemble Moderne, but was making his English debut at the Wigmore Hall in June. We had to be home for that. In a frenzy of optimism I booked air tickets to ensure we got back in time. Surely Arnold would be out of hospital by then?

It was a close-run thing. And our Mazda broke down irretrievably a few days before we had to leave, so we needed to rent a car to drive to the airport at LA. This was harder than I imagined. Cash – which I'd saved by not eating a great deal on my own – was unacceptable to Hertz, who demanded a credit card. We had been managing very well without one. Fortunately, I met Bobbie Louise Hawkins, one-time wife of Robert Creeley, who had just given a poetry reading at UCSD. She offered me hers with some generosity, since she would have been liable if we crashed the car. And so it was we were able to make our way up the road towards LA.

We stayed overnight with Jascha Kessler, an American English literature academic met a few years earlier at the Struga Poetry Festival on Lake Ohrid. He set up a poetry reading at UCLA for me on the day of our arrival, and the day after helped us to return the mercifully undamaged car to Hertz and then to catch our plane.

I felt such relief once in the air that the adrenalin which had kept me awake night after night left my bloodstream and I slept for most of the flight. I knew we would be unable to get into Park Parade for another month, but Fay had suggested we stay in her house on Ryland Road.

California had not been paradise, Arnold was still weak, and in a couple of months he would be fifty-nine. Very soon he would have to resign his position as Head of Department, and I had no idea what would come next. But at least I would be in England – and there were people who loved me in London.

*

CHAPTER 20

Poetry and Friends

Before I left for California, Emma Tennant advised me: "Write something every day. It will protect you." I must have believed her. Certainly, I came back from those lonely months in La Jolla with most of the poems which went into *Badlands*, including a long poem, 'The Water Magician of San Diego', which tells the story of the rainmaker Charles Hatfield and his Pied Piper revenge on those who doubted his powers. His downpour flooded freeways, brought down bridges and closed the banks. I don't think I felt the same contempt for materialism which fired Tsvetaeva in her *Ratcatcher*: my poem was more a celebration of those who live on their wits – "con men, poker players, poets". It was given verve by casually rhyming stanzas, with a regular – albeit unusual – rhythm. My poems had a new sound to them.

In *Badlands* I also wrote about the underside of my own life, using Virgil and the Greeks the while to disguise what I was doing. I abandoned that pretence as I began to admit my intense dedication to writing poems was in itself a betrayal of my role as supportive partner. Gender doesn't have much to do with this, but I suppose it is a selfishness more traditional in men.

In the difficult years after we returned from California, I was sustained by friends, the affection of children and poetry itself: writing it, of course, but also the electricity of sharing it with an audience.

It was not an excitement I shared with Arnold, though I showed him all my early poems. Almost the first time I met him – as I mentioned before – he brought me a poem of George Barker about a laughing, larger-than-life mother who reminded him, he said, of his own. I think he wanted me to recognize my mother in her, too, but I had to confess she was rather a quiet woman, unlikely to clutch a chicken or a gin bottle, and in no way resembling a brass band. (Nor, in fact, was his.) Still, I enjoyed the poem, and it was an important part of our getting together. I made the mistake of imagining poetry was important to him in the way music was. Not so. He came indeed rather to dislike it, though he encouraged me generously in the early years before I had published anything.

He distrusted the metaphysical poets of the seventeenth century – I once tried to tease out Donne's 'Air and Angels' for him, and he was outraged by the shifting logic – and he particularly disliked elegiac verse. In later years I heard him argue vehemently with Antonia Byatt on the same tack when she followed her reading of Tennyson's 'In Memoriam A.H.H.' with a poem by Henry King for a dead wife. Of the latter, Arnold complained the poem was all about the poet, not the woman lost. He was not mollified by learning the poem had been commissioned by a genuine mourner. It confirmed his worst suspicions.

All the more arresting then, one evening at dinner with Dannie and Joan Abse in their London home, to hear Arnold explain his attachment to a poem of Thom Gunn written about a close friend dying of Aids, from *The Man with Night Sweats*. Dannie, seeing his unusual enthusiasm, rather kindly left the table to fetch the book and asked him to read it. Arnold was taken aback, and for a moment looked as if he might refuse, but he did read it, rather shyly, first explaining that what he admired was the vivid presence of the sick man and Gunn's unobtrusive observation. I took good note of that when I came to write *Talking to the Dead* many years later. Some of his being, in words I have never forgotten, is present in every poem.

There was one early poem I never chose to read if Arnold was in the audience, a poem for a wedding anniversary from *The Magic Apple Tree*. This begins with a series of fanciful science-fiction transformations designed to force the recipient to admit how far people can develop outside marital expectations. He hated it, particularly the conclusion:

Listen, I shall have to whisper it
into your heart directly: we are all
supernatural   every day
we rise new creatures   cannot be predicted.

In those days, I still used the gaps and hesitations of Black Mountain poetry, but the assertion of freedom was as triumphant as a line of Tsvetaeva, whom I was translating at the same time. These days I prefer the flow of my voice to push against the boundaries of stanzaic form, though I still like unobtrusive rhymes.

I think now Charles Reznikoff was more useful to me than Charles Olson. Reznikoff was a leading figure in the Objectivist movement alongside Carl Rakosi and Louis Zukofsky. What I admired in him was the way he used detail to call up the physical presence of people he wanted to describe. People were his richest subject matter, as they were to me. And cities. What do I know of sea winds and seafarers? My own roots lie among the *Luftmenschen* of Europe, whose stamina brought my family to Britain.

Perhaps that is why I gave the voice of the title poem in *Gold* (2000) to Lorenzo da Ponte, Mozart's brilliant librettist. I delighted in his talent and resilience, and the ruses which took him, pursued by creditors and crooks, from his father's tannery to the court of Vienna. Baptism certainly made the transition easier – though he was always recognized as a Jew – and a Jesuit education helped, though he was not cut out for the priesthood. This long poem was a kind of holiday for me. My own life found a place in the short dark poems of the same book.

* * *

When Arnold left his position as Head of Department, there was only one upside: we could at last move to London. And so we sold the huge eight-bedroom house in Park Parade and for the same price bought a pretty two-bedroom flat in Belsize Park, a few hundred yards from where we had once lived before we were married.

Chalcot Gardens was a good choice. The flat was the whole floor of a Victorian house which stood behind a line of chestnut trees, shielding us from the traffic on England's Lane. Across the street stood a row of attractive shops and cafés. And we had come to a very friendly piece of London. As I was sticking stamps on a clutch of invitations for a house-warming party, John Lahr's then wife Anthea looked over my shoulder, and promptly invited me to the writers' teas they held every Friday. The Lahrs had the top two floors of a house a few doors along Chalcot Gardens, shared with the film director Karel Reisz and his wife Betsy.

Lahr had written a book about his father, Bert Lahr – the cowardly lion in the *Wizard of Oz* – and a biography of the playwright Joe Orton, which became a film directed by Stephen Frears. He knew about Hollywood and the New York theatre world, and was soon to become theatre critic on the *New Yorker*. Aside from his Friday teas, our old friend Jill Neville lived on Belsize Park Gardens with her new partner Professor Lewis Wolpert.

Jill was still a striking beauty with thick auburn hair, bold features and a full mouth, and had been a legendary figure in literary London long before I knew her as the wife of David Leitch. She left Australia on the same boat as Peter Porter and rapidly found a place among the copywriters of J. Walter Thompson, S.H. Benson's and other leading advertising agencies. She acquired a houseboat in Chelsea, which she shared for a time with Assia Wevill, the girl who led to the break-up of Ted Hughes's marriage. Wherever she met and married David Leitch, they shared a flat in the Marais while he was Paris correspondent for the *New Statesman* and then the *Sunday Times*. It was through David I came to know her, though in fact we already had several friends in common, including Fay Weldon and Elizabeth Smart. When she told us her story in Australia, I already knew much of it.

On my visits from Cambridge to see David at their Maida Vale flat in the Seventies, Jill and I talked at length if David was out. She was very funny, especially about sex. We knew each other's work, and I admired her first novel – which is, I am told, a thinly disguised account of an affair she had with the American poet Robert Lowell. She was already a lead reviewer on the *Sunday Times,* one of the judges for an important book club and, a few years later, the presenter of a television arts programme. I launched many of my own books in their many-roomed apartment, looking over boats on Little Venice.

I had never known her first husband, Peter Duval Smith, or indeed much about the open marriage of William and Hetta Empson, but it seemed to me Jill was lucky now to be happy with David. They had married in 1969. My memory of leaving them together contained a vivid image of David with his arm around her handsome shoulders. I was, however, quite wrong about the state of their marriage, as she was eager to explain. When I looked incredulous, she smiled ruefully.

"Yes, he is always affectionate until his friends go. Then it all starts again."

"What starts?"

She told me.

I was bewildered by her account of verbal abuse and occasional violence. I knew David drank heavily, ever since the days when he reported the Vietnam War. But this was a new side to him – and there was more. David now had a mistress who lived close by.

"A real Jewish American princess," Jill said, laughing the while. It was not a term I had heard before, and she had to explain it to me. David was quite open about the liaison, and enjoyed giving her details of the sexual experience. He rarely made love to Jill now, saying she was *too ugly.*

I found this last bit incredible, but she persuaded me.

"I really mind," she admitted, "because sex has always been my thing."

She was already pregnant when she confessed her situation to me, and had a son – Luke, now a fashion journalist at *The Telegraph* – a few months later. She lived with David a further eighteen months or so before leaving for the outback of Australia, as I have already described. David followed her there for a time, very much missing his son, and working on an Australian newspaper to finance his stay. When Jill returned to London she moved back into the Maida Vale flat, and though she and David now led completely separate sexual lives, they could still make one another laugh. They did not divorce until 1979.

Among David's new girlfriends was the formidable Rosie Boycott, one of the founders of *Spare Rib*, a '60s feminist magazine, who went on to become the editor of the *Independent* and the *Daily Express* – and, more recently, a confident panellist on BBC Two's *Late Show*. Rosie was a handsome woman, schooled at Cheltenham Ladies College, though she left before taking A levels. Her life had been filled with dangerous experiments, as she revealed with some candour in her 1984 memoir *A Nice Girl Like You*. David told me they met in a rehabilitation centre, where they were both recovering from alcohol addiction. I remember him adding, "You meet a very good class of people in bins."

Rosie adored David, and always welcomed us warmly as his old friends. I admired her directness and her air of worldly competence. She and David were married in 1983, and soon had an assured and precocious daughter, Daisy. We often visited the Maida Vale flat, where they continued to throw glittering parties, and sometimes entertained our old friend Tony Ward. David, however, proved a predictably difficult husband, and Rosie too left him, though she continued to be a good friend and did not divorce him until 1998 .

I don't remember Jill showing the least hostility to Rosie, as she continued to share a flat in Belsize Park Gardens with Lewis Wolpert. Sadly, she died of liver cancer far too young for a woman whose good health throughout her life had always seemed almost shameless in its exuberance.

* * *

Fay Weldon lived in Ryland Road, a few minutes from England's Lane, in two terraced houses refurbished to make a smartly lit office and luxurious living quarters. Ron and her sons remained in a large house in Shepton Mallet, Somerset, and she went back to them in the evening more often than not: she thought of her country residence as home. I often nipped down to Ryland Road for a chat, and quite soon her secretary, Jane Wynbourne, was working for me too.

I remember Ron came to London once when an art gallery near Cork Street decided to show some of his paintings. I congratulated him, but he shook his head. He was an attractive man, and his body seemed familiar to me, as if he were a relation of Arnold.

"Success is very bad for you," he said – a remark directed at Fay, but with half an eye on me.

"Failure is worse," I retorted.

* * *

I can't remember how I first met Elizabeth Smart. It may even have been in Cambridge. I knew her son Sebastian Barker, and he knew how much I admired her. I picture her now in her Suffolk garden, naming small flowering plants I could not recognize and seemingly more interested in the soil, colours and scents of the beauty she had created than anything in the world of literature. In fact, this absorption, though an important part of her, was also misleading. She had a sense of language which was at once precise and idiosyncratic, a control of tone and cadence that had, among other things, made her one of the cleverest writers of advertising copy in the country and brought her the editorship of *Queen* magazine. She retired to the Dell in Suffolk. Her most famous novel, *By Grand Central Station I Sat down and Wept*, which is frequently rediscovered and brought back into print, expresses her obsessive love for George Barker – and I recognized the truth in it.

* * *

My friendship with Michael Schmidt goes back long before I joined his poetry list. There was our early meeting at the Oxford English Club, when I transfixed him with a poem – 'Mother Love' from *In a Green Eye* – which mentioned baby shit smelling of curd cheese. And I remember watching him at the first Cambridge Poetry Festival, surrounded by a group of formidably assured young men, laughing and challenging each other. I was not part of that inner circle. Still, we had important friends in common. Donald Davie was a major influence on both of us, and Donald wrote in the *Listener* with indignant eloquence after discovering Larkin had not included me in his *Oxford Anthology of English Verse*.

My Tsvetaeva versions had already moved from OUP to Hutchinson, and had come out there alongside my biography of Tsvetaeva, *A Captive Lion*, before Michael and I had a professional relationship. The last book of poems I published with Hutchinson, *City Music* (1994), was orphaned when the axe fell on Tony Whittome's poetry list. I was aghast, since Tony had been a loyal friend for the whole of my publishing life since Dempsey left Hutchinson.

I gave Michael this news at a London party, and he suggested I come to Carcanet. I was delighted. His press had already grown into one of the most prestigious in the UK, with an international and modernist feel to it. He brought out my *Selected Poems* in 1994, with a cover painting by Vanessa Bell. Thus began a twenty-year friendship in which we exchanged racy detail of our own lives alongside literary gossip.

We met over coffee in Fortnum & Mason, had lunch in the Groucho and tea in the National Gallery many times over those years. I enjoyed the spice of his conversation, which was rarely malicious, though in other company the rapidity of his responses may have served him ill – and I have sometimes inherited his enemies.

Carcanet's list includes international stars like Les Murray and John Ashbery alongside poets who have a place in my own story: Donald Davie, Andrew Crozier, Robert Duncan and Ed Dorn. The press is based in Manchester, but in the last few years Michael has also worked as a Professor of Creative Writing in Glasgow University. He showed me around Glasgow's ancient university buildings with great pride on my first visit to give a reading there. Not many people would have the raw energy to direct a publishing house, edit *PN Review* and hold down a chair while writing fat books about the history of poetry.

Now that he has retired from the Glasgow chair, he is a Visiting Fellow at St John's College, Cambridge, and has taken to wearing a beard, which makes him look like a sea captain, perhaps in emulation of one of his sons, who cuts a dashing figure in the merchant navy.

I've enjoyed many other important friendships over the years: for instance, with wry, self-deprecating Daniel Weissbort, a close friend of Ted Hughes and the writer of some of the funniest letters I have ever received. His bumpy life seemed to have found a happy ending when he married Valentina Polukhina, his "pepper vodka" third wife, as I described her in my poem for their wedding. Sadly, he now battles with encroaching Alzheimer's.

Then there is Anthony Rudolf, a distinguished translator, notably of the great French poet Yves Bonnefoy, but also of Russian poets such as Alexander Tvardovsky – the editor of *Novy Mir* during the Thaw – and Yevgeny Vinokurov. Tony is the founder of Menard Press, whose many important booklets over the years include the first English translations of Primo Levi's poetry. Tony knew Primo well. I never met Levi, but there are few countries I have visited over the years where Tony has not had an interesting contact to give me. When I lived in Cambridge he brought Edmond Jabès, the French-Egyptian writer, to give a talk about *Le Livre de Yukel* in my upstairs living room to a group of notables including George Steiner. Later, I met Edmond in Paris and interviewed him for the *Sunday Times*.

Few days now go by without a telephone call between us. Tony is a generous spirit who gives help to anyone who asks for it, and I draw shamelessly on his encyclopedic knowledge of Jewish writing, French literature and contemporary painting. He is the boyfriend and long-term male model of Paula Rego.

* * *

Cambridge understood the importance of working in groups even in the Fifties. There were poets around *Delta* magazine – set up by Peter Redgrove and Roger Bannister – which included Philip Hobsbaum, a critic who had learned his discipline under Leavis at Downing. When Philip went down he held meetings of what became known as The Group in his bedsitter off the Edgware Road in London. Peter Porter and Edward Lucie-Smith attended them regularly. Ted Hughes went to some of these, though he had something else in mind when he set up the Arvon Foundation courses.

For me, poetry was essentially a lone activity. I remember after the birth of my first child waiting glumly for a bus on the Arbury Estate with a pushchair and a shopping bag while studying the trunk of a wet tree coloured by streetlights. When I got home I tried to find words to catch this experience with a sudden, almost forgotten excitement. It was like coming back to life.

If I had to say what has changed most in he poetry village over the fifty years since I first began writing I should point to the number of people who now write poems. How could there not be more of them, when creative writing forms a part of so many university courses? And among these new aspirant poets, many are women. Serious poetry was once thought to be male territory, even when women became successful as novelists. I wonder what exactly has happened. Certainly we now have a whole raft of excellent women writers in all genres, perhaps most surprisingly poets. What worries me a little is that society tends to downgrade the importance of areas where women predominate.

The expanding number of poets does not necessarily mean there are more readers, however. I doubt if the number of people who buy contemporary poetry has altered very much over the years. What has changed is the singular absence of kingmakers. No F.R. Leavis, of course, but also no Alvarez in the *Observer*, no magazine in which publication constitutes arrival. The closest we come to any such body is the Poetry Book Society. Being remembered by posterity – once a strong enough hope for John Keats to think, wistfully, of being "numbered among the English poets after his death" – may remain, but few take the interest of a future world for granted.

I began with *words*: thick, blunt words, which I could move about on the page as if they were lumps of clay. Now my poems come to me in *sentences*, spoken or thought, which seem to carry their own tune in them along with their syntax. This development seemed entirely organic, as if I had reached a new way of shaping my poems without any conscious decision on my part. Schmidt once remarked that no one setting my new work alongside the lyrics from *In a Green Eye* would necessarily recognize the same poet. I feel that the same sensibility runs throughout.

CHAPTER 21

Trips

Arnold and I were always happiest when we travelled together off the beaten track, preferably with some working aim in mind. We immediately became like two gleeful children on a jaunt. It was seeing that glee which led Jill Neville to murmur, as our marital crisis began to resolve, "I always thought you and Arnold would end up toddling off into the sunset together." Bolder, longer trips became feasible once Arnold retired.

I was invited to Singapore by Kirpal Singh, a Sikh friend of Brian Aldiss. Brian and I had been part of a group of English writers, funded by the GB-USSR Society and the Russian Writers' Union, who had been taken round the Soviet Empire in the early Eighties. We had struck up a friendship then, and corresponded intermittently over the years. He was far less acerbic than J.G. Ballard, though they had both made their way initially in the pages of the same science-fiction magazine alongside Michael Moorcock. Brian thought a trip to South East Asia might be just what I needed.

Singapore meant nothing more to me than shopping malls and the street of transvestite prostitutes we had visited on that stopover from Australia, and I was not at first at all enthusiastic. I knew the regime was totalitarian, and it was said you could be executed if you were caught carrying drugs into the city, however innocently. What drew me were Brian's descriptions of South East Asia, coloured by memories of Conrad, especially Bali and Sumatra.

About a week before our flight, Arnold set out in the rain for a local DIY shop to buy metal supports for a bookcase he was building in the hallway. The tiles outside the shop were wet and covered with leaves. He slipped, fell awkwardly and broke his ankle. The first I knew of the accident was his voice from A&E in the Royal

Free, and we both burst out laughing as he mimicked the anxiety of the Indian shop owner, who telephoned an ambulance at once, even though he clearly feared Arnold might sue him.

Unsurprisingly, with the bones of his ankle held in place by metal pins and his leg encased in plaster, the doctors were adamant that he could not fly out to Singapore in a week's time. I considered cancelling the trip altogether. There was no way I could have left him behind alone for more than two months. Fortunately, it proved possible to postpone the date of departure. So I rejigged the flights and we set off with a wheelchair alongside our luggage in the hold.

It was a long and sleepless flight, and I was exhausted as we collected our luggage and made our way out into the tropical night. I was surprised to be met by a photographer, who captured me in a wretched state, and a journalist who wanted to interview me. I remember *Loving Brecht* had just been published. The questioning on that was unexpectedly spiky. Why did I choose to centre a novel on a misogynist bully? How did this relate to my own life? I fended off the questions, crossly. Brecht's relations to his many women were history, weren't they? Did my interlocutor also think I could *sing* like the woman who told the story?

At the hotel a phone call from Kirpal was reassuring. He would meet us after we had slept, take us out for a meal and plan a few excursions. Singapore was not without glamour, I was reminded. Somerset Maugham and Noël Coward had chosen to live there. We too could enjoy gin slings in the Raffles Hotel, and would be astonished by the amazing multiplicity of food prepared in open-air Hawker centres.

We woke into a world of sunshine, cool air, ubiquitous wealth and modernity. Minions were on every hand to take Arnold around in a much superior hotel wheelchair. And in Singapore everyone spoke English. This was not, as I imagined, simply a relic of the Raj. The language was imposed by the current Singapore government: the streets of the city had run with blood twenty years earlier when the main ethnic groups threatened to tear it apart.

When I discovered in my first creative-writing class that English was the compulsory language of education, I asked: "What do you speak at home?" There was an embarrassed silence. At home they spoke Chinese, Bengali or Malay. English was a second language for all of them. They were a clever, hard-working group, but I soon discovered how vital it was for a writer to have a mother tongue.

* * *

Our first trip was to Bali, a Hindu country where in those days everyone smiled easily and banks had small vases of pretty flowers on their counters. Kirpal booked us into a guesthouse in Campuhan, far from the tourist coast, and there we found ourselves alone in a another century. An old-fashioned electric fan whirred in the ceiling, and the room was open to night noises. There were no mosquito nets, and the first night we covered ourselves with Deet, but there seemed to be no mosquitoes. We woke to find a lotus in the pool outside and an unfamiliar bird looking at us.

Bali is a green country, with that sharp young green you see in early spring leaves in England before they get used to the world. Many Balinese were farmers who did not depend on tourists. There was one distinctive local craft however: wood-carving. Talented young boys lived in their family compounds and learnt the skill from their grandfathers. We brought a magnificent image of Sita back with us. Arnold, marvelling at the perfection of every hair, separate and in its place, murmured: "I have never owned anything so perfect."

We were so happy together in Campuhan: we both found ourselves wondering exactly *why*. I found one of the answers in my poem 'Wheelchair'.

…we were both surprised
to find it rather soothing. And one day we surmised:
you needed an attention that I hardly ever pay
while I enjoyed the knowledge that you couldn't get away.

* * *

Sumatra was wild and unspoilt in those days: the beaches white sand fringed by tall trees, and several hundred tigers inhabited the forests at the centre of the island. When we visited a recently built university campus in Padang we were told of a workman attacked by a tiger when the foundations were being laid. Our guides seemed rather proud of that tiger, almost as if it were a legend. By the time my friend Ruth Padel visited Sumatra a decade or so later, the situation had somewhat changed. Swathes of forest trees had been cut down by logging firms, and beaches had been exploited for tourism. There were still tigers in the centre, however.

I had been invited to western Sumatra because the Minangs are one of the world's largest matrilineal societies, with a population of four million in their home province. All property descends through women, who might therefore be thought to have some political power. There is little sign of it. The English faculty of the university had invited me to speak about my D.H. Lawrence biography, and I was expecting to find a university visibly dominated by feminism. This was far from being the case. The professor was a man, and the only female lecturer was not only deferential to him, she was also the one delegated to accompany us round the island.

This was an unusually onerous act of hospitality. It was Ramadan. And Sumatra is hot. As infidels we were allowed bottles of juice and ice, but she and the driver, both observant Muslims, drank nothing and stopped to pray five times a day. Her English was good, and I tried to find out whether her ethnic culture clashed with Muslim practice. She had no sense that this was so. Minangkabau women generally kept to conventional roles, but when couples married,

husbands moved into their wives' homes and women shared decisions. The birth of a girl was considered good news, mainly because
when it came to marriage daughters had a higher market value. In
other respects, feminism clearly had some way to go.

There was only one hiccup in our Sumatran adventure. Arnold's
leg began to hurt with a new throbbing pain. We were deep in the
forest by then, and rather against my instinct he asked for a pair of
scissors and cut off the cast. We both saw at once he was in trouble.
Something was infected. A doctor was promptly summoned – but
this was not Singapore. Would the doctor even speak English?

The doctor was a woman, and fortunately she did. She brought
tablets and an ointment with her, and we looked at them narrowly.
Hoffmann-LaRoche, I think. English script assured us the products
contained high-strength penicillin. We blessed the global reach of
Swiss pharmacy.

* * *

The British Council had arranged for us to travel back through
Bombay so I could give another lecture on Lawrence to a university
there attended only by women. I planned to give the same lecture
I had given in Sumatra. We were staying in the splendour of the
Taj Mahal hotel, one of the grandest hotels of the world. Fruit and
flowers welcomed us to our room, and a complex of rich shops
and restaurants was enclosed within the hotel. Arnold thought he
would have a quiet day as I set off in a British Council car. I found
the dons at the college very impressive. Their carriage, and indeed
their hairstyles, reminded me most vividly of the paintings which
hang in Clough Hall at Newnham College. It was the only time I
felt at home in Bombay.

I have often been told that quite soon you no longer find the
pulsating shadowy throngs of beggars troubling. It may be so, but
both of us hated our hopeless encounters with emaciated children
and crippled women. Indeed, we decided the following day to give

the markets a miss and visit Elephant Island, with its ancient caves and carvings. It was a very tiring expedition, and we were glad to get back to the Taj for dinner and a comfortable bed.

As well we did, it turned out. We were woken the next morning by a phone call from our son Adam, who had read in his newspaper of a terrorist attack in Bombay. This we had missed by going to Elephant Island rather than the markets. Bombs had killed and injured hundreds – there had been no warning, and no one had claimed responsibility.

Later that evening we went by taxi to meet a Muslim writer and his wife, who told us the bombs were probably planted by the Hindu right wing in the hope that Muslims would be blamed. I asked him why, if there was such hostility in India, they did not prefer to live in Pakistan, but he shook his head at the thought of going to live in a rigorously Muslim state.

* * *

I can remember less clearly our months in Norway above the Arctic Circle, but I know how we came to be there. I was invited by Professor Andrew Kennedy, then teaching English and Drama at the University of Bergen. He was a friend from Cambridge days who often came to visit us when we were living there.

Bergen was a very pretty town, and after a weekend there we took a plane to the far north with some reluctance. Looking down from the clear skies we made out fjords which bit into the coastline and tried to imagine the loneliness of the villagers isolated in them.

Tromsø itself is a fair-sized town, the largest human settlement above the Arctic Circle. We arrived in the last week of winter, and although we were given a large and comfortable flat in the centre of town, both of us were disturbed by the unyielding darkness. Fortunately, the Norwegian spirit is hospitable, and quite soon we were part of a group of Tromsø academics. After only a few days spring arrived. It was very surprising. Trees came into leaf and bud as rapidly as Japanese paper flowers expanding in water.

We made good friends in Tromsø, notably Professor Roy Tommy Eriksen – a Swede indeed, but far from gloomy as the cartoonists have it – who spent half of the year in Rome. He was married to a red-haired, lively woman who pronounced herself an Inuit, a member of the very tribe Ed Dorn had celebrated decades earlier in his poem about Aklavik.

Once spring brought sunshine, Roy Tommy and his wife took us for a picnic on a snowy beach. The waters lapping the shore were bottle-blue and liquid, because of the Gulf Stream – but the land mass was still an icy white. Roy Tommy lit a fire, and we all drank schnapps and ate hot sausages in that unreal, dazzling landscape. As soon as the sun went down, though, we made haste to get into the car. We would not have survived long outside.

Just opposite our apartment was a tourist hotel which served very fine breakfasts of many kinds of fish, rye bread, cloudberries and a variety of egg dishes. At the door was a stuffed polar bear, which stood twice the height of a man. I have never been particularly sentimental about these great beasts, whose habitat is being destroyed by global warming. I enquired a little apprehensively whether there were any locally around Tromsø. We were with one of my students, an American, who replied with some relish, "Across the water, yes. And if you see one even a mile away *you are dead*."

"Even if you had a gun?" I asked.

"The Norwegians," he grinned, "do not let anyone shoot polar bears. The animals are an endangered species."

* * *

One exotic trip I took without Arnold was to a week-long festival held in Tampico, on the coast of the Gulf of Mexico. The town was not exactly a tourist destination, since the sea was extremely polluted. I arrived on the Day of the Dead, and the central plaza was filled with garish dolls and paper sculpture. A hot wind blew uneasily. The foyer of the hotel was rather shabby, the carpets badly scuffed and the chairs uncomfortable.

Tampico had its own interest, however. It was the town John Huston chose to set the opening of his film *The Treasure of the Sierra Madre*, and after breakfast next day we were taken to the very café where a desperate Humphrey Bogart decides to join the doomed group of gold-diggers. That was something Arnold would have enjoyed.

We saw very little of Malcolm Lowry country. When we passed his volcano on the way to entertain expats running an English bookshop, we could hardly make out the shape of it in the smog. I wasn't lonely. A charming Brazilian writer of detective stories soon established himself as my companion. But I missed Arnold.

CHAPTER 22

Resolution

When we came to London, Mark Pepys arranged a small MRC grant for Arnold, which came with a room in University College and a lab assistant; unfortunately he could not make much use of them. He had a series of unusual medical problems: he needed surgery on his parathyroid gland, for instance. Then he developed alarming fevers. These followed our visit to Malaysia, so he was taken away for tests to see if high temperatures signalled some tropical infection – but no, they were caused by Behçet's disease, an auto-immune disorder usually only suffered by Turkish peasants.

I was babysitting for Martin and Marina when he suffered a cerebral haemorrhage. I came in the flat's front door already a little anxious because he hadn't answered the phone, to find him lying on the floor with his face cricked so he could continue watching the television screen. The first ambulance came with a team of one man plus one woman – then a local union regulation. This made it impossible for them to lift a man of seventeen stone down the stairs, so we had to wait for a second crew. He was very patient then, though much less so in the Royal Free Hospital.

It was months before he could return to Chalcot Gardens – and, once home, although he sometimes praised me as a good nurse, he could not help resenting my preoccupation with my work when he so badly needed company.

Much of the lump sum he received on retirement he had already spent on a bronze Rover car, an uncharacteristic extravagance which arose, I think, from his conviction that he would not live much longer than a year or two. In the same spirit he bought us expensive tickets to the Opera House. When the lump sum was gone and his University College grant ended, it was up to me to find some means of keeping us afloat. As I began to search around for ways to do so, I felt as if I were putting my whole being into harness, like a horse. But that harness, paradoxically, gave me back my freedom.

Some of what I was doing was simply such fun. I worked for two years on three parts of a nine-part television series about the life of Bertolt Brecht, alongside Michael Hastings, who had written several successful plays, notably one about T.S. Eliot and his first wife Vivienne, and Jorge Semprún, the Spanish novelist who had worked for the French Resistance, by then minister of culture in a socialist Spanish government. There were jaunts to Paris – I cannot remember why – and meetings with the American John Fuegi, who had written the biography of Brecht we were given to work from.

After that, I wrote a six-part TV series about the life of Marie Stopes. I was paid handsomely for both projects, though neither series ever reached the screen. *The Edwardian Gentlewoman's Diary*, on the other hand, written with Dirk Campbell and also directed by him, went out all over the world, and still occasionally brings in royalties.

My many plays for radio – I love radio – attracted more critical attention, notably a trilogy of plays, *Foreign Girls*, about school friends who have Jewish roots in common but very different families: one European and sophisticated, the other conventionally adjusted to the English Midlands. Jenny Agutter played the more interesting girl, and was partly responsible for the plays' success, along with the meticulous direction of Marion Nancarrow.

There was a puppet play too, *The Bet*, written for the Almeida Theatre. This was commissioned by the Arts Council for Martin's ensemble, with music composed by Erika Fox. Then *Lear's Daughters*, workshopped by the Women's Theatre Group from an original idea of mine – a prequel to *King Lear* rather than a sequel. The play changed a good deal as the cast worked on it, however – the dead mother replaced by a jolly nurse and the stories largely drawn from the actresses who took part. Still it has been staged by universities across the world.

In the years that followed, I worked on a series of biographies. My *Bessie Smith* had been a short sketch, written fast and without any pretensions. My new projects were far more ambitious. After Tsvetaeva, I took on D.H. Lawrence, Alexander Pushkin, Ted Hughes and Anna Akhmatova. All were writers, since a writing life was the one I understood best. When friends observed with admiration that I was now amazingly prolific, Arnold usually remarked, "Well, of course. That's all she does!"

I swallowed the unfairness of this as I continued to shop and cook and arrange elaborate dinner parties. His unhappiness was so easy to understand. Sometimes at night he whispered, "What was it all *for*, Elaine?" And I knew he was thinking of the work he loved, the hours he had spent alone in laboratories at night, the opportunity he had thrown away so absurdly. Sometimes he sang an old folk song about "Poor Tom Bowling... gone aloft".

* * *

Arnold was always a vivid presence, and many people remember him with affection. With those who belonged to his old scientific community, he could always be charming and mischievous: many visitors remember relishing his conversation. More gently, he loved to explain scientific principles, especially to adolescents, and parents often watched with something like awe the unusual attention he won from their teenage children. When Arnold came to literary parties, however, he was mainly determined not to play the role of consort. Inside the flat his manner began to resemble the ferocity of his own father.

And he was not only fierce in the flat. I remember a dinner at a local restaurant with Fay Weldon and her new partner, Nick Fox, who rashly advanced theories about some biochemical discovery garnered, I think, from *Nature*. Arnold ridiculed these ideas impatiently. As Nick became indignant in his turn, I could not see how to intervene. After a while, Fay said, "Arnold, if you continue to be so unpleasant to Nick, we shall have to leave." The quiet tones of her voice calmed both men, but it was not the celebration we had intended.

When our children came to visit, the conflicts were far more painful. I knew he admired their talent, but he wished to appear judicious rather than doting. So he refused them the praise they had earned. He was more likely to argue loftily with Martin's replies to a Radio Four presenter on *Kaleidoscope* than compliment him on his spontaneity, and professed not to understand how Adam could enjoy his Malet Street editorial office, since most human contact was by telephone. As for Joel, then a lecturer in Pure Maths who did not yet have a long-term girlfriend, Arnold sometimes accused him of an unhealthy obsession with me.

I am well aware that this behaviour should not have been tolerated, but *taking a stand* always involved an argument that could last a whole day, which he would enjoy while I didn't. It was cowardly, because the children were hurt by my failure to defend them. Just recently, Joel reminded me that Arnold knew very well his remarks were hurtful. This confession followed an agitated exchange in which Joel had called him "needy". Arnold was brought to a pause, and began to explain that he retaliated only when he had sensible advice to give which he felt was being ignored. It may be so. It doesn't excuse my behaviour.

Friends often suggested I ought to leave him, since I wasn't after all dependent on him financially. But the trouble was I didn't *want* to. Arnold had been the love of my life for more than forty years, and I could not help believing that the companionship we had once shared would return. Until then, I had work to do: books and poems to write.

I remember David Leitch remarking that if Jill had been in my situation "she would have slept with every man between Maida Vale and the French Pub, just to show that she could". I brushed away the advice – or the invitation, whichever it was – without reminding him how long in fact it had taken Jill to leave Maida Vale.

* * *

It has always saddened me to remember that Arnold never lived to see Adam succeed as an author, though he did know he had been commissioned to write the first authoritative biography of Pablo Neruda for Bloomsbury. Arnold was mainly anxious about the opportunity, and did not live to see the spectacularly favourable reviews the book received on publication. Adam's excellent Spanish and love of Neruda's poetry had brought him the friendship of the Oxford don Robert Pring-Mill, who gave him access to his archive of Neruda papers and recommended him to all his own contacts in Chile. Adam gratefully followed up all the leads he was given.

Arnold knew nothing of Adam's second book, *A History of Autism: Conversations with the Pioneers,* commissioned by Dame Stephanie Shirley. This sprang out of the diagnosis of Adam's son, Johnny, with autism and his work for the Welsh autism organization, Autism Cymru. Researching the book took Adam to China, India, Latin America, the United States and all over Europe, including Russia. He received praise from the leading figures in the field.

Arnold always acknowledged Martin's musical talent, but he doubted his organizational skills and would have been surprised to see how he has created a baroque group of his own, large enough to put on annual Bach weekends for the Southbank Centre and able to fill the lovely new auditorium at St Martin-in-the-Fields regularly. Nor did Arnold have a chance to read the magnificent reviews of his discs in both *Gramophone* and *Fanfare.*

And he never saw Joel's children.

* * *

I think now it is unsurprising that Arnold once again fell into a depression. He did not dress in the mornings. He surrounded his chair with books and newspapers, and often fell asleep in it. He let me know that he had the means of taking his own life: digoxin, he said, would gradually stop his heart. Dismayed, I called in our GP – and soon Arnold was telling his story to a consultant at the Charter Nightingale in Lisson Grove.

I sat in on the consultation, expecting to hear that I was the source of his unhappiness. Instead, he was led to start with earlier memories, and the doctor elicited much information that was altogether unknown to me. For the first time, I understood Arnold's visits as a child to Great Ormond Street Hospital were to see a psychiatrist. And I learnt he had suffered a major depression long before we met, in his first year at university, during the war, when Queen Mary College was evacuated to King's College, Cambridge. He had never mentioned this early collapse to me.

This time he clamoured for ECT. They gave him a much longer course of treatments, and after one of them he woke, euphoric, and said: "Oh, Elaine, what a dance I have led you!"

* * *

Not much of this fed into my novels. In *Mother's Girl* I took quite a different tack. I was beginning to wonder about daughters who adore their fathers and undervalue their mothers as I had. It is the closest I came to questioning the childhood sources of my unusual loyalty.

The novel, two half-sisters come together on the day of their father's funeral and try to make sense of the family past. For Halina, her father Leo had always been the most exciting presence in her world; to Lucy he was a father she hardly knew. Halina describes the opulence of pre-war Budapest, the loneliness of childhood exile in England and her present solitary condition in London. Hers had been a life of academic success, sexual obsession and a doomed marriage. Her half-sister has lived a Californian exist-ence of promiscuity and drug addiction. The ghost in the book is that of Halina's mother, left behind in Budapest. The novel was shortlisted for the Los Angeles Times Fiction Prize in 1990, and Antonia Byatt found it "a major achievement".

No doubt *Loving Brecht* grew in part from my frustration at finding my three play scripts for TV were never going to be used – but it is not, in fact, a biography of Bertolt Brecht. I invented a talented singer-song writer, Frieda Bloom, whose character is in many ways similar to Halina in *Mother's Girl*. The novel is set in the smoky, sexy world of Kurt Weill and Lotte Lenya, in a Berlin made dangerous by the rise of the Nazis. Frieda tells the story: she is a sexually abused child who runs away from home and discovers her own strong voice in Thirties cabaret.

Her first experience of sexual pleasure is with Bertolt Brecht, and she continues to want him even as she becomes aware of the number of women who share his affections, his exploitation of them and his dependence on his wife, the great actress Helene Weigel. Although Frieda succeeds in tearing herself away from Brecht, their lives cross again: in Moscow, New York and post-war Berlin. I knew her stamina and resilience were qualities I needed for myself. The novel came out first from Hutchinson in 1992, but has been published by many others in paperback thereafter.

Dreamers came out two years later from Macmillan – a complex, many-voiced book with a dark secret at its heart, set this time in nineteenth-century Vienna. It was spoken of in several papers as a contender for the Booker, though historical novels were not then so fashionable as they are now.

I went on to try my hand at a literary sequel, a genre of which Emma Tennant had made herself a queen. She had an assured hand at pastiche and sophisticated insights into the social tensions of Jane Austen's world. I took a very different approach in *Lady Chatterley's Confession*. I wanted to explore what might have happened if Connie and Mellors had taken off to Italy together as Lawrence and Frieda did, and I told the story in Lady Chatterley's voice. It was a better novel than was realized by those who bought the foreign rights across the world hoping for pornographic thrills.

I had my own insights into the long battling marriage between Lawrence and Frieda, which I had already explored in my biography of Lawrence. Some of their friends saw the violent quarrels as a kind of sexual foreplay – I guessed a more obvious origin. The need to break away from female domination had by then become a central theme in Lawrence's writing, as Frieda became what he called a "Magna Mater" which "made it difficult to get the sexual relationship right".

We were staying in Gaiole in Chianti with our old friends Donald and Joyce Hope when, by chance, I ran into Frieda's daughter Barbara and her granddaughter Ursula, who lived in Tuscany. Donald knew Ursula well and admired her vivacity. (She had been the first wife of Al Alvarez.) Barbara remembered her father – Professor Ernest Weekley, whom Frieda left for Lawrence – with great affection, and was a source of fresh memories which had to be let into the story. The following year we returned to Tuscany and rented a huge flat in Barbara's house in Radda in Chianti, so I could talk to her at length.

* * *

One day, as I was strolling along England's Lane in Belsize Park, I was surprised to see Gerda Böhm, my Polish landlady from Hampstead Hill Gardens days, walking towards me. We hailed one another with astonishment and made our way to the Viennese Café with its gold-rimmed green cups and excellent pastries. She looked well, if more solidly built, enquired about Arnold, then hesitated, as if wondering about a question she wanted to ask.

It turned out that she knew Arnold's girlfriend, and was unsure if I knew about the episode. I have forgotten the exact connection which had brought the two of them to Gerda's new home at the height of their affair, but she was very glad to hear that Arnold and I were once again back together, assuring me I would have no further problems. I did not disabuse her. Her own intensity seemed to demand some explanation, and in a little while she began to talk freely about her own experience of jealousy. Her husband, it seemed, had been incorrigibly unfaithful.

"Never," she advised me, "*never* marry a short man."

I thought, but did not say, that whatever other problems Arnold had, *size* had not been one of them.

* * *

It was not my own idea to tackle a biography of Alexander Sergeyevich Pushkin, the fountainhead of Russian literature. Richard Cohen, who then had his own imprint, suggested it to me over a lunch on St Martin's Lane. We knew one another from the days when he had commissioned several of my books, including a UK version of my Tsvetaeva biography, for Hutchinson. The bicentenary of Pushkin's birth was in two years' time and, as it happened, most of the classical biographies were out of print. I knew that T. Binyon, an Oxford don, had been working away at one for many years and was not particularly keen to engage in a race, so I hesitated. Richard offered a decent sum, but even as I began to enjoy the possibility of writing the book, his own financial pressures led him to lower his offer, and Gill Coleridge took the book to Elsbeth Lindner at Weidenfeld & Nicolson.

Only when I went into the London Library, fired with enthusiasm for Pushkin's genius, did I realize the size of the task I had undertaken. There were shelves upon shelves of books about him, not only written by every Russian writer of note, but also contemporary scholars from all over the world. I only had two years to write the book.

So I needed to find a theme and structure the narrative around it. This turned out to be easier than I expected, since Pushkin had a family connection not widely known to an English-speaking audience: his great-grandfather on his mother's side was Gannibal, the African slave of Peter the Great. Gannibal's military genius advanced him to become an important general, yet Pushkin, in sketches of himself, strangely exaggerates his own African features. Although his father was an aristocrat, and he himself was the lover of some of the most beautiful women in Russia, Pushkin felt that he was *ugly*. He guessed that Gannibal, as a black man, had the same problem, and this he explores with cool brilliance in his unfinished novel *The Negro of Peter the Great*.

His poems make the point more lightly:

> While I, always an idle rake,
> Ugly descendant of a black
> Reared in a wilderness, can take
> No pleasure in the pains of love.

This thread lead me through a life as poignantly short as that of Mozart, whom in many ways Pushkin resembled. I loved the ease of his invention, the fizz of his wit and his impish courage. He remains a paradoxical figure, both urbane and without calculation – a man who could write marvellously of bookish heroines like the lovely Tatyana in *Eugene Onegin* and yet tease his mistress Anna Kern when she complained that he did not understand her character.

"You tell me that I do not know your character... Ought pretty women to have a character? The essentials are eyes, teeth, hands, feet."

In 1829 he chose for his wife Natalya Goncharova, a cold young beauty with no interest in literature and a passion for ball gowns and being admired. She brought no dowry, but she made him happy. She also trapped him at court, since the Tsar insisted on her presence there. A young French officer's pursuit of her favours led to the duel in which Pushkin died at only thirty-seven. The name of the officer, d'Anthès, is infamous in Russia as the killer of their best-loved poet.

Writing the book gave me much pleasure – all the more so as, quite unexpectedly, I had found a poet Arnold came to admire as much as I did. Indeed, I remember him telling the story of *The Bronze Horseman* with tears in his eyes; he even began to try and study Russian alongside me. We both learnt a few of Pushkin's short poems by heart, including the celebrated lyric which begins

Ya vas lyubil, lyubov yeshcho byt mozhet
V dushei moyei ugasla nye sovshem.

(I loved you once, and it may be that love
is not quite yet extinguished in my soul.)

The poem ends with ironic lines which suggest the woman would be lucky indeed if God let her find such a tender love again.

It was while writing that book Arnold and I began to regain something of our old affection for one another. I remember in Pushkinsky Dom in St Petersburg, where I had gone to meet the director Sergei Fomichev, Arnold asked a key question about the sketches scattered over Pushkin's manuscripts. Were they contemporary with the poems they accompanied? Fomichev was startled. "Good question," he replied – and indeed he had already put a great deal of work into trying to answer it.

My *Pushkin* was successful, and was included in the Cambridge University reading list for undergraduates studying Russian. Elsbeth Lindner wanted me to write another biography for her. So it was I undertook the life of Anna Akhmatova. On a recent trip to St Petersburg, Arnold and I had been fascinated by a visit to Anna Akhmatova's flat on the Fontanka.

The commission from Elsbeth Lindner, alongside an advance from Knopf in New York, made many other journeys possible. But I was thrown off my Akhmatova track by the death of Ted Hughes in 1998. I had not seen him in a while. There were rumours of illness, but he did not look sick when he was made OM, and was still handsome in press photographs of that occasion. It was a shock when Olwyn phoned us barely a month later with the news of his death.

It was a great effort for Arnold to set off by train to North Tawton, but we were determined to attend the funeral. I can't remember much about the service, except the enormous size of Ted's coffin. The family went off together with that coffin so the body could be cremated and Ted's ashes scattered. Carol, Olwyn and Ted's children Frieda and Nicholas were in the car, and perhaps also Ted's brother Gerald (though I may be conflating two occasions – Gerald was certainly present at the memorial in Westminster Abbey).

After the funeral, the rest of us milled around until it was time to make our way to Court Green. There was a huge press of mourners including Ted's old friends from Cambridge, many poets, including Seamus Heaney, and local fishermen and farmers. A gaunt but gallant Olwyn held the fort, while Carol tried to keep as far away as possible from the usual junketing.

About three weeks later Thomas Lynch, an Irish American writer I had met at a festival in Galway, phoned me out of the blue to ask whether I would be interested in writing Ted's biography for Norton. The perils of such an undertaking were clear enough. Carol believed Ted wanted *no* biography. But I knew there was a story to tell – his *own* story, rather than that of his marriage to Sylvia, which has been explored so many times: the shape of a life always dedicated to poetry, beginning in an ordinary Yorkshire home, which led to his appointment as Poet Laureate. His straightforward manner and genuine love of the English countryside allowed him to make close friends in the Royal Family, and he was sometimes invited to holiday at Balmoral.

Ted had sold many boxes of his papers to Emory University in Atlanta, Georgia, which remained on open shelves, so I could not feel he would have disapproved if I followed them there. On my first visit, Arnold came with me, and we stayed at a comfortable hotel on campus. Later, I interviewed many of Ted's old

Cambridge friends, such as Peter Redgrove, in Cornwall, and Daniel Weissbort in London. I spoke to Al Alvarez and his wife Anne, and corresponded by email with the lively Mike Boddy, in Australia, who threw a completely new light on set-piece occasions like the St Botolph party and Ted and Sylvia's first meeting in Rugby Street.

Olwyn was initially helpful about Ted's early years, introducing me to Donald Crossley, who had known Ted at primary school. Later, friends of Assia Wevill, including Fay Weldon, who knew her from her days in advertising, Suzette Macedo, who had been half in love with her, and Mira Hamermesh, who had known her from her adolescence in Israel, told me the story of Assia's suicide, alongside her child Shura, all with undisguised hostility to Ted.

The book came out in 2001, and the *Sunday Times* bought serial rights to three sections of it. On the whole, the book was generously reviewed, though there were certainly those who thought I ought to have criticized Ted's treatment of women more forcefully.

* * *

What I most liked about writing my next novel, *Dark Inheritance*, was the freshness of leaving my own life behind and entering a central figure who was independent, knowing and fearless. I enjoyed making her a gift of an Irish writer father. Moreover, the city of Rome was a rich new backcloth. I was there for a week while giving a lecture at the Keats-Shelley Memorial House in Piazza di Spagna, invited by Dannie Abse's niece, Bathsheba. I presented school prizes alongside the wife of the British Ambassador and then, after a reading, she took me off to have dinner on the terrace of the mansion which at that time was the ambassadorial residence. Isaiah Berlin and his wife were there as guests for the weekend.

The terrace was floored in yellow stone and overlooked a dark garden of poplars and birch trees. The air was warmly scented with jasmine and honeysuckle. Busy servants laid silver on a white cloth and lit tapers to repel mosquitoes. Berlin and his wife came down to join us after a while, and soon we were sitting at table together.

He was not a prepossessing man at first glance, but he was mesmerizing as soon as he began to speak. I could see how Akhmatova came to fall in love with him on that legendary night in Leningrad, when he visited her just after the war – an encounter she transmuted into poems. I longed to ask what they talked about, but I lacked the nerve to raise the subject with his wife at his side. The whole occasion was infused with magic: the terrace, the half-seen furry trees, the scents of southern vegetation, the brilliance of the night sky. The novel was born before I was back in my hotel bed.

Not only did I begin to write *Dark Inheritance* in Rome, but I was able to finish the book in Italy a year later. I was awarded a Rockefeller Foundation Fellowship to spend a month in Bellagio on Lake Como. Partners were welcome, and Arnold enjoyed everything about our stay: the beautiful house and grounds, the paintings on the walls and the delicious food. Most of all he enjoyed the group of interesting fellow guests who were always ready to talk to him about their special interests. There was a brilliant film scholar from Germany, then teaching in California, who was examining how the metaphor of shell shock played into early films such as *The Cabinet of Dr Caligari*, and a sturdy Israeli historian whose father had been an important figure in Ben-Gurion's cabinet. He was working on recently declassified cabinet papers which exposed the early years of battling to make a state. We all gave lectures on what we were doing – including Arnold, who had not given a lecture on molecules in years, but took some trouble to give an explanatory talk for the non-scientists there. Bellagio was a Magic Mountain.

Dark Inheritance went into a second printing; indeed, The Women's Press were keen to follow it up with another thriller with the same central figure as the detective. Sadly, the Press foundered before that became possible.

* * *

I returned to my Akhmatova biography only to find that three years moving in the clear waters of the English language had eroded much of the Russian vocabulary I had acquired while writing *Pushkin*. I determined to bring it back and to translate Akhmatova's poems myself, although there were already many excellent translations available. It would be my way of entering her being.

This was not so easy to do. Her beauty and stoic reticence put her in polar opposition to Tsvetaeva – or so I imagined. As I began to meet the poets who had once been protégés of Akhmatova in her last years and to read more widely, I came to understand how much I had simplified that opposition. Certainly, men fell in love with Akhmatova to the end of her life: she could never say, as Tsvetaeva did, that she didn't count much as a woman with men around her. Yet she knew the pains of rejection equally. Her first husband, the poet Nikolai Gumilev, pursued her through her adolescence, but once married to her was compulsively unfaithful. Her second husband, Vladimir Shileyko, a scholar of ancient scripts, was so possessive of her that he burned her poems in a samovar. Nikolai Punin, a brilliant art historian, with whom she spent her most passionate years, took a younger mistress towards the end of their time together and, if visitors began to praise her poems, sometimes sent Akhmatova to clean the herring. When she returned to Leningrad from Tashkent after the Second World War, her lover Garshin, whom she had agreed to marry, met her at the station to explain his plans had changed. But her worst grief was the anger of her son, who blamed her for his incarceration in the Gulag, and even more for her use of his suffering as material for her great poem *Requiem*.

Akhmatova's transformation from the "gay little sinner" of the Stray Dog Café in 1913 St Petersburg into the stalwart figure who became the voice of a whole people humbled me. As I began to push towards the end of the book, many years later, I had to go into hospital for surgery myself and thought ruefully of her physical resilience.

* * *

The only lengthy trip I took away from Arnold in those years was to the Wellington Literary Festival in New Zealand. Arnold had learnt to handle email by then. He had never enjoyed writing letters, but when I look now at the loving messages he sent me in Wellington, I find them almost unbearably moving: he so plainly missed me.

I did make short trips on the poetry circuit to major literary festivals as my books came out, and to read poems in Milan, Paris, Lisbon and Oradea in Transylvania, and to Cordova, where my poems were translated into Spanish (Arnold came with me there). All were fascinating to experience, but it is a later tour, a series of events organized by Sian Williams in 2004, called – perhaps a touch grandly – The Great Women Poets tour, with Carol Ann Duffy, Liz Lochhead, Nina Cassian and myself, which throws up now the single most vivid memory.

The tour was planned to end with a reading in a packed Purcell Room. Nina was a handsome woman in her eighties and a formidably expressive reader. She and I sat side by side while Carol Ann read, both of us a little unnerved by loud bangs from behind the curtain, which grew even louder and more desperate as it became my turn to read.

In the interval we discovered that those noises offstage were made by Liz Lochhead, who was trapped in the artists' lavatory. (I have been chary of using it ever since.) The door had to be broken down to release her in time for the second half.

* * *

When it became impossible for Arnold even to get up the stone steps to the front door of our house in Belsize Park, Martin and I set about finding another flat. We succeeded in buying the whole ground floor of a double-fronted Edwardian house in the Mapesbury conservation area. It was bright, recently modernized, with a garden you could enter both from the kitchen and the living room. He loved it. It was high summer, and we had breakfast on the patio. The new flat felt like a holiday.

> Coffee and grapefruit was the breakfast ritual,
> or boiled eggs eaten from blue terracotta.
> *Our paradise*, you called it, like a *gîte*
> we might have chosen somewhere in Provence.
> Neither of us understood you were in danger.
> Not even when we called the ambulance.

As autumn closed in, Arnold began to find it difficult even to get along the corridor from the bedroom to the kitchen. He was suffering from a blood disease, but we didn't know that then. One weekend, as he lay back against the pillows, I saw how much weight he had lost and was suddenly afraid. He wanted me to contact Mark Pepys, then Head of the Immunology Department at the Royal Free to explain his symptoms, and so I did – by email, since Mark was on holiday in Hawaii. It seemed an impractical way to find urgent medical help, and Arnold did not argue when I rang, weekend or no, for an out-of-hour doctor. He arrived more quickly than I expected, looked at the colour of the veins in Arnold's lower lids and pronounced him dangerously anaemic.

To Arnold's astonishment, he then called an ambulance, which arrived as if for an emergency in a matter of minutes. Arnold was given oxygen and blood on the way to the Royal Free, and by the time we arrived at A&E, he looked a little better. Mark had already contacted a friend to examine him.

By then I was seriously alarmed. I could tell he was far from out of danger

When I came in to visit him the next day, his face lit up with the lovely smile I remembered from our early days together. But he was not enjoying this stay in hospital. He had to sleep propped up on pillows, because his breathing was difficult, and the busy nurses hauled him about brusquely. He shooed them out when I arrived, saying, "Off you go. I'm talking to my wife."

We didn't talk much. He told me about the machine they used to lift him out of bed, and how much he had enjoyed being lowered into a bath. But he was drowsy, and as he felt himself falling asleep, he said, "Hold my hand. I feel I won't die while you are here."

I held his large gentle hand with a chill around my heart.

For all the transfusions he was given every three days, the haemoglobin count was evidently not improving. His red cells were being gobbled up, and the doctors seemed worryingly puzzled. Arnold revived a little when the problem was explained to him.

He had not lost his scientific ingenuity. He lay there thinking about the red-cell disappearance and came up with a method of finding out where the cells were going. He asked me to write down his suggestion carefully and send it over to Hawaii. Mark replied swiftly, both impressed and amused. Arnold, without any medical training, had independently invented a method already in general use. He had lost none of his imagination, his memory or his passion for life.

And he desperately wanted to come home. I could see there would have to be quite a support network to make that possible, but I too pressed for his return. I had been creating a garden with the help of two people recommended by an old friend at the Poetry Society. There were now trees of fig, cherry and plum along the wooden fence, a eucalyptus tree in the lawn and, close to the patio, bushes of winter jasmine and rosemary. The cumbersome boxes we had moved in with were safely sorted, and the living room was laid out like a stage set waiting for him.

When the hospital reluctantly agreed to let him leave, he wanted me to come and collect him in our car. I could not persuade the staff nurse to allow that, since the hospital would not be covered if he came to any harm. And when the ambulance men brought him in on a stretcher, I could see how frail he had become and how impossible it would have been for me to help him into the house. I had bought him an expensive toy: an electrically powered chair which could take him round the flat. He wanted to try it out immediately, and was soon steering it about the corridors and over to the window so he could look out at the garden. I brought him the list of plants that would flower in spring, and he enjoyed that.

He wasn't hungry and, when I offered him treats, asked: "Do I have to?" I offered him hot soup instead. All our boys were with us by then, fortunately, and were able to lift him in and out of chairs. (District nurses are instructed not to lift heavy patients.) There was oxygen to arrange. Martin did that. Joel stayed on for a few more days and helped me get him into bed at night. When we were alone again, however, this last proved an insoluble problem. I had to dial 999. Ambulance men came, lay him in bed and tucked him gently under the duvet.

That night he fell asleep as soon as I got in beside him.

"I feel so safe with you," he said.

I lay awake a long time, feeling the comfort of his warm body beside me, yet knowing he was not safe at all.

The next morning I was on the telephone to Brent Town Hall, trying to explain the difficulties, when two friendly nurses buzzed the front-door bell. I led them into the bedroom, where Arnold was still sleeping. As I came into the room, he gave a long sigh, as if he had been holding his breath until I appeared. The stertorous intake of breath which usually followed never came.

"Can't you help him?" I cried to the nurses.

But they looked almost embarrassed.

One said: "Why you don't call your son?"

So it was, ignorantly, desperately, that I tried to give mouth-to-mouth resuscitation.

Nothing.

I remember that ambulance men brought in a defibrillator – who called them? – and sent me to another room while they used it. I remember Martin and I setting off in his wife's car to Queen Mary's Hospital. I think Adam was already there. We all sat together in the waiting room.

Then one of the emergency team came back.

"I'm sorry. We're breathing for him, but his heart doesn't respond. We'll just clean him up, then you can go in to see him."

I went in first, and stood by the bed, looking at Arnold's peaceful face. He didn't look dead. I talked to him a long time, as if he were listening intently.

Of the funeral, I can remember nothing except the freezing rain.

CODA

In 2003, a year after Arnold's death, I was invited by the British Council to give a reading in the garden of the offices they once occupied near the centre of Jerusalem. At that time, I was not at ease anywhere much, except in the Mapesbury flat, where I could still sense Arnold's presence in the objects we had collected together over the years. Nevertheless, I accepted the invitation – partly, I think, because the solicitor I had once been engaged to long ago was now living there. I knew he was married. I was simply curious to know how life had treated him. The British Council sent him an invitation.

After the reading, I recognized him easily enough in the queue of people waiting to have their books signed. He was still handsome and well dressed. His wife was carrying a small pile of my books, and when they came up to me he said he had read everything I had written, which was flattering, but probably an exaggeration. Then he added:

"Didn't they all have *unhappy* lives, these Russian women poets you admire so much?"

I was puzzled by the tone of his voice. How could he fail to revere women of such iconic stature?

He wasn't interested in their place in history, however. He meant their *personal* lives, and perhaps the remark was aimed obliquely at what he guessed of my own. Certainly, he was almost right about theirs. Both had to face illness and starvation alone, and though Akhmatova usually found a friend to look after her, no one understood the opposition between poetry and happiness better than she did:

> If I can't have love, if I can't have peace,
> Give me a bitter glory.

As I looked at the couple in front of me in the Jerusalem evening, so comfortably together in their marriage, I guessed his remark was intended mainly to remind me of the joys of an ordinary life, if I had wanted that. So I nodded.

"It goes with the territory," I said.

ACKNOWLEDGEMENTS

The author is grateful to Carcanet Press for permission to quote from poems in her *Collected Poems* (Carcanet, 2002) and *Bride of Ice, New Selected Poems of Marina Tsvetaeva* (Carcanet, 2011) and fourteen lines from Ed Dorn's 'Thesis'; to Pollinger Limited for permission to quote five lines from Wallace Stevens's 'Sunday Morning'; to the Curator of Literary Collections, Thomas J. Dodd Center, University of Connecticut for permission to quote from Charles Olson's *Maximus Poems*; to Jeremy Prynne for permission to quote a verse of 'The Western Gate' from *The White Stones*; to Hana Amichai for permission to quote from Yehudah Amichai, *Selected Poems*, translated by Ted Hughes, Assia Wevill and others (Penguin, 1971); to Yevgeny Yevtushenko for three lines from 'Poet in a Market', in an unpublished translation by the late Masha Enzensberger.

I would also like to thank friends who read an early draft of this book and all those who lent me photographs for it. Most of all, I want to thank my sons who read this latest version with their own memories still vivid.

INDEX